D1303134

The Growth of a Personal Voice

The Growth of a Personal Voice

Piers Plowman AND *The Faerie Queene*

Judith H. Anderson

New Haven and London   Yale University Press

1976

Published with assistance from the foundation established in memory
of Henry Weldon Barnes of the Class of 1882, Yale College.

Library of Congress catalog card number: 75-43300
International standard book number: 0-300-02000-7

Designed by John O. C. McCrillis
and set in Bembo No. 270 type.
Printed in the United States of America by
Vail-Ballou Press, Inc., Binghamton, N.Y.

Published in Great Britain, Europe, Africa, and Asia (except Japan) by
Yale University Press, Ltd., London.
Distributed in Latin America by Kaiman & Polon,
Inc., New York City; in Australia and New Zealand by Book & Film
Services, Artarmon, N.S.W., Australia;
in Japan by John Weatherhill, Inc., Tokyo.

To Talbot

Contents

Acknowledgments

I wish to express my gratitude to scholars who read the manuscript of this book in whole or in part and generously offered their comments on it: Elizabeth D. Kirk, A. C. Hamilton, Rudolf Gottfried, E. Talbot Donaldson, A. Bartlett Giamatti, and Walter Henry Principe, C.S.B. To Elizabeth Kirk and Father Principe, I owe a special debt: the former for writing an extremely painstaking and informative critique of the entire manuscript; the latter, for looking over my translations of Scotus's references to the Hypostatic Union. Any errors in the following pages, I should hasten to add, are my own. This book was written in three countries and in four universities. The debts which I lack the space to mention outnumber those I acknowledge. At least the most important of these will appear in my footnotes, though I should also note here my particular gratitude to Harry Berger, Jr., who, if he did not first introduce me to *The Faerie Queene,* first led me to respect it. Another debt of very long standing is to my former colleagues Dorothy Mermin and Carol M. Sicherman, whose support and criticism proved invaluable at an early stage both of my career and of this book's.

Portions of three of my chapters on *The Faerie Queene* were previously published in another form—in two cases, a significantly different form. The editors of the following journals have kindly given me permission to rework these articles: "Redcrosse and the Descent into Hell," *ELH* 36 (1969): 470–92; "The July Eclogue and the House of Holiness: Perspective in Spenser," *SEL* 10 (1970): 17–32; " 'Nor Man It Is': The Knight of Justice in Book V of Spenser's *Faerie Queene,*" *PMLA* 85 (1970): 65–77; "The Knight and the Palmer in *The Faerie Queene,* Book II," *MLQ* 31 (1970): 160–78; "Whatever Happened to Amoret? The Poet's Role in Book IV of *The Faerie Queene,*" *Criticism* 13 (1971): 180–200; " 'Come, Let's Away to Prison': Fortune and Freedom in *The Faerie Queene,* Book VI," *JNT* 2 (1972): 133–37.

Perhaps only after again stating that any errors which follow are mine, can I acknowledge gracefully the person to whose humanity and intelligence I am most deeply indebted and to whom this book is dedicated.

Introduction

Piers Plowman reentered the literary and religious experience of English readers in the decade of Spenser's birth. There were two distinct editions and a third reprint of the poem by Robert Crowley in 1550, and another reprint of Crowley's last edition by Owen Rogers in 1561. Crowley's preliminary remarks to the reader suggest the reasons for Langland's popularity. Crowley, a Protestant preacher as well as a printer and minor poet, hailed Langland as a precursor of the Reformation, whose eyes "it pleased God to open ... to se hys truth" and whose heart God emboldened to "crye oute agaynste the worckes of darckenes." Crowley further described him as a "writer who in reportynge certayne visions and dreames, that he fayned him selfe to haue dreamed: doth moste christianlie enstruct the weake, and sharplye rebuke the obstynate blynde."

Crowley's editions and remarks alike indicate that he read *Piers Plowman* intelligently, understanding its language, the principle of its alliterative verse, and its "fayning" use of dreams.[1] The impact of his editions on other readers is evident in the subsequently increased occurrence of *Piers Plowman* as a term for the wise, just, dedicated man of earth—plower of fields, shepherd of flocks, and tiller of vineyards, both secular and sacred.[2] The figure of Piers in the May Eclogue of Spenser's earliest important poem, *The Shepheardes Calender,* expresses this tradition.

The Shepheardes Calender is a declaration of Spenser's calling as a poet and an indication of the kind of poet he was called to be. Appropriately, at its end he identifies the poetic tradition he would follow "farre off" and cautions his poem:

> *Goe lyttle Calender, thou hast a free passeporte,*
> *Goe but a lowly gate emongste the meaner sorte.*
> *Dare not to match thy pype with Tityrus hys style,*
> *Nor with the Pilgrim that the Ploughman playde a whyle. . . .*[3]

Allusion by imitation is a favorite Spenserian device. At the beginning of this quotation his allusion to Chaucer's *Troilus and Criseyde* is exact and explicit: "Go, litel bok, go, litel myn tragedye."[4] The name *Tityrus* in Spenser's lines refers to Chaucer, just as it has three times before in the *Calender.*[5] Since his final line starts with *Nor,* it obviously refers to a poet

I

other than Chaucer and does so in perfect alliterative verse (*aaax*). Allusion by imitation—stylistic as well as situational—therefore identifies the Pilgrim-Ploughman poet as Langland, the author of *Piers Plowman*.[6] The natural reading of the final line, that Spenser dares not match pipes with the pilgrim who played the role of plowman for a while,[7] makes good sense as a reference to *Piers Plowman,* and it means that Spenser not only knew Langland's poem but also knew it well enough to understand Piers as an aspect, a face, of Langland's narrator, which in fact Piers turns out to be.

Taking leave of the *Calender,* Spenser thus identifies Langland as one of the two English poets with whom he believes himself to be associated. Although the nature of Spenser's association with Langland alters as Spenser's art matures, the fact of his association never really changes, as an examination of the relationship between *Piers Plowman* and *The Faerie Queene* will make clear. In Spenser's epic, the Plowman, along with Redcrosse Knight and Colin Clout, becomes a metaphor for Spenser's past—his own past as the poet of *The Shepheardes Calender,* his past as an Englishman, and his past as a son of earth and of Adam.

Held close to *The Faerie Queene*—held, as it were, behind Spenser's poem—*Piers Plowman* looks in large structural and conceptual ways like a grid for it, a grid in part literary and in part intellectual. But although I am persuaded that *Piers Plowman* influenced Spenser's major work, it would be sufficient for my purposes if questions of direct influence were left in abeyance and apparent influence were considered the result of more general relationships and developments between the late Middle Ages and the Renaissance. In other words, I should be willing to have the grid interpreted as meaning intellectual history and literary tradition.

Or I should be *almost* willing, for without Langland's poem—his poem specifically—the grid would not be readily visible. Certain medieval elements that lie behind and within *The Faerie Queene* compose this grid, but Langland's poem proves a far more appropriate representative of the vitality and complexity of these elements than any of the nonliterary tracts or more trifling poems which could have been Spenser's direct source, even as a rooster is more sensibly compared to a peacock than is an omelet or a peacock's egg.

Our critical tradition still has more refined ideas about Spenser's use of Ovid or Vergil than about his use of the English past, which clearly held a fascination for him. A close look at *The Faerie Queene* together with *Piers Plowman* gives a better indication of the subtle, synthetic way in which Spenser used his sources, both direct and traditional. *Piers Plowman* is a monumental representative of the dream vision and therefore of a crucial type of influence on *The Faerie Queene,* for which no other source so adequately accounts. Because the exception introduces the larger category, the exceptional poem is indispensable to an assessment of Spenser's traditional sources.[8]

Langland's poem is an exceptional fulfillment of possibilities inherent in the dream tradition; it is the most complex, most sophisticated instance in pre-Spenserian English of the interiorizing and the more profoundly distinctive personalizing of allegory that derives from this tradition. His poem represents —clearly, impressively, and poetically—a way of organizing and conceiving experience, and a way of exploring the self while searching for Love and Truth, which are implicit in this tradition and without which *The Faerie Queene* would not be the inner, echoing poem, the imagined and remembered experience it is. J. V. Cunningham has observed that "What a writer finds in real life is to a large extent what his literary tradition enables him to see and to handle." He adds that the one term is tradition, "not unalterable but never abandoned" as "the other term is always experience."[9] I should extend these observations: in the hands of great poets, sources are likely to become analogues; and in the realm of ideas, every true analogue is potentially a source.

Besides belonging to England's poetic past, *Piers Plowman* belongs to the history of thought and belief. It centers on the character Will and reflects some of the more radical statements formulated in the Middle Ages to affirm the freedom and responsibility of the will, yet it also proves to be progressively reconcilable with *The Faerie Queene,* a poem informed deeply by Protestantism, indeed by a faith showing Calvin's influence. Taken together, these poems readjust a number of our presuppositions, simplified by catch-words like *free will, predestination, justification, Catholic* and *Protestant, medieval* and *Renaissance,* which have got in the way of understanding. Many years and many differences in taste and outlook separate these two poetic *summas*; but to the extent that *Piers Plowman* seems an unlikely match for *The Faerie Queene,* it is because Langland's poem is the grandfather of Spenser's and not because his poem is a different species. The theological differences between the poems are in significant ways more superficial than their likenesses, as is actually the case with the systems of thought—even Scotus's and Calvin's—behind them. We shall find these facts important in assessing relationships between the poems, for in both of them method evolves simultaneously with meaning.

The poet's role in these poems, for example, shifts concurrently with changes in the nature and location of Truth (Reality). Within each poem and, historically speaking, between the two of them, we find an expansion of the personal voice of the poet and the development of characters more fully personal in themselves. We therefore meet an instance of the evolution of forms, both poets' and characters'. As the poems become in their varying degree more personal, and in this sense more fully and directly experiential, central conceptions in them such as "nature" and "life" will not hold still.

In the hands of these poets, the fundamental concerns of philosophy and theology also become progressively personalized: in varying degrees, philosophy and theology, like literary dream-forms and fairy landscapes, begin to lose their objective status. Their truths become more subjective and more relative to one person than before. They start to look like autobiography projected into other forms, whether animated abstractions, characters, or symbols, whether feigned dreams or poetic visions. By this same process, allegory itself becomes more personal. Both poems suggest, though Spenser's alone really shows, that this process will, carried further, mean the end of allegory, or rather its endurance in so altered a form that it is, if not entirely unrecognizable, then likely to be called by some other name. It is difficult here not to think of the personal symbolism of Romantic poetry, and particularly of Wordsworth's.

Both *Piers Plowman* and *The Faerie Queene* are major achievements, both relatively early, allegorical, narrative, Christian, moral, English, and long—indeed endless. Both are profoundly original in their manipulation of allegory as an exploratory rather than a hortatory mode. Together they illuminate the special problems of the evolving narrative consciousness in an allegorical poem, both the form it takes and the effects it has on allegorical expression. In referring to the evolution of a narrative consciousness, I seek to comprehend the poet's role and those of his characters and symbols and, from another view, to embrace both the narrator and his story.

All these terms—poet, character, symbol, narrator, story—are more interchangeable in Langland's and Spenser's major works than in Chaucer's, a fact inseparable from the more dramatically autonomous role of the Chaucerian persona. Both Langland and Spenser use the psychology of projection in a more direct and obvious way. An element of directly personal realization distinguishes their poems, incidentally also removing them from the vast majority of other contemporary allegories in English. The vexed problem of the persona and a related issue, the nature of characters (or of other characters) in the narrative, raise peculiar difficulties of interpretation and definition in either poem. These are not difficulties present in all allegorical poems, nor precisely the difficulties the same issues raise with Chaucer and Milton, both writers of more dramatic narratives. Inevitably, of course, these difficulties are also relevant in various ways to the writings of such other poets.

Piers Plowman and *The Faerie Queene* are more explicitly—perhaps more

literally—concerned with the workings of the mind, with its play on the
world and its self-reflective play, than are other English poems of their
centuries. This is not an exclusive or identically expressed concern in the
two poems, but it is a vitally important one. Neither poem gives us a character who is objectively real and autonomously self-conscious the way King
Lear or Rosalind or Criseyde, the Pardoner, or even Milton's Satan is. Both
represent the action of the mind more abstractly and symbolically than do
these other works. They give it a more disembodied form than would, until
quite recently, a good novel or play, but they also represent it more immediately, more extensively, and in some ways more freely. They achieve an
order of realism which particularly engages the intellectual side of our
imaginations.

In the strangely fluid surfaces and insubstantial stories of these poems, ideas
are transformed and systems altered. Attitudes take shape gradually, but when
they do, and often as soon as they do, their shape is modified. Early events
return in the poems like voices from the past to threaten, to expand, or to
complete the present. Dimensions of meaning and reference shift swiftly
and subtly: landscapes thicken, recede, or become interiorized; not only
symbols but also words continually evolve, interact, and even merge; both
narratives contract to focus on the poet himself and enlarge to include mankind. Through their shifting, cycling, echoing movements, these poems
realize a process—or better, a life—of thought, of perception and recognition,
in their efforts to achieve awareness of truth.

Before turning to the body of this study, I should raise explicitly some
issues of approach and method which have hitherto obscured the nature of
the relationship between Langland's and Spenser's poems. These issues are
troublesome precisely because they are generally inexplicit and involve
unspoken assumptions or aesthetic preferences. Even A. C. Hamilton's
essay on *Piers Plowman* and *The Faerie Queene,* which is an admirable and
important pioneer effort to relate the two poems, manifests the biases of
theory and sensibility that make their relationship elusive; it can therefore
serve to clarify these biases for us.[10] Thinking of Sidney's " 'right Poet,' "
Hamilton explains that Spenser " 'nothing affirmes' " and that "In contrast,
Langland does seem to affirm truth." He adds, however, that we see Langland's Dreamer "as a character who functions within a poetic drama; and
since what he 'affirms' is expressed chiefly through fragments of himself in
Thought and the rest, we are at two removes from simple affirmative statement." This curiously hesitant extension of the name of poet to Langland
follows logically from Hamilton's position that Spenser's "whole effort
through his poem is to render clearly defined, exact, and visual images." In

this way the "literal level" of Spenser's poem becomes metaphor, "a radiating center of meaning which organizes whole areas of human experience," and thus his fiction "triumphs over any supporting framework of morality and belief."

No one would want to reverse the observation that Spenser's poem is more "visual" in Hamilton's sense than Langland's, but many readers would not now say that Spenser's whole effort is to render exact and visual images.[11] Hamilton's remarks illuminate a distrust of abstraction which, although not unknown to Spenser or even to Langland, is not shared by them to the same extent that it is likely to be by us. A criticism that starts from the image rather than from the word—and the word is, after all, by definition more abstract than the image—will identify the visual with the fictional and with the metaphorical in too limited, indeed too literal, a sense. It will not find that Spenser and Langland have very much, certainly not much that is profound, in common. If it is true that Spenser's poetry can be described as more "visual" than Langland's, such a criticism is not invalid, though it cannot be primary in an effort to explore relationships between *Piers Plowman* and *The Faerie Queene*. This effort will have to make more use of principles of development in the poems which are less visual and spatial—at least in the literal sense—and more temporal and audible.

Hamilton's remarks, sensitive to the visually rich experience of Spenserian allegory, suggest the difficulty of talking about two poems without simply deciding that one is better than the other, without employing an approach derived from an understanding of one poem but less congenial to the other. This sort of judgment can elucidate a critical principle or preference but is likely to compromise one of the poems, especially if both are good. It has been my intention to respect the radical individuality of both poems, and my attempt to do so has influenced the methods and organization of this book. I have kept the two poems apart while trying to hold them together, and have treated them more descriptively than prescriptively. Instead of obscuring the genuine critical and historical issues that comparison raises, such a procedure clarifies them more usefully.

For perfectly sensible reasons, either Spenser's or Langland's poem has generally dictated the organization of books about it. Both poems are massive, and their development is protean. Although it is also episodic—literally incidental—a Book, event, stanza, line, or word loses meaning in the same proportion that it is divorced from its encompassing context. Interpretations of *The Faerie Queene* usually proceed Book by Book or treat single Books or sequential sections of the poem, and *Piers Plowman* invites the same procedure. In a discussion of both poems, the question of their relationships and the limitations of space remove the usual option. I have had to be more selective and to rely on the reader's having a good acquaintance with the poems. For reasons succeeding chapters will clarify, I have taken considerable selections from both poems, more or less in the order they come, rather than limiting discussion to a single section of *Piers Plowman* or to a single Book of *The Faerie Queene:* Spenser's first two Books are closer to Langland's poem in subject matter, but it is the whole of *The Faerie Queene* which is, in its progressive movement and concerns, analogous to *Piers Plowman* in the most interesting and fundamental ways.

The first section to follow discusses similarities in subject and technique in Langland's Prologue and Visio and in Spenser's Books I and II: the Wandering Wood, the Descent into Hell, Contemplation, the Cave of Mammon. The second section deals with the development of awareness and its concerns in Langland's Vita de Dowel and in Spenser's Books III and IV. The last section, like the first, touches on similarities of conception but stresses the growth of a personal voice in both works: Passūs XV to XX and Books V, VI, and the Mutability Cantos.

One difficulty about the text of *Piers Plowman* remains to be mentioned. My choices were to use readings from the new edition of the B-text by George Kane and E. Talbot Donaldson, from Crowley's B-text, or from Skeat's B-text, which is closer to Crowley's than is Kane-Donaldson.[12] I have used Skeat because his edition is more accessible to the majority of readers than Crowley's, but I have made the following exceptions: (1) if Crowley varies significantly from Skeat I have used Crowley's reading; (2) where I am not trying to make any case for verbal similarities between *Piers Plowman* and *The Faerie Queene,* but am trying to make a point about Langland's poem which Crowley's variant obscures, I have retained Skeat. (In these few instances Skeat is in essential agreement with Kane-Donaldson.) I record Crowley's variants from Skeat's text whether they are shared by all three printings, or only two, or only one, when they are relevant to the terms of my discussion. Any Crowley variant I adopt is also noted.

Part I

Narrator, Dreamer, and Dream

Foreword to Part I

The beginnings of Langland's and Spenser's poems recall the materials of traditional moralities, and it is part of their strength that they do. Langland's poem introduces mankind, chiefly gainserving and sinful, working and wandering in a field that lies between Good and Evil. The setting of Spenser's first Book is likewise conventional: the Christian Knight, accompanied by Truth, loses himself in the wood that will lead him to Error and prepare him for falsehood, duplicity, disunity. The distinctive concern of both poems at the outset is rather with awareness than with instruction, and the familiarity of their initial situations makes this concern clearer. In both poems the initial event is perceptual and as a result a little unnerving. It is (in both senses) a critical experience that brings the reader up sharply against the condition of mankind, a condition not to be separated simply from his own.

1

Langland: Prologue and Passus I

The Prologue of *Piers Plowman* takes only ten lines to identify a Dreamer and get him to sleep before remarking the presence of the high "toure" and the dark "dongeon" and focusing on the "felde ful of folke"—laborers, tramps, beggars, swarms of hermits, merchants, palmers, and minstrels. With the narrator's attention, ours is drawn to humanity as it actually obtrudes itself on the human consciousness and, beyond that, to the simple fact that it is doing so: "As I bihelde in-to the est . . . I seigh a toure on a toft . . . A faire felde ful of folke fonde I there bytwene . . . Bidders and beggeres fast aboute ʒede . . . I fonde there freris, alle the foure ordres . . . There preched a pardonere as he a prest were." The Prologue dramatizes the responses of the mind to the world and its seemingly inextricable involvement in it. Perhaps for this reason the Prologue presents a narrator who speaks now as if he were vividly living the dream:

> Cokes and here knaues crieden, "hote pies, hote!
> Gode gris and gees, gowe dyne, gowe!"
> Tauerners vn-til hem tolde the same,
> "White wyn of Oseye and red wyn of Gascoigne,
> Of the Ryne and of the Rochel, the roste to defye."

and now as if the dream were over:

> Al this seiʒ I slepyng and seuene sythes more.

[225-30]

The narrator's awareness is a double one. It sees the experience as an experience, and without neatly rationalizing its meaning, makes clear the fact that meaning is there. This is satire, but it is also discovery. If it is affirmation, it is close to denial, and if it is moral, then it is deeply ironic as well.

As the Prologue develops, it rapidly draws into its field of vision the various orders of action and being—social, political, and religious, natural, moral, and theological. A reference to one order evokes thoughts of another, indeed seems actually to contain them within itself. Nothing stays still. Distinctions become as elusive as those between sleep and waking. Perceiving the corruption of Churchmen, the narrator also perceives how Peter left his power with love

> Amonges foure vertues, the best of alle vertues,
> That cardinales ben called and closyng 3atis
> There crist is in kyngdome to close and to shutte
> And to opne it to hem and heuene blisse shewe;
> Ac of the cardinales atte Courte that cau3t of that name
> And power presumed in hem a pope to make,
> To han that power that Peter hadde, inpugnen I nelle . . .

[103-09]

A pun based on the derivation of the word *cardinal* (*cardo* = hinge) becomes a double pun on the title of the Cardinals of Rome; in this way a figure for the relationship of the cardinal virtues to heavenly reward subsides into papal reality. The narrator moves from a word through its associated meanings to orders associated in thought, though as he views this world in the Prologue, perhaps merely thought to be associated. His movement through associations is so condensed, so fast, so allusive, that it seems at once inevitable and capricious, at once controlled and uncontrolled. Its effect is simultaneously to dissociate these orders and to relate them.

Instead of rationalizing this effect and thereby distorting the reality he presently discerns, the narrator begs off because he "can and can nau3te of courte speke more" (111). From the papal court he turns to the right interaction of the king with the commons. As before, his reflections again come to focus on the relation of words to actions—"*Dum rex a regere dicatur nomen habere, / Nomen habet sine re nisi studet iura tenere*"—until they lead to the maddening irony, the duplicitous meaning, of words in themselves: "*Precepta Regis sunt nobis vincula legis*" (141-42, 145).[1] Throughout the Prologue, the narrator's associations persistently make a kind of sense, but he does not stop to make sense of them for us. If we try simply to rationalize his associations, we fail to account for the abrupt interruptions, the apparent tangents, the dramatic leaps in time, space, and context which characterize the surface of the Prologue, making it seem both experiential and erratic. Overlooking these, we miss what makes Langland's Prologue distinctive.

At the beginning of Passus I, Lady Holy Church descends from her castle and addresses the narrator as a dreamer: "Sone, slepestow; sestow this poeple" so "bisi . . . abouten the mase?" (5-6). Like the Prologue itself, her comment is curiously double-edged, on the one hand suggesting that in

sleep the Dreamer really can see what the world is about (Do you sleep; do
you see them?) and on the other, that in sleep he really cannot (Do you
sleep; don't you see them?). The Dreamer replies with an apt, if simple,
question of his own which comprehends his experience to this point and, I
should think, the bemused reader's as well: "what is this to mene?" (11).
The problem of meaning, interwoven with that of morality in the Prologue,
becomes explicit in Passus I, and in the Passūs that follow, the narrator undertakes an often bewildering search for truth, in every sense a search for the
reality of the word. This is not a search just for words, still less for dogmatic
answers, but for awareness, the ability to know what words and traditional
answers can really mean, given human nature and the nature of this world.

The Prologue is the introduction to this search and the initial context of it.
There the narrative voice records a world with its eyes largely shut to the
values which have given it order, purpose, and meaning. At the same time
that voice expresses these values, sometimes directly but more often implicitly
through irony. Although the narrator plays a satirist's role in the Prologue,
he also dramatizes, relives, refuses, perhaps even fails to distance and to
rationalize his experience as a dreamer. The field of action in some sense
remains his own mind, his dream, the reflection in his mind of a world fast
sleeping. The satirist thus implies ideal possibilities yet makes them real by
weaving them inextricably into the sinful world his dream pictures; the
Dreamer realizes the way of the world in his dream, yet he realizes it,
ironically, in himself. The dream is his, its action also inside him. Half awake,
half asleep, half writer, half Dreamer, the narrator we hear in the Prologue
stays elusively in-between. The restless movement of his mind—or words—
depicts the waking-sleeping state of mankind, and as Lady Holy Church
seems to tell him, it is his own state as well (1.5–6). This is the state of awareness and bewilderment, of fragmentation and wholeness. As Lady Holy
Church observes, it is a question of seeing the way things actually are, a
vision that at this point makes profound sense—and makes none at all.[2]

The beginning of any poem has an intrinsic importance, and the beginning
of a long poem revised repeatedly, like Langland's, or projected and refined
for many years, like Spenser's, is likely to be especially careful. The dislocations of Langland's Prologue skillfully prepare us for a poem that will finally
make "Vnite" the explicit object of its search (XIX–XX). Like *The Faerie
Queene,* the whole of *Piers Plowman* is a search for *unified* meaning, for a
continuity of being and experience. It proves a search in which we begin to
see the reality of the word becoming relative.[3] We shall see the same process

in *The Faerie Queene* further advanced and more calmly developed, because in the later poem it is enshrined from the start in a more personalized belief of the sort which Langland has yet to discover. Before turning even to the first of Spenser's Books, however, we need a more representative sampling from the initial stages of *Piers Plowman*.

No other Passus of *Piers Plowman* duplicates the experience of the Prologue, nor once knowing the poem should we ever expect it to. Many Passūs consist of conversations between characters, or more exactly of discourses delivered by one character with others taking active and responsive parts. In this simple sense, the first Passus of the poem, an extensive exchange between Holy Church and the Dreamer, is analogous to numerous passages in *The Faerie Queene*, perhaps most memorably to the exchanges between Redcrosse and Despair or Redcrosse and Contemplation, but also to those between Duessa and Night, Guyon and the Palmer or Mammon, Britomart and Glauce, Calidore and Melibee. When such exchanges occur in either poem, the characters are stationary, and we listen primarily to the action of their voices. Inevitably, in poems such as these the role of the narrator comes into question.

If ever there was an occasion to tempt Langland to the affirmation of truth, it must have been when he let Lady Holy Church open her mouth, but the situation in which she is found and the quality of her statements in Passus I produce a different result. However minimally dramatic her conversation with the Dreamer is, the fact that it actually is an exchange is important, for it provides the setting, the condition of a double awareness within the dream. Yet the part the Dreamer's personality plays in realizing this condition in the early stages of the poem is easily overemphasized. The quality of his awareness, indeed the nature of his presence, will change significantly in the course of the poem, but in Passus I he is perhaps inevitably, and even rightly, something of a straw man. Our impression of what Lady Holy Church is— or says, which amounts to the same thing in this Passus—is nevertheless modified by her relation to the Dreamer. The relation between them is human, and that is its point. More than a name and something less than a person in Passus I, the Dreamer is on the dramatic level of the holy Lady herself, and our impression of him is similarly influenced by our impression of her.

When Lady Holy Church begins to utter her truth, the Dreamer does not at first know who she is, and without her help, it is worth noting, neither do we. His ignorance at least fleetingly touches our own. The Dreamer naturally recognizes the wisdom of the Lady's words but fails to identify its source. She does not appreciate at all what seems to her his obtuseness:

> Thanne had I wonder in my witt what womman it were
> That such wise wordes of holy writ shewed,
> And asked hir on the hei3e name, ar heo thennes 3eode,
> What she were witterli that wissed me so faire.
> "Holicherche I am," quod she, "thow ou3test me to knowe . . ."
>
> [1.71–75]

The humor of this passage is pointed. One reason the Dreamer does not recognize her immediately might well be that he has never seen her this way before. His recognition of her is gradual and touched with the slightly comic, slightly incredible dismay of a confirmed believer, or rather, of a believer who might have thought he was confirmed. His wide-eyed, wondering recognition makes us ask why he failed to know her sooner. Inadvertently he manages to cast her in an ironic light. Shortly thereafter, moved by knowledge of her, he succeeds just as well in casting that light on himself:

> Teche me to no tresore, but telle me this ilke,
> How I may saue my soule, that seynt art yholden?
> "Whan alle tresores aren tried," quod she, "trewthe is the best . . ."
>
> [1.83–85]

Lady Holy Church's reply gently exposes the worldy values which the Dreamer's stated alternatives suggest, yet its firmness also limits any impulse we might have had to associate ourselves exclusively with his point of view. As they continue to speak, her exasperation with the shortcomings of his comprehension increases: " 'Thow doted daffe,' quod she, 'dulle arne thi wittes; / To litel latyn thow lernedest, lede, in thi 3outhe' " (1.138–39); and as it does, the pace and complexity of her utterances increase as well.

Especially in view of the Dreamer's apparent need for clarity, the quality of Lady Holy Church's statements is puzzling. They are sequentially more difficult to follow, perhaps more associative, than most other sections of the poem after the Prologue. We nod in agreement when we read them, but after twenty or thirty lines we are likely to want her to retrace her steps, beginning to feel that we might have missed some connection. We need her to stop, to pick up the threads, and to tie them together more neatly. For some reason, she does not or else cannot, but then if she could, Passus 1 would really be the end of the poem. There would be no search.

Lady Holy Church holds forth at considerable length, speaking all but twenty-odd lines in a Passus of over two hundred. When she does break into the public address of a sermon, however, the change is immediately notice-able: "For-thi I rede 3ow riche haueth reuthe of the pouere; / Thou3 3e be my3tful to mote, beth meke in 3owre werkes" (173–74). Such a change brings to mind more explicitly the form Holy Church's message usually takes and the preacher she herself becomes in an actual social context. But it also reminds us that someone is reporting her words; it recalls the intrusive narrator of the poem who stands just behind her.

In Passus I Lady Holy Church is the repository of truth and the spokesman for it, the embodiment of a series of words, ideas, and associations that issue in recognizable phrasings and arguments. Her statements have a distantly remembered and—in view of the Dreamer's presence—an overheard quality. This results largely from the fact that they sound so familiar, like something we know, doubtless, but also like something we have actually heard in Scripture, prayer, or sermon before:

> Whan thise wikked went out wonderwise thei fellen,
> Somme in eyre, somme in erthe, and somme in helle depe;
> Ac Lucifer lowest lith of hem alle;
> For pryde that he pult out, his peyne hath none ende;
> And alle that worche with wronge wenden hij shulle
> After her deth day and dwelle with that shrewe.
> Ac tho that worche wel, as holiwritt telleth,
> And enden as I ere seide in treuthe, that is the best,
> Mowe be siker that her soule shal wende to heuene,
> Ther treuthe is in Trinitee and troneth hem alle.[4]
> For-thi I sey as I seide ere, bi si3te of thise textis,
> Whan alle tresores arne ytried, treuthe is the beste.
>
> [I.122–33]

A generation more frequently exposed to the teaching of working and wandering clerics would have found no fewer echoes in these lines than we.

There are process and growth in the course of Lady Holy Church's discourse, though they amount to a step (a *passus*), not an answer. She starts her counsel with the basic morality of temperance—"Mesure is medcyne"—enumerates biblical exempla, and talks of David, Christ, and Lucifer. Finally, with the Dreamer's somewhat inept prodding, she centers on love:

> For trewthe telleth that loue is triacle of heuene;
> May no synne be on him sene that vseth that spise,
> And alle his werkes he wrou3te with loue as him liste
> And lered it Moises for the leuest thing and moste like to heuene
> And also the plant of pees, moste precious of vertues;
> For heuene my3te nou3te holden it, it was so heuy of hym-self,

Tyl it hadde of the erthe yoten it selue,
And whan it haued of this folde flesshe and blode taken,
Was neuere leef vpon lynde li3ter ther-after
And portatyf and persant as the poynt of a nedle,
That my3te non armure it lette, ne none hei3 walles.
For-thi is loue leder of the lordes folke of heuene
And a mene, as the maire is, bitwene the kyng and the comune;
Ri3t so is loue a ledere and the lawe shapeth,
Vpon man for his mysdedes the merciment he taxeth.
And for to knowe it kyndely it comseth bi myght,
And in the herte, there is the heuede and the hei3 welle.[5]

[1.146–62]

The eye of lover, lunatic, and poet could hardly glance with more comprehension and compression from heaven to earth, from earth to heaven than
it does in this passage. This, the finest sustained poetry that Holy Church
utters, is "imagination all compact," a description the poem will cause us to
bear in mind. Her passage seems to be spoken in nearly one breath and over-
flows with verbal suggestion. It is not an easy passage to analyze because it
sees love as a continuous act. The passage treats of incarnation, incorporating
the inanimate with the personal and the material with the supernatural. In
it Langland uses words, as later he will use symbols more fully formed, to
achieve a process of realization.

The passage begins with the witness of Truth—a word used in every conceivable sense, God, reality, integrity—to the sovereignty of love, the
medicine for obduracy and the remedy for weakness and all other ills. Its
lines move easily, gracefully to the action of love in the Old Testament and
settle on the plant of peace, on Old Testament image which prefigures the
New. As described in the fifth line, the plant of peace is love, the most
precious of all the virtues and, with the Latin sense of virtue (*virtus*) present,
the most powerful and most efficacious as well. In the context of incarnation,
an act which in the third line extends to creation, the biblical image of a
plant suggests natural growth and historical origins: "alle his werkes he
wrou3te with loue ... lered it Moises for the leuest thing ... the plant of
pees."[6]

In the lines that follow these, the implanting and growth of love produce
a sense of love's copiousness—"heuene my3te nou3te holden it, it was so
heuy of hym-self"—and with good medieval logic, a sense of its heaviness,
too. Heaviness falls naturally to earth, to alloy, to the Incarnation.[7] But
heaviness also leads with breathtaking ease to lightness and to the power to

penetrate armor, high walls, human society, and heaven itself (154–58). Alloy, the mixing of a precious metal with a baser one, dilutes but paradoxically strengthens; a metallic image, likely to carry suggestions of hardness and heaviness, is transformed to suggest lightness and penetration: "portatyf and persant as the poynt of a nedle." Piercing, permeating love becomes a remedy for obstruction—for obduracy, fear, hostility, possessiveness, self-enclosure; it becomes an antidote to its opposites, armor and high walls, whatever their origin.

Lady Holy Church concludes that a natural knowledge of love, by God's might—indeed, by Love's power—commences "in the herte, there is the heuede and the hei3 welle." The heart is where the head, the leader, is and the head, Christ, where the heart should be. In the head is the source, and in the heart is the beginning, "the hei3 welle," but potentially there, too, is the high wall, the obstruction. Both possibilities are present in the echoing word-play of this line.

Lady Holy Church's speech is a perceptual drama, an act of seeing, and in it love is positively alive. The meaning and role of love will not be restricted to single definitions in her speech because she perceives love as a continuing process, or as I called it earlier, a continuous act. When she speaks, bearing witness to what "trewthe telleth," love exists, takes form, in her words or more simply, if you will, in the word. Her remarks about high walls and the high well are made to a Dreamer who was quick to recognize her wisdom but had begun to think that he had no natural knowledge ("kynde knowyng") of truth.[8] They suggest that the word used as it is in her speech might be a remedy for his obstructing obtuseness as well.

Impressed by the truths which Lady Holy Church utters, we can easily forget that she is Langland's creation. She belongs to the narrator's dream and has no personal subsistence outside it. She is one half of his experience in that dream, and the Dreamer is simply the other half. Her speeches embody an act of perception, and they read like a process of thought. When combined with the Dreamer's queries, they resemble an internal dialogue or debate or a dramatized meditation. Though projected into art and shaped by it, the exchange between Lady Holy Church and the Dreamer imitates what is essentially a process of understanding.

In Passus I the Dreamer represents in a simplified and more rational form the narrator's confusion, instability, and sense of loss and indirection in the Prologue. His responses frame Lady Holy Church's, showing at once how accessible and how inaccessible her truth is. She embodies, and therefore is, an act of creative recollection made self-consciously and honestly by the narrator of the Prologue. In this act he reaches out to recover a touchstone in a new, or perhaps merely in a renewed, light. But he touches it without turning his back on the other half of his experience in the Prologue and, indeed, of his present condition, the wandering, wondering Dreamer, half awake, half asleep. The narrator's special stand-in, his chosen image of himself, the Dreamer is figuratively—spiritually and physically but not literally —like him. The one is awake and talking in a dream, the other in a dream while awake and writing. The boundary between them is no more distinct or constant than that between sleep and waking.[9]

2

Spenser: Book I

Coming from Langland's Prologue and first Passus to the first Book of
The Faerie Queene, we might easily feel that Spenser knows more clearly
what truth is and where it lies than Langland would ever have dreamed. This
impression arises largely from the fact that the action in Spenser's poem has
moved to a more professional and artificial stage. The plot is denser, more
continuous. The narrator's focus on it is steadier and characterization is
fuller. *The Faerie Queene* has a more deliberative rhetorical structure and
more narrative autonomy than does *Piers Plowman.* Langland's poem
impresses us as a more immediate and personal transcription of thought,
although his repeatedly revised work should be called "unstudied" only
with care.

The Faerie Queene opens with a formal invocation of its Muse and an
address to the reigning sovereign. Instead of telling us that he has had a
dream, the poet addresses his readers to tell about the kind of poem he is
going to sing. He announces a deliberate, if also an inspired, fiction in the
Proem without pretending that it is an event which actually happened to
him, and his announcement is rightly said to indicate the more self-consciously
literary role of a Renaissance poet. Assenting to this fact, however, we should
recall that Langland's adoption of the familiar medieval convention of a
dream poem effectively signals a literary mode with, at the very least, an
ambiguous relation to actual occurrences. Spenser's Proem is different,
though not so different in this last sense, from the opening of *Piers Plowman.*

As his Proem suggests, Spenser's relation to his fiction when the cantos of
Book I begin is also different but not incomparably different from Langland's. He steps farther, though neither entirely nor always to the same
extent, behind his characters; if anyone dreams in this Book, it is Redcrosse.
The action of the mind is centrally present in Book I, but it is less directly
and immediately presented as the poet's. Yet it is easy to overlook the fact
that Spenser's Proem does a little more than identify a poet now turning in

good Vergilian tradition from pastoral to epic.[1] This fact becomes evident
when we try to talk about its first lines with someone who has never read,
perhaps never heard of, *The Shepheardes Calender*. For a reader who knows
the earlier poem, these lines have a more personal and immediate dimension.[2]
Slight, indeed conventionally personal in the first Proem, this dimension is
also actual in view of *The Shepheardes Calender*. It is a dimension that will
become increasingly vital in *The Faerie Queene*, particularly toward its close.

Spenser's pastoral beginning, to which he refers in the first Proem, parallels
the rustic background of the Redcrosse Knight which Contemplation reveals
to him in canto x. In other figurative ways this beginning corresponds to
the natural limitations Redcrosse experiences in Book I. Spenser's roots as a
poet lie in a pastoral poem which is finally tied to the natural order to an
obvious extent (January, February, and so on) that *The Faerie Queene* is not.
Although *The Shepheardes Calender* intimates an order beyond the merely
natural, it consistently backs away from realization of the power this higher
order implies, and is therefore limited.[3] Spenser reminds us of his pastoral
beginnings even as he turns from pastoral to epic in the Proem to Book I,
and then proceeds to use pastoral imagery arrestingly in the very first canto,
when he describes Error's attacks and Redcrosse's weakness—the inherent
weakness of Everyman's nature—in terms of the natural cycle and natural
world. In at least a qualified sense, his description signals his own involvement
in these events. In later Books, most clearly in Book VI, Spenser employs
pastoral more extensively to explore the potential for strength, as well as
for weakness, in human nature. Here, too, in a way provocatively similar to
Langland's practice, the poet as Colin Clout, his pastoral persona, has a
role inside the fiction itself, when on Mount Acidale the Graces appear to
him, if not in a dream, then in a vision.

The narrator of *Piers Plowman* is inside the action of his poem, for his
mind is its immediate field and the Dreamer who participates directly in its
action is explicitly identified first as an aspect, later as the determinant aspect,
of him, namely Will. In the first Book of *The Faerie Queene*, the poet's
presence takes another form, but it is a form significantly comparable to
Langland's. In fact, *Piers Plowman* offers an unusually pertinent example of
the dream tradition which informs Spenser's practice throughout *The
Faerie Queene* and especially in Book I. This tradition is present both in his
narrative posture and in the inner, remembered quality of experience
which is characteristic of the poem. It is further noticeable in the fact that
this quality and Spenser's narrative role are not at crucial moments easily
separable.

When Spenser's narrative role is mentioned, most of us probably think of the brief introductions to cantos where as guide or reflective commentator he is likely to address us directly, much as he does in the first Proem.[4] This is his most obvious and most public role, and it is one with some parallels in Langland. Awake, Langland's narrator tells us at the beginning of Passus I, "What this montaigne bymeneth and the merke dale / And the felde ful of folke I shal ʒow faire schewe" (1–2); or he treats us at some length to his reflections on the Pardon Scene, again addressing us directly. The very fact that both poems have varying narrative postures within them is worth remarking. The waking voice or the voice addressing the audience directly is important in both, but it will not be my major interest except when its tones start to mingle with those of other voices, particularly later in the poems.

Another voice, a narrative presence which enters the fiction, is my immediate concern. In reading *The Faerie Queene,* we sense this presence subtly more often than we meet it directly or with sudden force, but it is close enough to the surface of the fiction to appear suggestively in Redcrosse's battle with Error and more unmistakably in his descent into hell, and even to break into the middle of the fiction, as it does in the tenth canto of Book I and with redoubled energy and insistence in later Books. In *Piers Plowman,* characters and situations, verbal, figural, and rhythmic surfaces, display a freedom (occasionally a license) which the mind effects on its own terms; a similar freedom touches the heart of Spenser's poem. As in *Piers Plowman,* its expression varies as the poem develops.

Such freedom characterizes the narrator's presence within his fiction in Books I and II, where it accounts for the disembodied quality that his voice generally affects. The narrator of these Books sets his characters moving as if to have their own experiences and so define their fates, but we soon notice, indeed eventually have to notice, his voice modulating itself into their experiences and his presence shaping itself to theirs. I have said earlier that the relationship of narrator and characters in Langland's and Spenser's poems is simply closer, one of greater mutual interdependence, than it is in more purely dramatic narratives, like Chaucer's; it makes for a more pervasive narrative presence but for one less explicitly individualized than his. Spenser's narrative presence in Books I and II shares something of Langland's ventriloquism, while it remains generally less obvious and more self-effacing—in fact less willful—than Langland's.

It is this narrative presence which makes the initial event in *The Faerie Queene* perceptual. Once Redcrosse and Una have been introduced and their quest identified, they encounter the rainstorm that "enforces" them to take shelter in a wood. Their forward movement is for a moment suspended, while the narrator describes the landscape they are to enter:

> Enforst to seeke some couert nigh at hand,
>   A shadie groue not far away they spide,
>   That promist ayde the tempest to withstand:
>   Whose loftie trees yclad with sommers pride,
>   Did spred so broad, that heauens light did hide,
>   Not perceable with power of any starre:
>   And all within were pathes and alleies wide,
>   With footing worne, and leading inward farre:
> Faire harbour that them seemes; so in they entred arre.
>
> [I.i.7]

The narrator's description becomes an integral part of their action by transforming its meaning. With these lines the landscape deepens; the poetic surface becomes densely suggestive, attracting our attention and drawing it to the wood. These qualities result largely from gratuitous elaboration, beginning in line 4 and culminating in the second half of the penultimate line: "leading inward farre." This phrase has a particularly haunting resonance, in part because it is not truly end-stopped, and in part because it is so clearly irrelevant to the simple fact that Redcrosse and Una have to get out of the rain.

A spiritual dimension becomes potential in the fifth line—*heauens light*—and the purely natural and innocent meaning of *pride* in the line before, namely, "prime," "flowering," "splendor," becomes potentially sinful and similarly shades our reading of *loftie trees*.[5] The negative suggestions enforced by the rhyme linking these lines seem all the more deceptively ominous given the fluency of these verses: balanced phrases, an absolutely regular metre, alliterative connections between the two lines. Yet the negative suggestions of *pride* are triggered retroactively (if almost instantaneously) by *heauens light,* not because we have been imperceptive, careless, or unregenerate readers, but because we had no particular reason and no real right to invoke the negative meaning earlier. Narrative vision, like Redcrosse's and Una's, is here limited, allied to sequence and to experience. As readers, we also have to suspend suspicion, not to mention judgment, until we reach the phrase *heauens light,* and this is no more than unmistakably suggestive. It surely is not so precise in intention as the phrase *God's light* would have been.

The final clause of this stanza puts an end to these dilemmas of perception. The narrator turns from surveying the wood to focus directly again on Redcrosse and Una and reminds us rather sharply of their need for action: "so in they entred arre." So simple, so decisive, so quick, this clause heavily echoes the sound and the rhythm of the penultimate line—"and leading inward farre." With these echoes Redcrosse and Una enter a new context. An altering veil of meaning has fallen over the figures we watch. As they enter the wood, their progress thus participates in its significance. If we cannot say simply that this stanza expresses the action of the poet's mind, we surely can say that its lines contain the result of his narrative presence.[6] They replace the participation of the narrator in a dramatic or personal role, and yet they express the mind perceiving. The landscape they describe becomes a realization about the world and about the very nature of experience in it.

The narrative in this stanza conveys the impression that Redcrosse and Una are getting into more than they know when they enter the wood; at the same time it reminds us that they need shelter—indeed, that they have enough sense to come in out of the rain. As they pass through the catalogue of trees in the next two stanzas, it becomes clearer that they have entered a wood latent with meaning but a meaning they do not, or cannot as yet, grasp.[7] It is in its present form not fully accessible to them, no more than it was to us on first reading. In these stanzas their carelessness is a matter of omission rather than of conscious rejection, a lack of constant direction rather than the wrong direction. They are in a wood of human possibilities rather than choices, and they are experiencing an emblematic landscape, a topos, instead of being primarily engaged in decisive action. Their one choice, if it is a free one, lies in their being in a wood in which the possibilities are all limited to the natural order, but we have seen how circumstantial—or "natural" in view of the rainstorm—that choice is.[8] Just by being there they invite temptation, and by lingering they make the invitation stronger, but in these stanzas they simply are not as yet in Error.

By stanza 10, Redcrosse and Una are wandering "too and fro in wayes vnknowne" to the extent that they "doubt, their wits be not their owne." Echoing the Bible and anticipating the House of Pride, the next stanza continues, "That path they take, that beaten seemd most bare," and it is this path which leads them to the cave of Error.[9] Yet even with the biblical echo, these two stanzas momentarily leave us asking whose fault it has been; exactly what and where they have done wrong; in short, why has it happened? It appears precisely the poet's point to bring these questions to mind. In stanza 28, at the conclusion of the battle with Error, we read that Redcrosse "with the Lady backward sought to wend; / That path he kept, which beaten was most plaine."

The final word is striking; despite the rhyme scheme, we are likely to anticipate the more expectable word *bare,* especially right after *backward* and *beaten.* With regard to the bare path that leads to Error's cave, the substitution of the word *plaine* suggests the whole question of vision in canto i: *bare* has in its context a more physical, phenomenal import than a perceptual one. (Paths are beaten bare by feet, not plain or clear.) Error herself is "wont in desert darknesse to remaine, / Where plaine none might her see, nor she see any plaine" (i.16). With Error defeated, we realize in this stanza that the whole incident has been a matter of perception, and it is in this light that we read the description of the Wandering Wood the next time.

DREAMER AND DREAM POEM

Before proceeding, it will be useful to reassert that the terms *poet* and *narrator* are virtually interchangeable as they apply to Langland's and Spenser's poems. Narrating is one of the poet's functions in these poems; the narrator or narrative presence (a more appropriate term for Spenser's early role within the fiction) is an aspect or extension of the poet. Emulating Spenser, I shall use *poet* in my general intention and *narrator* in my particular. The combination "narrative presence" asserts that both the poet and his characters are inside the poem, and that there are definable relationships between them important to its meaning.

The relationship of poet to poem becomes discernibly more intimate as Book I unfolds. His narrative presence becomes less indirect and impersonal than we have seen it to be in the first few stanzas, and as it does, the dream tradition bears more influentially on the narrative action, both the poet's and his characters'. Taking cantos from the first half of Book I, we can trace the transformation of the dream mode and observe the poet's more definite involvement in a kind of projection or, to use my earlier word, ventriloquism.

The character of the poet's involvement, his presence in the fiction of Book I, develops and deepens with Redcrosse's own. This is not to say that the *poet* suffers a fall and runs off with a whore named Duessa. Still less than Langland's narrator is to be simply equated with the rather stupid Dreamer of Passus I, and his poem literally equated with a dream, is Spenser's narrator to be equated with Redcrosse and Book I with the poet's personal experience. In the first half of this Book, however, the poet's ventriloquism does become more dramatic and personal. His presence within the fiction becomes more definite, more audible, more fully formed, although we do not as yet hear within these cantos what might be described as the poet's own voice, one that is not specifically or primarily narrative but is immediately experiential. That voice comes later, briefly in canto x.

It is hardly atypical of Spenser's poem that the most informative introduction to the subject of dreams in Book I should actually be found in Book IV,
where the narrator recounts Scudamour's experience in the House of Care.
In this instance, as in so many others, Book IV proves a close companion
piece to Book I:

> So long he muzed, and so long he lay,
>> That at the last his wearie sprite opprest
>> With fleshly weaknesse, which no creature may
>> Long time resist, gaue place to kindly rest,
>> That all his senses did full soone arrest:
>> Yet in his soundest sleepe, his dayly feare
>> His ydle braine gan busily molest,
>> And made him dreame those two disloyall were:
>> *The things that day most minds, at night doe most appeare.*
>
> [IV.v.43; my italics]

The narrator might as well be explaining Redcrosse's experiences in the
first two cantos of Book I, especially his dream of a false Una; the similarities
in Redcrosse's and Scudamour's physical and psychological conditions,
reinforced here by verbal echoes, strongly suggest that, at least in an in-
directly remembered way, he is.[10] The first two cantos of Book I include
Redcrosse's story from the time he battles Error until he abandons Una
(Truth, Unity) and, reasonably enough, then joins Duessa (*Duo-esse:* double
being, duplicity, falseness). In joining her he finds a fragmentation and
dislocation reminiscent of qualities we have already observed in the narrator
of Langland's Prologue. Redcrosse's battle with Error and his subsequent
dream at Archimago's hermitage in cantos i and ii of the first Book crucially
prepare him for the much greater dislocation, worse dream, and more engulfing illusion of the descent into hell in canto v. Like the poet and Redcrosse, we must proceed to the dreams of Book I by first looking more
closely at Error.

Pointed references to the natural world, inseparable from the dilemmas of
perception in Book I, intervene extensively in Redcrosse's battle with Error.
Like the arresting stanza which takes Redcrosse and Una into the Wandering
Wood, they not only attest to the narrator's special presence but do so more
clearly, more noticeably, and with more self-conscious artistry. Though
Redcrosse defeats Error, such references become in a sense the legacy of
battle, to recur in canto i as well as in later cantos. For these reasons, stanza
21 must be quoted in full:

As when old father *Nilus* gins to swell
    With timely pride aboue the *Aegyptian* vale,
    His fattie waues do fertile slime outwell,
    And ouerflow each plaine and lowly dale:
    But when his later spring gins to auale,
    Huge heapes of mudd he leaues, wherein there breed
    Ten thousand kindes of creatures, partly male
    And partly female of his fruitfull seed;
Such vgly monstrous shapes elswhere may no man reed.

This stanza, initially puzzling in its combination of repulsion and attraction, extends the description of Error's vomit from pamphleteers, Inquisitorial torturers, and eyeless toads, to the fertility of nature herself. The following stanza strengthens a grossly physical presentation of Error, which is now associated directly with the diabolic. From "her hellish sinke" the "feend" now disgorges

Her fruitfull cursed spawne of serpents small,
    Deformed monsters, fowle, and blacke as inke,
    Which swarming all about his legs did crall,
    And him encombred sore, but could not hurt at all.

The surprising suggestion in the final line is further developed in stanza 23:

As gentle Shepheard in sweete euen-tide,
    When ruddy *Phoebus* gins to welke in west,
    High on a hill, his flocke to vewen wide,
    Markes which do byte their hasty supper best;
    A cloud of combrous gnattes do him molest,
    All striuing to infixe their feeble stings,
    That from their noyance he no where can rest,
    But with his clownish hands their tender wings
He brusheth oft, and oft doth mar their murmurings.

Together, stanzas 21 (Nilus) and 23 comprise the first extended reference in the poem to the teeming world of nature, distorted in stanza 22 by Error. In the opening lines of stanza 21 we meet a description of natural fertility which, however qualified (pride, old age, slime), still offers too positive a point of reference for Error's "filthy parbreake" (1.i.20).[11] We confront a surprising shift in tone at the beginning of stanza 21, but as the stanza progresses we are made increasingly aware, not so much of the positive energies of natural generation, as of the ugly by-products, the dregs and excrescences, which such energies leave in their wake. This second perception begins in line 5 and by the final line leaves the source and primary cycle of natural fertility largely innocent. Stanza 22, specifically describing Error's actions and relating the simile of Nilus to them, then intervenes between Nilus's monsters and the shepherd's gnats, and it seems to attract to itself the repugnant excrescences of the natural world. What is left by stanza 23 are first the mere annoyance (v. 7), then the attractively tender delicacy (v. 8), and finally the soothing harmony of the natural world (v. 9). We are far from seeing the natural world itself as merely an evil in these stanzas; yet it is in terms of the natural cycle and the natural world that we are asked to see Error's attacks and Redcrosse's weakness.

It is in these same terms, finally and most arrestingly pastoral, that our attention is drawn to the self-conscious artistry of the poet's narrative presence. His extended epic similes in these stanzas increasingly call attention to themselves, even while they expand and actually transform the significance of Redcrosse's battle with the serpent-lady Error. Intervening in the action of battle, they are simultaneously and inseparably a part of its significance. They are at once an integral part of the narrative and an expression, even an assertion, of the poet's own involvement in its meaning.

The battle with Error generates and releases themes and images that recur in Redcrosse's visit to Archimago's hermitage, following immediately on the battle. Here numerous parallels between Redcrosse's waking experiences and the elements of illusion clearly indicate that Archimago is a force within as well as outside him. There are the various images of water near the hermitage, in the dream, and even in the narrator's comments about the ways of the world.[12] There is also the more explicit paralleling of Redcrosse and Morpheus, indicating that Morpheus is an aspect of Redcrosse's nature. Like Redcrosse, Morpheus is "drowned deepe / In drowsie fit." A trickling stream lulls him to sleep, and he mumbles softly, "As one then in a dreame, whose dryer braine / Is tost with troubled sights and fancies weake." Until Archimago's sprite wakes him, he slumbers on, "of nothing . . . [taking] keepe," cast in a daze by "a murmuring winde, much like the sowne / Of swarming Bees."[13] Some nine stanzas after the extended reference to nature in stanzas 21 to 23, we first hear Una counsel Redcrosse to get some sleep, because, after all, "The Sunne that measures heauen all day long, / At night doth baite his steedes the *Ocean* waues emong"; in another six stanzas, with Redcrosse "drownd in deadly sleepe," legions of sprites "like little flyes" begin to flutter around Archimago's head; and in three stanzas more, the winds murmur like bees around Morpheus. It all seems very natural.[14]

Nearly every instance cited in the preceding paragraph appears in the initial stage of sleep and illusion (1.i.36–44), and it is worth noting how carefully the poet establishes a relationship between Redcrosse and the dream in

this stage. Morpheus, as an aspect of Redcrosse and as the source of the
knight's false dream, explicitly connects natural sleep with illusion. Once
relationships between knight and dream, sleep and illusion, have been
established, Redcrosse experiences three more stages of temptation, or
illusion: the dream of Una surrounded by the Graces and crowned by Flora
(i.46–48), the apparition of a false Una (i.49–55), and the sight of false Una
with her squire (ii.3–5).[15] Each stage marks a gradual blurring of the distinction between the states of waking and sleeping and a concomitant weakening
of Redcrosse's rationally conscious will. By the final stanza of canto i, for
example, key words, such as *spright,* are in context ambiguous enough to
suggest that Redcrosse's battle with illusion may finally be self-defeating.
In this stanza the sprite troubled and the sprite troubling are not easily
distinguished:

> At last dull wearinesse of former fight
> Hauing yrockt a sleepe his irkesome spright,
> That troublous dreame gan freshly tosse his braine,
> With bowres, and beds, and Ladies deare delight:
> But when he saw his labour all was vaine,
> With that misformed spright he backe returnd againe.

Presumably the word *he* in the penultimate line refers to the "dreame," on
which it confers a personifying force; but with personification so weak,
pronominal referents so vague, and the pressures of a context in which
Redcrosse gradually gives in to illusion, we think momentarily in the penultimate line of Redcrosse himself. At several points, the lines concluding canto
i afford an instance of that blurring of dream with the sprite that embodies it,
and of sprite with Redcrosse himself which recurs increasingly as the temptation progresses. This is a technique Spenser uses again, notably in Book IV,
and one for which we shall find pertinent precedents in Langland's work
(see chapter 4).

If we consider again the end of canto i—"That troublous dreame gan
freshly tosse his braine"—we also find a blurring of the states of sleep and
waking: in fact, we begin to wonder precisely when Redcrosse woke up.
Are the first three lines of stanza 49, for example, part of the dream?

> In this great passion of vnwonted lust,
> Or wonted feare of doing ought amis,
> He started vp . . .

And if they are not, then in what sense can we say that Redcrosse is truly awake? The knight wakes to more and more fully illusory experiences; he wakes to find falsehood more and more true. Once he has clearly established a relationship between Redcrosse and the dream in earlier stanzas (36–44), the poet presents the deeper content of illusion in more dramatic or objective terms. To put it another way, the poem moves more and more deeply into an inner landscape; and as it does, the figures which people this kind of landscape become clearer, more complete, more "real" (the progression from Morpheus and the sprites to the false Una, to Duessa, for instance).

We read unequivocally near the outset of canto ii that Redcrosse wakens (ii.4, v. 4), but by this point we know that he wakens to an inner world—a world which is losing touch with realities outside its own self-reference, a world which will increasingly reflect and embody the Knight's own passions. Seeing the false Una and her squire, Redcrosse experiences the "bitter anguish of his guiltie sight," and when he flies from that sight, he is "flying from his thoughts and gealous feare"—in short, from himself (i.ii.6, 12). As before Redcrosse's dream, we now get a narration of his actions, but the meaning of these actions has been transformed by the intervention of the dream, and Redcrosse as actor has come to embody a new significance. In the course of Redcrosse's dream, spiritual and natural, moral and physical meanings—so precariously balanced before the dream—have simply broken apart. For Redcrosse there has been an inversion, a turning inward, of meaning: to dream seems now to be awake; and to waken, now to be in a deadly sleep.

"Sone, slepestow . . . ?" What Redcrosse could use now is the intervention of a Lady Holy Church, and in a sense—a sense less objective and institutional, hence more subjective and personal than Langland's—that is exactly what the Spenserian narrator gives him. In the first stanza of canto ii, the narrator pauses briefly on the threshold of sleep and waking. Right in the midst of Redcrosse's dream about the false Una, just before the final temptation, he remarks:

> By this the Northerne wagoner had set
> His seuenfold teme behind the stedfast starre,
> That was in Ocean waues yet neuer wet,
> But firme is fixt, and sendeth light from farre
> To all, that in the wide deepe wandring arre . . .

These lines, given prominence by their position at the opening of a canto, serve to locate Redcrosse's current experience with respect to the rest of the world, and especially to those realities he is most in danger of forgetting—those outside or beyond his own passions. The star, a recurrent image in cantos i and ii, here suggests resources both within and beyond nature, at once manly force and something "more then manly force." These lines also draw our attention, with the narrator's, specifically to the hour and to the physical heavens, and in this sense they stand outside the dream. They involve our drawing back from the dream precisely at the moment Redcrosse is giving in to it (1.i.55), and they suggest his need similarly to pull back.

Even in these lines, however, there is a movement from outer to inner, from the Ocean to the "wide deepe." Picking up the images of water that have woven both through Redcrosse's waking experiences and then through his dream, the narrator himself recapitulates the movement from outer to inner landscape in the first canto. He locates the "wide deepe" in its relation to the outer world and then to us all. From our first sight of Redcrosse in the Christian's armor, we of course knew that he was, in a general way, Everyman's surrogate. But it is only at the beginning of canto ii that, in a much more precise way, the narrator invites us to recognize the inner landscape as our own. This is not to say that we suddenly acknowledge Redcrosse's erotic fantasies as our own. The occasion remains specifically Redcrosse's; but his dream embodies an expression of the "wide deepe" that is familiar to us all, and at the beginning of canto ii we acknowledge this last fact explicitly. Our relationship to the events in canto i—like the poet's— has been dynamic and progressive. We are drawn in progressively as Redcrosse himself is, and it is progressively an inner landscape into which we are drawn.

The nature of this landscape emerges more clearly in canto v, particularly as this canto moves from Redcrosse, wounded by Sans Joy but resting in the House of Pride, to hell, where Sans Joy, defeated but not destroyed by Redcrosse, has been concealed. Events which precipitate the actual descent into hell remind us in a persistent, if elusive, way of passages we have read before in Book i—a woman, and a serpent, the Nile, the night, a knight in bed, light gleaming before a cave, a sharp cry of encouragement to Redcrosse, a body conveyed from sight and "fro me hid."[16] We are able only with conscious effort to account for this strange sense of recognition—the blurring of illusion with waking reality, the dilemmas of sight and perception, the persistent echoes in this canto of the Redcrosse Knight's earlier experiences, especially of his battle with Error and his dreams and illusions at Archimago's hermitage: "The things that day most minds, at night doe most appeare." Evidently they reappear relentlessly the next night, too.

Redcrosse's illusory experiences at Archimago's hermitage might be seen as dramatizing the shifting meanings present in the derivation and definitions of the word *dream* itself. This word has etymological ties with words like *deception, delusion, ghost, apparition, deceptive appearance,* and *illusion;* and sixteenth-century meanings of *dream* listed in the *OED* read like a description of the progressive stages of Redcrosse's illusion: [1] "A train of thoughts, images, or fancies passing through the mind during sleep; a vision during sleep; the state in which this occurs. *Waking dream,* a similar involuntary vision occurring to one awake. . . . [2] *fig.* A vision of the fancy voluntarily or consciously indulged in when awake."[17] All Redcrosse's experiences from canto ii to canto v have illusory qualities, but they are not dreams in the same sense that they are at Archimago's hermitage in canto i and at Lucifera's House of Pride in canto v. In a figurative and spiritual sense, we can say that Redcrosse is dreaming progressively from the time he abandons Una and begins to accept the reality (truth) of falsehood, but he sleeps literally and physically, as well as figuratively and spiritually, at Archimago's; if he is not quite so literally asleep at Lucifera's, the difference is a slight one, involving degree rather than kind of experience. If Redcrosse's visionary experiences begin with a waking dream in canto v instead of leading up to one, in this knight's condition the difference is only, and ironically, natural.

We know that Redcrosse is in bed in canto v, but we are not told explicitly, as we are in canto i, that he is asleep. It should not be surprising that we are less pointedly "in on it" in canto v, because we are already more so. Partly because the dream at Archimago's exists as a precedent and as a point of allusion, the illusory experiences in canto v are not, and do not have to be, so explicitly and literally a dream as in canto i. Indeed, if they were so explicit, they would suggest that the poem is presenting exactly the same level of experience as before. This is a principle of precedent and allusion, of using accretively significant parallels and echoes, which is familiar to readers of poems in the dream tradition, and it is one Spenser will use in various ways again.

The stanzas recounting Redcrosse's seeming victory over Sans Joy, which stand at the threshold of his dream in canto v, render illusion and reality, states of sleep and waking, almost indistinguishable (15–17). Redcrosse's bewilderment at the fading away of Sans Joy is never resolved; without transition it is just covered over by the adulation and buoyancy of the crowd, which as quickly fade into the solitary grief and inner agony of Redcrosse. Stanza 17 alone moves from a rhythm of triumphant affirmation (v. 1), to an emphasis on Redcrosse's sickness, and at last to a scene more befitting a deathbed (vv. 5–9) than the return of a hero.[18] This same stanza first sees Redcrosse "laid in sumptuous bed"; then, with a swift, smooth shift in perspective, his condition is compared to that of the "wearie traueller" who "strayes," of all familiar places,

By muddy shore of broad seuen-mouthed *Nile*,
Vnweeting of the perillous wandring wayes,
[And] . . . meet[s] a cruell craftie Crocodile . . .

[i.v.18]

Explicitly comparing Duessa's role to a crocodile's, this simile transfers the
focus of narrative attention from Redcrosse to Duessa, Sans Joy, and Night.
Throughout Book i darkness and night have been threats, and it is perhaps
inevitable that as we get to the pitchy, filthy center of Night herself, the
description of her "coleblacke steedes" and "darkesome mew" should seem
at least vaguely familiar. But when in stanza 21 we hear that Night, seeing
"*Duessa* sunny bright,"

. . . greatly grew amazed at the sight,
And th'vnacquainted light began to feare:
. . . .
And would haue backe retyred to her caue,

we hear distinctly parodic echoes of Error's initial response to Redcrosse in
canto i (14–16). Duessa, as we soon learn, is not only the daughter of Deceit
and Shame but also the distant offspring of Falsehood and Night herself
(26–27). Coming first into view right after Redcrosse and Una have been
"diuided into double parts" (ii.9), Duessa expresses the fragmentation of
Redcrosse's psyche. She makes a fitting emissary to bridge the gap between
Redcrosse's grief and agony to his dream, to the recovery of his Joylessness,
to hell.

The strongest echoes of Redcrosse's earlier experiences come, as before
in canto i, in the initial phase of his present dream, roughly stanzas 18 to 21
of canto v. This time, however, the relation of the initial phase to earlier
experiences is chiefly one of inversion and parody rather than one of parallel
and analogy. The first dream is a temptation, structured with four recognizable stages; the second, far more loosely structured, manifests a consuming
sickness within. The first dream has in Archimago and, beyond him, in
Error an origin at least partially external to Redcrosse; the second dream,
evoked by no single agent, has virtually none (unless it is the first dream).[19]
In terms of physical fact, Redcrosse wakes up twice in the first dream, and
he finally gives conscious consent to temptation; in the course of the second,
he never wakes up at all. If the second dream is a much more dangerously
engulfing experience, if it more nearly takes over the narrative surface and
erodes its rational structure, it emerges from deeper within the psyche. Sans
Joy embodies a Joylessness belonging to the surface of despair, the symptom

of a worse and deeper sickness. The dream and descent of canto v express this sickness within, a despair of which Redcrosse will not be fully conscious until he meets the actual figure of Despair in canto ix.

Recalling the buzzing insects and the "lumpish head" of a Morpheus quaking in canto i, we might be surprised by some of the tones and concerns evident in the exchange between Duessa and Night. This exchange combines elements of the grotesque with humane responses and traditional values. The result is parody, but of a deadly serious sort. In stanzas 20 to 21, Night is a beastly black shape and Duessa, a witch. The elevated rhetoric of Duessa's address to Night in the next stanza is not precisely what we might have anticipated:

> O thou most auncient Grandmother of all,
> More old than *Ioue,* whom thou at first didst breede,
> Or that great house of Gods caelestiall,
> Which wast begot in *Daemogorgons* hall,
> And sawst the secrets of the world vnmade . . .

This rhetoric, serving to assuage Night's fears, retains some of the haunting dignity of traditional addresses to an elemental power, and it contrasts sharply with the quality of exchange between Morpheus and the sprite in canto i: Archimago "bids thee to him send for his intent / A fit false dreame, that can delude the sleepers sent" (i.i.43). Values subsequently invoked by Duessa—"And now the pray of fowles in field he lyes, / Nor wayld of friends, nor laid on groning beare" (i.v.23)—draw on deep, even primitive, human responses as much, of course, as they draw on well-known classical texts. Duessa's "feeling speeches" move even Night to "some compassion" (24), at which point Night gives voice to the classic theme that overshadows the next four cantos to culminate in the presence of Despair:

> But who can turne the streame of destinee,
> Or breake the chayne of strong necessitee,
> Which fast is tyde to *Ioues* eternall seat?

The exchange between Duessa and Night continues so long, attracting to itself so many powerful statements, that we begin to feel we have reached an impasse. Duessa and Night do most of the talking, which is punctuated by no other action and by a bare minimum of narrative commentary. In terms of physical movement, the poem simply stops. Duessa and Night are the focus of attention, and their statements begin to look interesting for their own sakes, virtually without reference to what has preceded or to what will follow them.

The poem invites us to read these "feeling" speeches out of context—
"Vp then, vp dreary Dame, of darknesse Queene, / Go gather vp the reliques
of thy race" (v.24)—to hear their emotional appeal and respond to their
values. At the same time, however, we recall, or the narrator reminds us of,
the character of the speakers and the object of their debate (23, v.7; 24, v.8–9).
Then the debate strikes us as being out of its narrative context, and their
statements, resonant with human sentiment, seem strangely isolated from
their customary moral authority. The debate conveys at once a sense of
familiarity and of irrelevance. Its effect is dislocating, and reading it we have
just enough time to forget pretty thoroughly about Redcrosse.

It is with a start that we are suddenly returned with Night and Duessa to
earth (v.27, verse 9) and to the presence of Sans Joy, earlier identified with
Redcrosse's condition and now, like Redcrosse, lying "Deuoid of outward
sense, and natiue strength":

> His cruell wounds with cruddy bloud congealed,
> They binden vp so wisely, as they may,
> And handle softly, till they can be healed:
> So lay him in her charet, close in night concealed.[20]

The last phrase for a moment de-personifies or unmasks Night. Through
the paralleling of situations and the sudden, double sense of the word *night,*
we are brought back to Redcrosse's despair in the night, which *is* this dream.
The next stanza describes Night and firmly locates her action on earth:[21]

> And all the while she stood vpon the ground,
> The wakefull dogs did neuer cease to bay,
> . . . .
> The messenger of death, the ghastly Owle
> With drearie shriekes did also her bewray;
> And hungry Wolues continually did howle,
> At her abhorred face, so filthy and so fowle.
>
> [I.v.30)

Coming between Duessa's debate with Night and hell proper, the final level
of the dream, this stanza is the closest parallel that we find to the opening of
the second canto, where the narrator located Redcrosse's first dream with
respect to the exterior world ("By this the Northerne wagoner had set . . . To
all, that in the wide deepe wandring arre"). In the present stanza, however,
we have no sense of a distinction between the landscape of dream and that
of the exterior world. Anticipating the setting of Despair in canto ix, this
stanza belongs to a wholly inner landscape and to a world of sleep. Here the

exterior world has been assimilated into the dream; indeed, it is just a different level within that dream. The narrator does not address us so directly now as he did at the opening of the second canto, and he does not invite us so explicitly to draw back from Redcrosse's immediate experience. His voice as an external commentator on the action has also been swept progressively into the dream.

After a stanza relating hell to earth—"there [living] creature never past, / That backe returned without heauenly grace" (I.v.31)—there follows the actual descent into hell and a description of the infernal landscape. At the "furthest part" of hell, Night and Duessa find Aesculapius's cave, and with him, at the very bottom of hell, we find the story of Hippolytus.

It is often remarked that the descent into hell closely imitates, indeed parodies, the descent in *Aeneid* VI. But parallels in landscape or ironic relationships between Aeneas's reasons for being in hell and Redcrosse's do not really tell us why such parody—and so much parody—should come precisely here. I should even more simply ask why canto v gives us a hell so markedly literary. In comparison with the dream in canto i, the reliance in canto v on a literary art more imaginative and less magical than Archimago's conjurings suggests a progression. The art in canto v is paradoxically less faked yet more artificial; it helps to shift our attention from the weaknesses and failures of our physical senses to the grander and more sophisticated delusions of our pride. In doing so, it raises yet another question: what about the Vergilian poet of the Proem to Book I of *The Faerie Queene,* who turned from pastoral to epic? As the poet's art so clearly recalls Vergil's in canto v, it perhaps signals a special involvement on his own part in this canto.[22]

The unmistakably classical character of hell's landscape (as before of Duessa's addresses to Night) serves to compromise the whole classical view—both its self-sufficient values and its forms. The same implication becomes explicit when noble and wicked classical heroes are heaped together in Lucifera's dungeon.[23] Descent to a Vergilian netherworld also suggests a realm of death far more real—because more fully elaborated and more clearly human—than do the references to "deadly sleepe" in canto i (36). Canto v more fully dramatizes such a phrase as "deadly sleepe," pushing the analogy of sleep with death further toward the final identification of the two terms in the speeches of Despair:

> Is not short paine well borne, that brings long ease,
> And layes the soule to sleepe in quiet graue?
> Sleepe after toyle, port after stormie seas . . .
>
> [I.ix.40][24]

The extended treatment of Aesculapius, interrupted by the story of Hippolytus, raises more explicit questions about the nature of hell's "furthest part" and the poet's involvement in it. At the end of stanza 36 we hear that Aesculapius has been imprisoned "in chaines remedilesse, / For that *Hippolytus* rent corse he did redresse." Then, before we have reason to suspect that the poem will treat Aesculapius at any greater length than the other overreachers, stanza 37 begins, "*Hippolytus* a iolly huntsman was, / That wont in charet chace the foming Bore," and for two more stanzas we read Hippolytus's story. The beginning of stanza 37, let alone the extension of this story for three stanzas, is startling: whose voice are we hearing? Even in the pastoral context with which canto vii opens, the poet will flash a narrative signal to introduce a similar digression: there, the stream from which Redcrosse drinks is enervating, and "The cause was this: one day when *Phoebe* fayre . . ." (I.vii.5). We find nothing comparable in the story of Hippolytus. Further, our awareness of the lack of transition is heightened by the fact that the story is presented in a plain, fast narrative mode. Put another way, we sweep into this story before we know it.

The story of Hippolytus expresses those complementary processes of suppression and emergence (control and lack of control) characteristic of Redcrosse's present condition. We come upon the story as part of a purely associative sequence, a display of imaginative virtuosity which is not responsible to any sort of rational structure. When the story is taken by itself, however, it displays a rapid and concise narrative surface. This surface reflects the relentlessness of Hippolytus's fate, even while strangely distancing its agony: his limbs were "Scattered on euery mountaine, as he went, / That of *Hippolytus* was left no moniment" (I.v.38). Going beyond an obvious allusion to classical story, the very introduction and treatment of Hippolytus's story are strongly reminiscent of Ovidian narrative: restless shifting from subject to subject or from story to story—the smooth surface movement of a story with violent passions welling below. Much more overtly than any earlier passage, the story of Hippolytus proves dislocating. We are startled at being switched still further into another world, startled by the fleeting impression that we are reading Ovid. We are led to question both the nature of the narrator's involvement in the story of Hippolytus and the relation of this story to Redcrosse.

As before in the dream of canto i, the specific occasion of illusion remains Redcrosse's; in canto v, however, we have already noted that the occasion itself is less specific and far more suggestive in motivation, location, and symbolism. The story of Hippolytus comments on Redcrosse's condition by expressing it directly. This story is so completely an expression, an embodiment, of Redcrosse's psyche, that a narrator in any way explicit (i.e. flashing narrative signals or even talking about his actual characters in the third person) has dropped from sight. The story of Hippolytus therefore comments on Redcrosse's condition only by being itself. It *is* his condition, and it is also a direct expression of the poet's narrative presence, far more direct than when Redcrosse and Una entered the Wandering Wood. It is the immediate, dramatic presence in the dream of an experiencing narrative voice. It reads *as if* it were a figurative transcription of personal experience. This is not to say that the story is such a transcription—except, perhaps, in the same sense that we might say Langland's whole poem is a dream, and his narrator, in a dream while awake and writing.[25]

The specific relation of Hippolytus to Redcrosse is appropriately suggestive and shifting. Consider in sequence the emotional elements of Hippolytus's story: "loue . . . to hate," "treason false," "gealous," "rage," "dread," "rash" (I.v.37–39). These responses are coupled with an emphasis on chastity and on the monsters which rise from a "surging gulf." It is clearly possible to take the story in two ways. On the one hand, Redcrosse, like Hippolytus, is "too simple and too trew" (I.ii.45); he is the chaste victim pursued by monsters, and in his eyes Una is lustful, untrue, treasonous (cf. I.vi.2). On the other hand, Redcrosse is lustful, faithless, rash, jealous, wrathful, and Una is the chaste and innocent victim threatened by the monstrous forces of a hostile world. It is supremely ironical that the "double parts" of Redcrosse and Una should be thus united—or rather, should impinge upon one another at the bottom of hell. This netherworld mirrors unity and wholeness with the distortion of parody.

The story of Hippolytus intervenes on the road to lust, defeat, and total despair (I.vii–ix). As we notice in the story elements of fear, guilt, torment—self-inflicted or inflicted by an outside force—and of agonizing destruction and fairy-tale cures, these elements keep realigning themselves into new combinations. We are not supposed to be able to fix these shifting combinations into a single rational structure, commentary, or judgment. Approached from a slightly different angle, for example, the story of Hippolytus becomes a psychomachy. In this case Una becomes irrelevant to the story, and Redcrosse takes all the major roles: the raging, wrathful Theseus; the lustful, treasonous, tormented Phaedra; Hippolytus, too simply chaste.

Seneca's *Hippolytus* is not the only source for Spenser's treatment of the story, but it illustrates this last point most clearly.[26] It is difficult not to suspect that Seneca's play informs Spenser's presentation of an interior world when we hear Theseus's response to news of his son's innocence: "while, as stern avenger, I was punishing an unreal crime, [I] have myself fallen into true guilt. Heaven, hell, and ocean have I filled up by my sin." Or even more, when we hear the exchanges between Phaedra, tortured by a lawless passion, and her Nurse: " 'No rest by night, no deep slumber frees me from care. A malady feeds and grows within my heart, and it burns there hot as the steam that wells from Aetna's caverns ' . . . ' [But] what of the ever-present penalty, the soul's conscious dread, and the heart filled with crime and fearful of itself?' " Oppressed by the fatal curse of her parent Pasiphaë, Phaedra, like Redcrosse, gradually gives in to her passions. She tries to imply that there is a relentless logic and a dignified resignation in her surrender, but her logic is false, and her resignation misleading. Both serve to mask the despair which now festers beneath her calmer questions: "What can reason do? Passion has conquered and now rules supreme."[27] If we can say that in a perverse sense Redcrosse's experiences touch Una's in Spenser's story of Hippolytus, we can also say that in this story Redcrosse catches up with his fragmented self. In any case, it is obvious that within the context of Book I the elements of Hippolytus's story invite several readings, and the narrator, our customary guide, here withdraws from an interpretive role in favor of a role that is more directly experiential.

THE POET

In *Piers Plowman,* Lady Holy Church's words about love serve as a touchstone for the entire poem, but *The Faerie Queene* is a more autonomously narrative work, both less compactly conceptual and less abstractly verbal than Langland's, and no single short passage serves adequately as a touchstone corresponding to Langland's first Passus. Book I is full of passages that will echo and reëcho through the changing contexts of *The Faerie Queene,* as we shall see more fully later on. At this stage, however, we need a third passage from Book I which relates, perhaps more closely than any other, to Passus I of *Piers Plowman,* and it comes in the tenth canto.

Despite a conceptual similarity to Spenser's Una, Lady Holy Church's role has a more striking resemblance to Contemplation's, the figure whose counsel concludes Redcrosse's trip to the House of Holiness. Once Redcrosse finds Contemplation, the significance of both these characters evolves as their relationship alters. Their spoken exchange also realizes a perceptual act involving the meaning of symbols. For Redcrosse, we might say that their exchange is an immediate process of self-definition; for the narrator it actually becomes a dramatized meditation.

Unlike Langland's first Passus—or even Spenser's first and fifth cantos—canto x is not a dream. The basic fictional situation is unalterably different. The narrative framing of Redcrosse's conversation with Contemplation is far more extensive than is the framing of Passus I, and the narrator's control of his two speakers is more direct and explicit. The phrase *quoth he* (or its equivalents) enters either character's speech like a refrain. This phrase is so common elsewhere in *The Faerie Queene* that we tend, and in fact try, to ignore what might at first seem its annoying insistence in this passage. I am not trying to suggest that the narrator's presence is much more than subliminal when Redcrosse and Contemplation speak, but to point out that it is more noticeable and explicit, more concentrated, than *in* many other arresting conversations—for example, that between Duessa and Night and that between Guyon and Mammon. It is a kind of presence which, we shall see, should not, out of misplaced critical politeness, go unnoticed. There is plenty of precedent for it in Langland.

Spenser's tenth canto provides the conditions not only of a double awareness in the exchange of Redcrosse and Contemplation, but also of a triple awareness, for it includes the narrator himself in a role that frames, and briefly even surpasses, his characters'. When the waking narrator who quickly introduces Langland's first Passus and whose voice blends into both Lady Holy Church's and the Dreamer's is added to these two characters, the conditions in this Passus are at least superficially analogous to those in canto x; but Spenser's narrator realizes them much further. He introduces, twice qualifies, and so helps to define, Contemplation. He also reveals himself as an active participant in the canto before Contemplation ever appears. As so often in Book I, he is inside Redcrosse's experience in this canto, and also in some ways outside it. But this time, in taking an active role within the canto, he eventually moves beyond that experience; this time he moves beyond the specific occasion that belongs to Redcrosse.

Introducing the tenth canto, the narrator assumes his customary public role. As a commentator he points the significance of Redcrosse's progress thus far: "What man is he, that boasts of fleshly might, / And vaine assurance of mortality . . . If any strength we haue, it is to ill, / But all the good is Gods, both power and eke will." Then he begins to describe Redcrosse's spiritual rehabilitation, keeping the knight silent and in the background for nearly two-thirds of the canto. Redcrosse is primarily acted upon in this section of the canto, because Holiness is something he no longer embodies and it has to be restored, given back, to him. At the beginning of the canto the narrator does not locate himself within Redcrosse's consciousness because Redcrosse is not properly conscious of virtue. The narrator reports far more than he participates in the early operations of Faith, Hope, and Charity on the knight. When characters such as these are introduced, they are abstractions external to Redcrosse's condition. In fact, they do not even recognize

him at first: "They seeing *Vna,* towards her gan wend" (x.15). After the
bewitching rhetoric of canto ix, the narrator is reaffirming truth in this canto.
Redcrosse has to learn his theological lesson before the dragon fight, and it
could not be more fitting emotionally and better motivated psychologically
than for him to learn it right here. These considerations weighed, a large
proportion of canto x nevertheless remains an exposition of truth, much like
a sermon, and until Contemplation's appearance, it has less perceptual life
and dialectical movement than most other cantos. Its form differs from that
of Langland's first Passus, but reading it we can still be reminded of the
earlier portions of Lady Holy Church's speeches:

> The moste partie of this poeple that passeth on this erthe,
> Haue thei worship in this worlde, thei wilne no better;
> Of other heuene than here holde thei no tale.

[1.7–9]

As Caelia addresses Una early in canto x, the narrator's voice quietly
blends into hers:

> . . . So few there bee,
> That chose the narrow path, or seeke the right:
> All keepe the broad high way, and take delight
> With many rather for to go astray,
> And be partakers of their euill plight,
> Then with a few to walke the rightest way;
> O foolish men, why haste ye to your owne decay?

[I.x.10]

Caelia's direct address in the alexandrine differs only slightly from Lady
Holy Church's shift into the address of a sermon: "For-thi I rede ȝow riche
haueth reuthe of the pouere" (1.173); and like that shift it brings to mind the
narrator who stands behind one of his spokesmen. The unhurried apostrophe
in line 9 resembles many other incursions of the narrator's own voice within
the cantos of *The Faerie Queene,* incursions often more surprising because
they do not find, or are not meant to find, so ready a spokesman as Caelia
present in the fiction. But canto x reveals fundamentally and distinctly
another form that the narrator's role takes in Spenser's poem, and as the
canto proceeds, that form becomes increasingly noticeable and engaging.

When the narrator describes the Corporal Works of Mercy, he seems about
to turn canto x into a formal meditation. Describing the fourth and fifth
works, he speaks of God's forgiving "vs" and of "our dying day"; then he
turns to address mankind directly: "O man haue mind of that last bitter

throw; / For as the tree does fall, so lyes it euer low" (40–41). As he speaks
of the sixth work, he refers directly to himself—"Ah dearest God me graunt,
I dead be not defould" (42). Here the poet appears to address God in a
moment of formal prayer. With the subsequent introduction of Contemplation, his role becomes visionary and, inevitably it would seem, more spontaneous and personal. Recollecting three mountains on which inspiration
was realized, he compares the Mount of Contemplation to them, first to
Mount Sinai and then to Olivet and Parnassus. The Mount of Contemplation
is such a one,

> . . . as that same mighty man of God,
> That bloud-red billowes like a walled front
> On either side disparted with his rod,
> Till that his army dry-foot through them yod,
> Dwelt fortie dayes vpon; where writ in stone
> With bloudy letters by the hand of God,
> The bitter doome of death and balefull mone
> He did receiue, whiles flashing fire about him shone.

> Or like that sacred hill, whose head full hie,
> Adornd with fruitfull Oliues all arownd,
> Is, as it were for endlesse memory
> Of that deare Lord, who oft thereon was fownd,
> For euer with a flowring girlond crownd:
> Or like that pleasaunt Mount, that is for ay
> Through famous Poets verse each where renownd,
> On which the thrise three learned Ladies play
> Their heauenly notes, and make full many a louely lay.
>
> [I.x.53–54]

His comparisons suggest a fullness of meaning and an inclusiveness of
reference that have previously been lacking in canto x, but we get only a
glimpse of this fullness.[28] Almost immediately the vision retracts; the poet
pulls back from this experience, and we hear an apology so simple and so
humble that it might strike us as being abrupt and a little flat.

He says that he will not describe the New Jerusalem, the ultimate site of
vision, because no "wit of man can tell" it; for it is, he adds, "Too high a
ditty for my simple song" (55). A simple song is not what the Proem to
Book I led us to expect, nor what the descriptions of Sinai, Olivet, and
Parnassus actually are. In these descriptions we find an unexpected burst of
insight and imagination that must then be restrained or simply ceases. We

hear a new voice, specifically identified as the poet's ("Too high a ditty . . .
my simple song"), which outstrips the special guidance of the character
Contemplation, and we become aware of a vision that breaks out of the
form of canto x. The suddenness, extent, and evocative richness of this
vision prefigure a unity and complexity of experience at odds with the
precise and abstract outlines still dominant in this canto.

The poet's description of these mountains and the loss of power which
follows it introduce Redcrosse's preception of the New Jerusalem and
Contemplation's comments on it. Both Redcrosse's and Contemplation's
views are apparently restricted to the limitations the poet has perceived, or
else their views in some way enable him to avoid these limitations, as once
more he modulates his personal voice into his agents' and his personal vision
into theirs. Both views mark the renewal of a participation in the knight's
experience which is more self-effacing for the poet. At the beginning of his
exchange with Redcrosse, Contemplation expresses himself in a curiously
pastoral idiom: "Now are they Saints all in that Citie sam, / More deare
vnto their God, then younglings to their dam" (x.57). Contemplation's
rather witty pastoralizing of Revelation at this point, immediately before
Redcrosse himself starts to speak for the first time since canto ix, brings him
down toward earth, makes him sound more accessibly human, brings him
closer to the knight. Yet the pastoral idiom comes as a mild surprise; it
seems a little understated, even quaint, coming from Contemplation at
precisely this point. The poet's imagined Mount, just three stanzas earlier,
is noticeably fuller and more affective than Contemplation's vision.[29]

The narrator's initial presentation of Contemplation, which precedes this
character's first words, also qualifies him. The narrator exalts the power of
Contemplation's spirit, as "quick and persant . . . As Eagles eye, that can
behold the Sunne," and acknowledges the completeness of his self-sacrificing
devotion, but at the same time he lays a singularly heavy stress on his physical
decrepitude. Contemplation is deficient in some aspects of humanity. His
"earthly eyen" are "blunt and bad"; they have lost their "kindly," or natural,
sight. More remarkable, Contemplation's is a "carcas long vnfed."[30] Seeing
Mercy and Redcrosse approach him, Contemplation "At their first presence
grew agrieued sore," and "had he not that Dame respected more . . . He
would not once haue moued for the knight." For a moment the narrator
allows Contemplation's unkindly sight to seem a little unchristian. It strikes
us as being too single-minded, perhaps inhumanly so. Contemplation's
lying in a "litle Hermitage" by a chapel, his bad eyesight, his age and resemblance to "an Oke halfe ded" start further complicating eddies of remem-
brance for the reader of Book i. They recall Archimago's little hermitage by

a chapel, Ignaro's blindness, Orgoglio's club, and the whole theme of fleshly nature, earlier connected with Fradubio, and thereafter with the imagery of trees in Book I (cf. the Wandering Wood and even Arthur's helmet).[31] Contemplation is a salutary treatment for the ills of Book I but by himself no panacea. The narrator's qualifying treatment of Contemplation invites our seeing in him not an answer for Redcrosse but an essential step in reaching one (x.47–49).

Prior to Contemplation's presence and the subsequent brief occurrence on the mountain of the narrator's personal vision, there are few shadings and no depths in the surface of canto x: events and their significations are reduced to a single meaning, narrowed to a single plane. Narrative and fictional voices blend single-mindedly (10, v. 9). But as the voices of Redcrosse and Contemplation take over, they bring with them contradictory and ambiguous points of reference, sets of values, and even meanings of words. Half the time the two speakers talk on different frequencies, and while they do, the narrator withdraws to the background, yet signals his presence by the peculiar insistence of that phrase, *quoth he.*

Redcrosse speaks of his regard for "Ladies loue," and Contemplation counters with a dismissal of "loose loues." Redcrosse then desires to live apart from the world "whose ioyes so fruitlesse are," and Contemplation tells him that he cannot as "yit / Forgo that royall maides bequeathed care . . . Till from her cursed foe . . . [he has] her freely quit." Particularly coming from Contemplation, these statements leave us wondering whether Una is here supposed to be a lady or whether she is Truth, and whether the cursed foe is one dragon or all dragons. Temporal references, especially dense in these stanzas, only add to such blurring: "Thenceforth," "after all," "at last," "yit," "Till," "soone," "shortly" (60–64). The perspectives of time and eternity oscillate here enigmatically.

The exchange between Contemplation and Redcrosse is a moment of poise, of suspension, before Redcrosse discovers who he is (65) and returns to earth (68). Nothing, in a sense, is happening: the figures are just talking, poised on the Mount of Contemplation between two worlds. Their words point both ways; perspectives in stanzas 60 to 64 are about equally mixed. The passage belongs to a middle state, corresponding to no state of actual existence in the world (or in another world) but to an act of perception that achieves and expresses a resolution of doubt and fear.

While the words of Redcrosse and Contemplation dramatize this act, they have less ambiguous referents within the context of the poem. The "royall" maid refers not to Una as lady, love, or Truth but to what she has been in the poem so far, no one of these elements nor just their sum. Outside

the poem a Una might not exist any more than does a Lady Holy Church
(let alone a Piers Plowman), but within the poem Una symbolizes the unity
of these elements. She is seen both in process (as continuity) and, at least
briefly and incompletely, as an end. As a symbol she therefore suggests a
union of journey and destination, of process and end. In canto x, this union
inevitably appears more elliptical and enigmatic than in canto xii: the special
quest of Book I has yet to be accomplished; even this phase of the poem has
yet to be fulfilled.[32]

Like the first Passus of *Piers Plowman*, the exchange between Redcrosse
and Contemplation involves a process of self-debate. Revealing Redcrosse's
ordination to "a blessed end," Contemplation sounds almost enthusiastic:

> For thou emongst those Saints, whom thou doest see,
> Shalt be a Saint, and thine owne nations frend
> And Patrone: thou Saint *George* shalt called bee,
> Saint *George* of mery England, the signe of victoree.

> [I.x.61]

Redcrosse's reply brings us back rather sharply to the present, to the knight's
state of emotional response, to the way a man in Redcrosse's situation must
feel: "Vnworthy wretch (quoth he) of so great grace." Following immediately Contemplation's prophecy of sainthood, these words emphasize
Redcrosse's feeling of unworthiness so heavily that for a moment they seem
an overstated response, a reply that is strangely out of sequence.

Conversely, Redcrosse's response to Contemplation's dismissal of "loose
loues" seems at first reasonable—"O let me not (quoth he) then turne
againe / Backe to the world, whose ioyes so fruitlesse are"—until we realize
that Redcrosse is not responding to what Contemplation has actually said:
it is Redcrosse, not Contemplation, who identifies "loose loues" with the
joys of this life. Upon reading further, we realize that Contemplation, seen
first by Redcrosse as an escape from human conditions and from oneself,
is the knight's final temptation. Redcrosse's replies spring really from fear
of reinvolvement with life of the kind he has recently experienced:

> But let me here for aye in peace remaine,
> Or streight way on that last long voyage fare,
> That nothing may my present hope empare.

> [I.x.63]

It is to these lines that Contemplation replies, "That may not be," at least
not until you have "freely quit" Una "from her cursed foe." Apparently

Contemplation hits exactly the right note, for Redcrosse, his fears gone, instantly rejoins:

> Then shall I soone, (quoth he) so God me grace,
>   Abet that virgins cause disconsolate,
>   And shortly backe returne vnto this place,
>   To walke this way in Pilgrims poore estate.
>   But now aread, old father, why of late
>   Didst thou behight me borne of English blood,
>   Whom all a Faeries sonne doen nominate?
>
> [I.x.64]

Comprehension of the enigmatic terms and symbols Contemplation has used, and an acceptance of his own destiny, are implicit in Redcrosse's resolution. Quite simply, this is faith, and Spenser probably could not or did not wish to go any further in rationalizing it. After Redcrosse's hatred of the world and of himself—a hatred which led to despair in canto ix—it has taken the simplicity, austerity, and abstraction of canto x to lead him back to himself and to his purpose in the world. We could put it another way and say that he has had to get out of nature in order to get back into it. Now, in returning, he brings a new dimension.

Given Contemplation's effect on Redcrosse, we might look more closely at his means of achieving it. Contemplation appears first in the poem as a kind of signpost, the extreme manifestation of one pole in a clearly stratified universe—a world of ladders. He comes into relation with Redcrosse when he talks to him and when the knight begins to respond. Necessarily, in explaining to Redcrosse the meaning of what he sees, Contemplation relates it to the knight's experience: we can thus speak of a development of the meaning of Contemplation, a dilation of significance, a broadening of relevance. Finally, Contemplation does not so much explain as imply Una's significance to Redcrosse. This is the turning point in the whole exchange between Contemplation and Redcrosse, the point which leads directly to the knight's resolve. Contemplation perceives the spirit as it quickens nature —not merely a lady or Truth, but neither and both, a unity, Una herself. Originating in a universe that is rigidly hierarchical and opposed to mere nature, Contemplation finally reveals to Redcrosse the possibility of a unity of being.

As Contemplation becomes pertinent to the experience of Redcrosse, his own significance as a figure is affected. He shifts or develops, and implicit in this development is his own humanity. Put another way, with Redcrosse's gradual realization of his own destiny, Contemplation becomes more human. At the end of the canto, with Redcrosse's voice (and intelligence) now fully restored, Contemplation begins to sound for all the world like the kindly old shepherd or ancient retainer, even the Merlin, who reveals a secret of the hero's lineage: "For well I wote, thou springst from ancient race / Of *Saxon* kings . . ." (65). In Contemplation's development and relation to the knight we find a movement fundamental to *The Faerie Queene:* we see the supernatural permeating the forms of this life and a religious form permeating a romance one. We further see, as we did in the dreams of cantos i and v, medieval forms of thought and literary traditions reborn in a Renaissance poem.

Canto x is markedly impersonal at its beginning, but it is at the end of this canto that Redcrosse finds out who he is—*Georgos,* the man of earth, found by a Plowman in a furrow and raised by him "in ploughmans state to byde, . . . Till prickt with courage, and . . . [his] forces pryde, / To Faery court . . . [he came] to seeke for fame" (66). Redcrosse's development, like Contemplation's, participates in a single process of revelation that is fundamentally sequential and committed to time.

The poet, too, has participated in this process, and we can see the developing relationship between Contemplation and Redcrosse as a paradigm of his own relation to his poem. The poet who moved from pastoral to Faerie court in the Proem to Book I has evidently realized enough in Redcrosse's exchange with Contemplation to take his characters to the next stage. But the poet's distancing and even his backing away from his own vision, as in the stanzas of inspiration in canto x, will recur in *The Faerie Queene,* as they do in many of Spenser's other works and as they also do in Langland's poem. The poet's treatment of fear and doubt in canto x has already echoed the words of Night, or of a night (and a knight), in hell (I.v.43) and the words of Despair in canto ix:

> The lenger life, I wote the greater sin,
>
> . . . .
>
> For he, that once hath missed the right way,
> The further he doth goe, the further he doth stray.
>
> [I.ix.43]

And it will be heard echoing again from the depths of this poem—and, indeed, from the poet's mind. Perhaps in their recollection of Redcrosse's conversation with Contemplation, the final stanzas of the Mutability Cantos tell us most clearly where the poet was while his two characters spoke to one another. He refers in these stanzas to the sway of Mutability,

> Which makes me loath this state of life so tickle,
> And loue of things so vaine to cast away;
> Whose flowring pride, so fading and so fickle,
> Short *Time* shall soon cut down with his consuming sickle.
>
> [VII.viii.1]

These lines recall an earlier meditation, the one in canto x; and their verbal ambiguities (*loath,* a verb or an adjective; *vaine,* an adjective or an adverb)[33] reflect its dilemmas: its questions—"must I at last be faine, / . . . Ladies loue to leaue so dearely bought?"—its replies—"As for loose loues are vaine, and vanish into nought"—and its resolution: "Then shall I . . . shortly backe returne vnto this place."[34] The poet's final plea for a site of rest and vision, "O! that great Sabbaoth God, grant me that Sabaoths sight" (VII.viii.2), stirs even more powerful memories of the Redcrosse Knight's earlier plea:[35]

> O let me not (quoth he) then turne againe
>   Backe to the world, whose ioyes so fruitlesse are;
>   But let me here for aye in peace remaine,
>   Or streight way on that last long voyage fare,
>   That nothing may my present hope empare.[36]
>
> [I.x.63]

The knight's experiences in Book I reverberate through the remaining Books, much as the Dreamer's do in Langland's poem, and for much the same reason. For these poets allegory is a habit of mind and a way of thinking—if you will, a continuous act. Behind each character, though not always at the same distance, there is present in the fabric of their poems a single perceiving mind whose unifying consciousness of what has gone before enters new situations, enriching or darkening each new conceit.

The Faerie Queene is not a dream, though it is occasionally about dreams and has conventional qualities, whatever their origins, in common with them.[37] It is an image, a creative reflection in words, of life; and that is what *Piers Plowman,* for all Langland's feigning of dreams, is too. Spenser, like Langland before (and Shakespeare and Milton after) him, knows that the line between living and dreaming is not very distinct and is, perhaps, not real at all. For better and for worse, the line is relative, not absolute: "We are such stuff / As dreams are made on"—a harshly ironic reflection on our nature if we think of Redcrosse's false Una, or Langland's friars or Lady Meed, but an ideal reflection, a hope and a faith, if we think of the Faerie Queene or Piers Plowman, neither of whom appears in these poems except in a dream.

3

The Cave of Mammon and the Visio

The poet's posture, his relation to the poem, evolves both within and between every section of *Piers Plowman* and every Book of *The Faerie Queene*.
In both poems the narrator can recede from the foreground, appear briefly
in it as a commentator, or engage more directly in its action. He seems to
treat his story as he chooses, often with a disregard for formal consistency or,
if form is to be rigidly defined, then with a freedom from its imaginative
and intellectual restrictions. We might say that he manages his story as he
sees it and that he is found—as a character, as an allusion, as a voice—where
he sees himself.

In Passūs II through VII of the Visio or first section of *Piers Plowman,*
the narrator has with few exceptions the role of an observer and recounter of
dreams.[1] At least to appearances, his role is more passive than it is in the
Prologue and first Passus. He does not take so direct and outspoken a role
in the poem himself. Inside the dream, the Dreamer, his stand-in, stays
generally silent and still, though intently watchful. On the whole the narrator does not intrude directly in the dream action; he, too, stands to the
side, though he makes several notable exceptions, including himself, in the
Repentance of the Deadly Sins, and specifically as the Dreamer, in the direct
perusal of Piers's Pardon; he also disrupts the dream action vigorously in
Passus III, when he evidently cannot contain himself within it once Meed's
bribery takes the form of glazing friary windows.[2]

The narrator's "pilgrimage," his active search, properly starts with a
choice, rather than with an examination, and with the more personal and
interior action of the Vita de Dowel, the second section of the poem. It is at
the beginning of the second section when he meets two friars, the walking
(and waking) embodiments of Holy Church's teaching in the actual world,
that his choice is precipitated. The Visio, which precedes this choice, provides
the background for his hostility to the friars and the foundation for his
deciding to take a more active and interior role.

Lady Holy Church having had her say, the Visio turns to examine what
actually happens to conscience and reason when in various guises and in-

creasingly human forms they face the desires, especially the greedy and material hungers, of mankind. This section concentrates on what is wrong with society in general rather than with the particular self, and finds it in the cycle of wanting and wasting, of real and gross misuse, which characterizes human hunger and desire. The Visio views this cycle from a middle distance, somewhere between privileged knowledge and frustrating self-awareness, between satirical observation and sympathetic involvement, or, to put it more succinctly, between the righteous and the damned.

In these respects the Visio resembles the second Book of *The Faerie Queene*, a Book less tightly correlated to the acts of a single knight's psyche than Book I and specifically concerned, in the Cave of Mammon, with the lusts which feed materialism and corrupt the very foundations of life. The Faerie hero of Book II is a representative character, a symbolic presence, in ways that make him look like the watchful but rather passive Dreamer of the Visio. In the second canto of this Book, Guyon picks up the burden of human nature when he lifts Mordant's armor, and in the remainder of the Book he finds out what it means to have done so. Unlike Redcrosse, Guyon never experiences the willful betrayal of truth but instead explores the nature of the burden he adopts until he has reached into its depths and has exhausted the significance his human creator has given him.

The narrator of Book II is located less specifically inside the hero than is the case in the crucial sections of Book I. Guyon does not dream the Cave of Mammon, the parallel to Redcrosse's hell. It is not Guyon's function to reenact the biblical Fall as such, but to experience its debilitating effects and, in terms as merely human as possible, to resist them. The special companion of enlightened reason, not of religious truth, Guyon, like the Dreamer of the Visio, observes more than he initiates; he is more of a response and a measure than a cause. His story progresses from abstract, emblematic situations—the Castle of Medina, the fettering of Furor and Occasion—to those which embody a consciousness more deeply and complexly human.[3] Its movement, like that of the Visio, is dialectical and perceptually vital in this sense, and it precedes a further modification of narrative action in the Books which follow. Guyon's story is not the Dreamer's to the extent that the Redcrosse Knight's might at first glance seem to be, but its thematic emphases and development have so much in common with the Visio that they warrant our looking more closely at them both.

THE CAVE: "For stonde he neuere so styf he stombleth ȝif he moeue ..."

The Proem to Spenser's second Book signals a change of pace and a redirection of focus. The poet acknowledges that by some "this famous

antique history . . . th'aboundance of an idle braine / Will iudged be . . .
Rather then matter of iust memory." He avows the justness of recollection,
the exactness, rightness, and completeness of memory, present in his poetic
material and fends off short-sighted misjudgments of it. He points to the
recent discoveries of "th'Indian *Peru*," of "The *Amazons* huge riuer," and
of "fruitfullest *Virginia*" to suggest man's limited knowledge of the world
he inhabits. Though the poet refers here to real geographical places, he does
so to suggest the reality, or the justness, of Faerie itself. He will similarly
include America and India in the mythical domains of Guyon's elfin an-
cestors near the end of canto x. In the Proem the poet obviously plays with
other than geographical senses in which human awareness of the world is
limited. With both the physical world and Faerie in mind, he goes on in the
Proem to ask, "Why then should witlesse man so much misweene / That
nothing is, but that which he hath seene?" His wonder at man's failure of
wit reverses a question that Mutability will ask many Books later: "But
what we see not, who shall vs perswade?" (vii.vii.49); and it underscores
issues of sight and location, of reality and relevance, which the poet did not
raise this outspoken way in Book i. Essentially these are issues of judgment,
and they pertain to the whole of Book ii, though perhaps most clearly, and
for my purposes most usefully, to Guyon's experience with Mammon.

The teasing treatment of sight in the second Proem introduces a Book
in which Guyon's seeing, his perceptual experience, will lead to the crucial
faint that follows his tour through the Cave of Mammon.[4] To be sure,
Guyon's experience in the Cave has resemblances to the earlier experiences
of the Redcrosse Knight, and the narrator of canto vii is at some pains to
have them noticed. Guyon's initial approach to Mammon recalls Redcrosse's
approach to the Wandering Wood: "At last he came vnto a gloomy glade, /
Couer'd with boughes and shrubs from heauens light" (3), and more than
once the terrain and persons of the Cave recall those of the House of Pride
or of hell in Book i. These resemblances underscore relationship rather than
duplication. The tone of Spenser's second Proem would have been inappro-
priately playful as an introduction to Redcrosse's more directly spiritual,
more emotional experiences; and as it would suggest, Guyon's perceptual
experiences differ considerably in meaning from those of Book i.

Without seeing this difference, we miss the rationale for reading the Cave
of Mammon. When Redcrosse went into the Wood, the limits of his vision
were tested, and his vulnerability to deceptive appearances was established.
Characteristically, thereafter he was tormented by "his guiltie sight," and
he flew "from his thoughts and gealous feare" (i.ii.6, 12). He saw, or thought
he saw, something wrong outside him when he was really seeing the result

of something wrong within. The case with Guyon is different as he enters the Cave, though

> ... vew of chearefull day
> Did neuer in that house it selfe display,
> But a faint shadow of vncertain light;
> Such as a lamp, whose life does fade away:
> Or as the Moone cloathed with clowdy night,
> Does shew to him, that walkes in feare and sad affright.

[II.vii.29]

Guyon, unlike Redcrosse, does not walk in fear; the simile concluding this stanza keeps it at one remove from him. The site of the Cave is not specifically his mind, and although it is right and just for him to see the Cave, that site is not a precise corollary of his own condition. These facts are important ones, for they raise the question of what he is doing there.

Unlike Redcrosse in cantos i and v, Guyon is awake and in control of himself when he enters the Cave. His values and his self-confidence—his faith in himself—are being tested, but his perception of deceptive appearances is not. Little is deceptive about Mammon or his Cave. Both are immediately and powerfully repellent:[5]

> [For] all the ground with sculs was scattered,
> And dead mens bones, which round about were flong,
> Whose liues, it seemed, whilome there were shed,
> And their vile carcases now left vnburied.
> . . . .
> Therein an hundred raunges weren pight,
> And hundred fornaces all burning bright;
> By euery fornace many feends did bide,
> Deformed creatures, horrible in sight,
> And euery feend his busie paines applide,
> To melt the golden metall, ready to be tride.

[II.vii.30, 35]

Mammon never speaks with the emotionally transfixing rhythms of a character like Despair, and Guyon never wavers in his rejection of Mammon's offers once he sets eyes on them. Guyon sees with wonder, not with greed. He is not the occasion of an internal struggle but of an appraisal and a devastating recognition of the selfishness and greed which stoke the fires of materialism. The narrator keeps his distance from Guyon in canto vii, just having him look, listen, answer, and learn. His single, short cry of sympathy for Guyon—"Eternall God thee saue from such decay" (34)—is spontaneously responsive to his character's situation, not a direct part of it or an explanation of it or in place of it.[6] His cry indicates the role of an intent, concerned, but rather helpless onlooker. When Guyon enters the Cave, his judgment rather than his faith is at stake, and his awareness, his perception of dark human depths, is being educated profoundly.

Just before entering the Cave, Mammon tells Guyon that he keeps his horde "in secret mew" safe "From heauens sight" (19). Incredulous, Guyon asks him, "What secret place . . . can safely hold / So huge a masse, and hide from heauens eye?" His question involves a subtle shift from the ambiguous phrase "heauens sight" (heaven's own sight, one's sight of heaven) to an uncompromising, if also instinctual, emphasis on heaven's all-beholding eye; it holds no quickening interest in Mammon but a challenge to his assumptions. It suggests Guyon's skepticism and the surety of his control. Guyon's second question, following on his first, enforces this suggestion: "Or where hast thou thy wonne, that so much gold / Thou canst preserue from wrong and robbery?" This question, like the first, has more wonder and disbelief in it than naïve or sinful curiosity. It leaves open the meaning of wrong and theft, the question of whether they harm Mammon or someone else, and it thus suggests the possibility that they could as easily dim the glitter of Mammon's gold in Guyon's view as merely diminish the size of his horde. To Guyon's challenges, Mammon delivers an ominously simple challenge of his own, "Come thou . . . and see," and together they enter the site of unrighteousness.

Guyon's movement into the recesses of the Cave is a progressive realization, not of sins he has committed, but of what Mammon's nature really is. We shall have to let the paradox involved in this statement unfold gradually with the action of the canto. Guyon moves from the surface of materialism, the rooms full of gold, to the source of its power, where he learns more clearly its deadly price. What is frightening and sobering in the Cave is the comprehension of its evil, the spread of its cancerous effects. Mammon's "secret place," his home, is the heart of unrighteousness, and it is unrighteousness in a sense which embraces misuse, deformity, distortion, and injustice, for it finds its roots in a materialism that suffocates the spirit; it deadens truth, as "th'vniust *Atheniens* made to dy / Wise *Socrates*" (vii.52) and kills Life, as Pilate, "the falsest Iudge . . . And most vniust,"

> . . . by vnrighteous
> And wicked doome, to Iewes despiteous
> Deliuered vp the Lord of life to die . . .
>
> [II.vii.62]

The unrighteous theft or "bloud guiltinesse" (19) which Guyon suspected might be in the Cave before he entered it leads finally, at the heart of the Cave, to Tantalus and Pilate. As Guyon sees, it is the one's greed and the other's injustice which destroy or deny anything higher than themselves. Both express the Mammon of unrighteousness, materialism in its broadest and most basic sense.[7]

The power of the Cave is not unlike the Bower of Bliss's. It debases by materializing the spirit in created nature. In its garden grows the archetypal "goodly tree" laden with fruit, with golden, glistering apples, which "On earth like neuer grew, ne liuing wight / Like euer saw, but they from hence were sold" (54). This is the false paradise unrighteousness aggressively seeks, taking from Mammon, but really taking away from what truly belongs to life and to the Lord of life. The Cave acts parasitically on life to deform the right use, and hence the nature, of its materials. Mammon himself is early associated with rust (4). Guyon's journey through the Cave progresses through a distorting house of mirrors, and its disorienting pressures bear down on him. Mammon's fiends "wonder at the sight" of Guyon (37) as much as he wonders at the sight of them. The knight who has been "disdainfull" to Phaedria (vi.37) now shows disdain for Mammon, who has shown disdain for him (vii.7, 39); then he meets Disdain, who "did disdaine / To be so cald, and who so did him call" (41), and has to be pacified in his response to Disdain by Mammon's "reason": "For nothing might abash the villein bold, / Ne mortall steele emperce his miscreated mould" (42–43).

Disdain of virtue cannot be destroyed or even forced from sight by Guyon who has to hold back his "hasty" hand and pass patiently onward. Mammon's counsel to Guyon is the reasonable response in the fundamentally irrational condition of his Cave. Mammon repeatedly usurps a higher power than the Palmer's reason by offering his "grace" to Guyon and by presenting himself as "the fountaine of the worldes good" (38). He offers Guyon his daughter Philotime (Love of Honor), who, like everything else in the Cave, deforms what was created good. In the narrator's words, "Nath'lesse most heauenly faire in deed and vew / She by creation was, till she did fall" (45), and in Mammon's:

> The fairest wight that wonneth vnder skye,
> But that this darksome neather world her light
> Doth dim with horrour and deformitie . . .
>
> [II.vii.49]

The Cave is not Guyon's condition as such but it progressively touches and

affects him. He is neither of the Cave nor willfully responsible for its existence; but now he is in it, ever more deeply into it, and his shining armor
begins to look a little dimmed, too.

The realization of Mammon's unrighteousness is necessary for Guyon,
although it is also degrading and literally disgracing to him. His look into
these depths must come because they exist; they are there in the human past
and in the human present. No solution that failed to acknowledge them
could be realistic or complete, for they, too, are "matter of iust memory,"
matter of which the righteous man must be mindful. Guyon is in the Cave
without his Palmer's abstractive and idealizing Reason, but he nonetheless
has reason to be there. He is not there to destroy the Cave, as he later will
the Bower of Bliss, but to see it. He is there to face it, to be ruined by it only
if he acts, either reaching for its glitter or obliterating its threats, either de-
siring what the Cave is or denying that it is.

Recognition of the debasing power of materialism educates Guyon's consciousness but also exhausts it. His "vitall powres" run down through a
lack of "food, and sleepe," through the natural material needs of his body.
His spirit weakened, his life starts to slip away:

> But all so soone as his enfeebled spright
> Gan sucke this vitall aire into his brest,
> As ouercome with too exceeding might,
> The life did flit away out of her nest,
> And all his senses were with deadly fit opprest.
>
> [II.vii.66]

The rejection of materialism, however heroic, has sensible limitations, for,
ironically, man's material nature, if only his most basic wants, will reassert
themselves. Where these wants exist, there exists also the matter on which
Mammon naturally preys. In depicting Mammon and his "house" (viii.3),
Spenser clearly recalls such a figure on his scaffold in the old morality plays.
Mammon is not merely the "Money God," as Guyon disdainfully calls him
(vii.39), but the distorting, deforming "God of the world and worldlings,"
as he calls himself (vii.8). Without supernatural assistance, Guyon escapes
the site of materialism, which is, after all, to some extent an image of this
world, only to lose consciousness. He faints; his success itself momentarily
seems as suicidal as surrender.

The narrator's comments at the opening of canto viii, following instantly
on Guyon's faint, hardly make sense if we see them applying to anything
which "the good *Guyon*" (viii.4) could really avoid, rather than to something which as a vehicle of meaning he has been created, shown, "used" to

realize. If they did, the narrator would be unfair to Guyon and to his own meaning; readers have often enough found him so, when he asks:

> And is there care in heauen? and is there loue
> In heauenly spirits to these creatures bace,
> That may compassion of their euils moue?

Answering that there is, he then marvels,

> . . . But O th'exceeding grace
> Of highest God, that loues his creatures so,
> And all his workes with mercy doth embrace,
> That blessed Angels, he sends to and fro,
> To serue to wicked man, to serue his wicked foe.

The narrator's rhetorical questions, exclamations, and repetitions enforce an emotional response to the seventh canto. He shows himself overwhelmed by what the Cave has revealed, not about man's strength, but about his frailty, or rather, by what he has realized—though not necessarily just dis-covered—about human nature in depicting the Cave. Guyon's strength in the Cave is now unimportant to him, and Guyon is now helpless, his heroism useless unless it can be fully assimilated to the larger drama of the Fall and Redemption.

The question of whether or not Guyon sins in entering the Cave seems to me misleading because it misses the point of what he sees once inside and why he should be sent there. On the one hand, Guyon does abide in the house of Mammon, a fact sufficient to sully the credentials of Everyman in any morality play; but on the other, his experiences in the Cave allude to the temptation of Christ's humanity in the wilderness, a fact that makes his trial seem noble, necessary, humanly inevitable. Guyon gets through the Cave without falling, but when he leaves it, he faints and literally falls. He is Christ-like, he is erring; he is strong in himself, but he is weak. He should never have entered the Cave, but since he carries the burden of human nature, he has to see the place. Guyon, in the tradition of Reformed theology, has to face and thus to acknowledge, though not to indulge, human depravity before he can find saving grace. He is in the Cave for this reason.

This reason is a commonplace of Reformed theology and a premise fundamental to the central doctrine of justification by faith. Calvin's ex-planations of it read like a commentary on Guyon's experience in the Cave: "But that primal worthiness cannot come to mind without the sorry spectacle of our foulness and dishonor presenting itself by way of contrast . . . From this source arise abhorrence and displeasure with ourselves, as well as true

humility" (1); and again, "First . . . [a man] should consider for what
purpose he was created and endowed with no mean gifts. . . . Secondly, he
should weigh his own abilities—or rather, lack of abilities. When he perceives this lack, he should lie prostrate in extreme confusion . . . reduced to
nought. The first consideration tends to make him recognize the nature of
his duty; the second, the extent of his ability to carry it out" (3).[8] Reading
Calvin, we think of Guyon's feeding himself with the comfort of his own
deeds and virtues at the beginning of this canto and then of his figure prostrate on the ground at its end.

Guyon's conversation with Mammon outside the Cave further clarifies
why, through Guyon's eyes, the narrator should have explored so memorably
and so uncompromisingly a "secret place" and a dark past which at first
have no relation to the workings of Guyon's consciousness—which, in fact,
he at first skeptically doubts could exist. Guyon hardly finds a figure whose
appearance is misleading when "in secret shade" he first stumbles on Mammon telling over and over the mass of coin in his lap and surrounded by
pieces of gold which "in their metall bare / The antique shapes of kings and
kesars straunge and rare" (3–5). Yet Guyon seems to know nothing of
Mammon's nature and initially recognizes its relation neither to man nor
to the world. Doubtful, he asks Mammon, "What art thou man, (if man at
all thou art)" that "these rich heapes of wealth doest hide apart / From the
worldes eye, and from her right vsaunce?" (7). If in all innocence (or ignorance) Guyon wonders *wide-eyed* at the sight of Mammon, that depraved
figure is more than ready to disillusion him, proclaiming his godhead in the
world and of the world:[9]

> Riches, renowme, and principality,
> Honour, estate, and all this worldes good,
> For which men swinck and sweat incessantly,
> Fro me do flow into an ample flood,
> And in the hollow earth haue their eternall brood.
>
> [II.vii.8]

Mammon's association with the earth, his corrosion of the basic and base-
elements of life, is already evident, though not so overwhelmingly clear as
it will become inside the Cave.

Guyon rejects Mammon's first offer of wealth because "Regard of worldly
mucke doth . . . low abase the high heroicke spright" (10), but his disdainful
reply contains the roots of self-contradiction. The phrase "Regard of" can
mean "attention to," even "awareness of," as well as "respect for," and
"worldly mucke" is not far removed, except in Guyon's present unworldly

attitude, from the "*Aegyptian* slime" which the wall of the House of Alma most resembles (ix.21).[10] The tangles of self-contradiction draw tighter as Guyon adds that the high heroic "spright"

> ... ioyes for crownes and kingdomes to contend;
> Faire shields, gay steedes, bright armes be my delight:
> Those be the riches fit for an aduent'rous knight.

[II.vii.10]

"Vaine glorious Elfe," begins Mammon's reply, and his address brings to the surface the contradictory possibilities in Guyon's statements.

Although the rest of Mammon's answer is ugly and immoral, we might say that it brings Guyon's lofty "spright" down to earth. Mammon also scores in this exchange, as he scornfully points out that money can supply what Guyon does desire, "Sheilds, steeds, and armes" (11). Money, he adds, can "crownes and kingdomes to thee multiply," and with sinister logic suggests that his fortune and Fortune's wheel work to one end in determining the succession of rulers, indeed that they are one:

> Do not I kings create, and throw the crowne
> Sometimes to him, that low in dust doth ly?
> And him that raignd, into his rowme thrust downe,
> And whom I lust, do heape with glory and renowne?

[I.vii.11]

Guyon forcefully rejects this claim to sovereignty, basing his rejection on the immorality of Mammon's power, but for the first time, in doing so he tacitly admits the existence of that power.[11] He suddenly seems to remember Mammon's effects on the world and in fact begins to show considerable knowledge of them. With a little prodding from the corrosive Mammon, he proves to be aware of unrighteousness after all (12–13). Guyon defines riches as the "roote of all disquietnesse," but Mammon counters with a question based on observation of the world; he argues from the undeniable actions of men:

> ... And why then, [Mammon] said,
> Are mortall men so fond and vndiscreet,
> So euill thing to seeke vnto their ayd,
> And hauing not complaine, and hauing it vpbraid?

[II.vii.14]

In rebuttal Guyon argues first from a moral ideal and soon quite simply from myth:

> The antique world, in his first flowring youth,
>   Found no defect in his Creatours grace,
>   But with glad thankes, and vnreproued truth,
>   The gifts of soueraigne bountie did embrace:
>   Like Angels life was then mens happy cace . . .
>
>   [II.vii.16]

But the pride of later ages, Guyon continues, abused her plenty and began to exceed "The measure of her meane, and naturall first need."

> Then gan a cursed hand the quiet wombe
>   Of his great Grandmother with steele to wound,
>   And the hid treasures in her sacred tombe,
>   With Sacriledge to dig. Therein he found
>   Fountaines of gold and siluer to abound,
>   Of which the matter of his huge desire
>   And pompous pride eftsoones he did compound . . .
>
>   [II.vii.17]

Mammon's answer is in its tone disarming and frustrating, even maddening, in its effect; but in its content it is experiential and in a worldly sense, totally realistic:

> Sonne (said he then) let be thy bitter scorne,
>   And leaue the rudenesse of that antique age
>   To them, that liu'd therein in state forlorne;
>   Thou that doest liue in later times, must wage
>   Thy workes for wealth, and life for gold engage.
>
>   [II.vii.18]

Mammon fails to convince Guyon, but he drives him back from idealization to the basic, practical moral questions that apply to everyday life, and back from myth to Aristotle.[12] Implicit in Guyon's new tack is a further acknowledgment of Mammon's existence, of the raw fact of vast material wealth:

> Me list not (said the Elfin knight) receaue
>   Thing offred, till I know it well be got,
>   Ne wote I, but thou didst these goods bereaue
>   From rightfull owner by vnrighteous lot,
>   Or that bloud guiltinesse or guile them blot.
>
>   [II.vii.19]

Guyon's final questions, in contrast to his first, appeal not to the world's eye but to a higher power, the eye of heaven (20), and they express his doubts, still genuinely strong, about Mammon's complicity with human nature:

> What secret place (quoth he) can safely hold
> So huge a masse, and hide from heauens eye?
> Or where hast thou thy wonne, that so much gold
> Thou canst preserue from wrong and robbery?
>
> [II.vii.20]

The voices of Mammon and Guyon have independent force throughout this conversation. Mammon is the spokesman for worldly reason, Guyon for idealism, and both make extended speeches. Their exchange lacks the concentration and intensity of Redcrosse's talk with Contemplation. It explores issues in the intellectual way which pertains to rational assessment rather than to visionary insight, to reason rather than to faith.[13] We have far less sense of the narrator's presence in this debate. Certainly the phrase "quoth he" does not function as a virtual refrain but, when it recurs, as the emphasis added to a challenge (20). The narrator steps back in this controversy to maintain a posture consistent with his role as a basically knowledgeable Christian.

It might clarify this last statement to recall Langland's Dreamer in Passus I, something of a straw man before Lady Holy Church's truths but thereafter a careful, comprehending observer in the Visio (II–VII). There is, perhaps, a little of this straw man in Guyon, the Faerie figure who progressively and with increasing complexity manifests human nature in the course of his quest in Book II.[14] The poet's own religious position conceivably might have been reflected in the occasional awkwardness of his narrative posture in Book II. Presumably, the Protestant with any real kind of faith could no longer doubt—could not have failed in some way to experience—the depravity and helplessness of natural man. With this recognition, saving faith wakens; but this recognition comes first. (The example of Calvin, although extreme in its certainty of salvation, is handy: after the second step to knowledge that Calvin describes, namely the realization of our moral impotence, the elect are ready to know justification, a further realization which is in essence irreversible, even if the elect are subject on occasion to weakness or error.) In view of this sequence, the poet's knowledge of Mammon's Cave, though not his poetic fulfillment of this knowledge, would be a priori to a degree that his sense of closeness to, or communion with, God (as in I.x), or even his emotional security in God (I.v), might not be. It is difficult to see how, as a man of faith, the poet could participate immediately or fully in Guyon's discovery—indeed in his education—in the Cave; that is, how he could participate without our becoming distinctly aware of some qualifying distance in his narrative attitude, whether as participant (presence) or as master of ceremonies (his more public role; e.g. vii.34, viii.1).

Before Mammon and Guyon enter the Cave, they are not properly engaged in a dialogue with self or in private meditation, but in an externalized disagreement that might better be compared to a game of chess. Using pieces of different value, each character scores some and loses some until they reach an impasse and in fact begin to repeat themselves (7, 20). Guyon's basic reasonableness then leads to their exploration of the Cave, where he faces a religious paradox not entirely (or merely) rational, the relation of the father's sins to the innocence of the son. As the same paradox is put by Dame Study in *Piers Plowman:*

> . . . thise lordes gynneth dispute,
> "Of that 3e clerkes vs kenneth of Cryst by the gospel;
> *Filius non portabit iniquitatem patris . . .*
> Whi shulde we that now ben for the werkes of Adam
> Roten and to-rende? resoun wolde it neuere;
> *Vnusquisque portabit onus suum . . ."*
> Suche motyues thei moeue, this maistres in her glorie,
> And maken men in mysbileue that muse moche on her wordes;
> Ymaginatyf her-afterward shal answere to 3owre purpos.
>
> [x.109–15]

These disputatious men fail to grasp how such biblical quotations can be reconciled with the doctrine of Original Sin. They fail to understand that the innocence of Adam's sons can be real only by its relation to that of the Son and only when it has been realized fully in the Redemption. Their disputes recall the difficulties readers have had in interpreting the combination of Guyon's virtue with his fall to earth. Guyon imitates Christ's humanity and also the weakness of Adam resulting from the Fall. Alone, his strength in the Cave cannot save him in the narrator's eyes or in ours, but it looks ahead to—in fact must lead us to expect—the redemptive action of canto viii. Guyon's relation to the historical Redemption cannot be fulfilled in the Cave of Mammon, from which he emerges as individually uncompromised, paradoxically good but generically fallen. It is only fulfilled in canto viii when he is rescued through Arthur's agency and by God's love.

At the beginning of this chapter, I referred to the wakened Dreamer's meeting two friars at the threshold of the second section of *Piers Plowman,* shortly after Piers has torn the Pardon, in effect ending the Visio. The friars have some sound instruction for him, despite the evident contradiction of their knowledge by the lives they lead:

> "Lat brynge a man in a bote amydde a brode water,
> The wynde and the water and the bote waggynge
> Maketh the man many a tyme to falle and to stonde,
> For stonde he neuere so styf he stombleth ʒif he moeue;
> Ac ʒit is he sauf and sounde and so hym bihoueth,
> 35 For ʒif he ne arise the rather and rauʒte to the stiere,
> The wynde wolde wyth the water the bote ouerthrowe,
> And thanne were his lyf loste thourgh lacchesse of hym-self.
> And thus it falleth," quod the frere, "bi folke here on erthe;
> The water is likned to the worlde that wanyeth and wexeth,
> 40 The godis of this grounde aren like to the grete wawes[15]
> That as wyndes and wederes walweth aboute.
> The bote is likned to owre body that brutel is of kynde,
> That thorugh the fende and the flesshe and the frele worlde[16]
> Synneth the sadman a day seuene sythes.
> 45 Ac dedly synne doth he nouʒt for Dowel hym kepith,
> And that is Charite the champioun chief help aʒein synne,
> For he strengtheth man to stonde and stereth mannes soule . . ."
> [VIII.30–47]

This passage is close to the heart of Spenser's second Book. Even present is the imagery of wind and water, so dominant in that Book, and the emphasis on man's need to keep moving, his inability to keep Occasion in fetters, to stop time or, for that matter, history. Lines 34 through 37 of the friar's parable apply better, perhaps, to Guyon's journey by boat to the Bower of Bliss than to his progress through the Cave, the episode in which Spenser so emphatically establishes man's final helplessness without God's intervention. Even in the Cave, however, Spenser presents such helplessness without compromising man's natural obligation to endure in the face of temptation. Guyon's will is actually stronger, even if his helplessness is finally greater, than those of the "sadman" (steadfast man) in the friar's parable. The doctrinal difference between the friar's parable and canto vii, like that between Aquinas and Hooker or between Augustine and Calvin, is not really so great. Consider the opening of canto vii:

> As Pilot well expert in perilous waue,
>   That to a stedfast starre his course hath bent,
>   When foggy mistes, or cloudy tempests haue

The faithfull light of that faire lampe yblent,
And couer'd heauen with hideous dreriment,
Vpon his card and compas firmes his eye,
The maisters of his long experiment,
And to them does the steddy helme apply,
Bidding his winged vessell fairely forward fly.

So *Guyon* hauing lost his trusty guide,
Late left beyond that *Ydle lake,* proceedes
Yet on his way, of none accompanide;
And euermore himselfe with comfort feedes,
Of his owne vertues, and prayse-worthy deedes.

Guyon's celebrated self-righteousness, like his bearing in the Cave, is a source of strength and a cause of weakness. His own virtues do nourish him. Their nourishment is opposed to what Langland's unselfconscious friar calls "lacchesse of hym-self" (his own negligence, but also negligence with respect to himself); and by Aristotelian standards, it is thoroughly righteous.

But of course their nourishment is not enough.[17] As canto vii develops, its context *becomes* increasingly Christian, and does so in a manner very familiar to readers of *Piers Plowman.* (See chapters 4, 6). As Guyon moves through this canto, we might say that time, or history, unfolds. The context of his movement does not become explicitly and undeniably Christian until its end, where we read of Pilate, of Christ, "the Lord of life"; and also of Mammon, no longer just the world but now the traditionally Satanic "Guyler" (62, 64).[18] Such dimensions are earlier hinted at, foreshadowed, but they are not fulfilled. Once they are—and not until then—we realize that Guyon's nourishment partakes not only of virtue but also of self-love, the self-regard which Langland's Dreamer has already heard can harden the heart and cause a man to lose sight of Truth (v.610–26).[19] Like Guyon's faint, self-sufficiency leads to a loss of self and a loss of true consciousness because it is not founded on and fulfilled by dependence on a loving God. If, then, Guyon sins by entering the Cave—and I do not find that he does—his sin is wanting the knowledge of it without which he cannot be saved.

Before turning to discuss *Piers Plowman* at greater length, I should add a final word about the passages from this poem which I have just used to clarify issues in the Cave of Mammon. The coincidence of ideas and imagery in the two poems at these points is noteworthy, although it need not prove that Langland is Spenser's source. The burden of the father's sins and the hardening of the heart and subsequent loss of Truth are so thoroughly biblical that Spenser did not need Langland or anybody else to call them to his attention. Langland's use of a boat in the friar's parable is also traditional, an image for the body and in a more general sense, for life. Spenser might have found it in any number of sources, among them Erasmus's controversy with Luther on free will, surely a text relevant to his treatment of Guyon in cantos vii and viii.[20]

I hardly want to deny that Spenser's Cave of Mammon is surprisingly reminiscent of *Piers Plowman* (especially of the Visio) or to suggest that the identification of possible echoes is not important. But such echoes will not tell us enough about what might have made Langland's passages peculiarly memorable to another poet or what it is that has caused readers to think of *Piers Plowman* when they read Mammon's Cave.[21] The Cave recalls *Piers Plowman,* not merely because they both echo a whole library of common texts and commonplaces, but because they also share essential features which countless other works treating similar issues do not. These features are what concern me now.

THE VISIO: "For want of food, and sleepe, which two vpbeare,
     Like mightie pillours, this fraile life of man . . ."

The passages from *Piers Plowman* cited in connection with the Cave of Mammon occur in Passūs which follow closely on the Visio; these Passūs pertain to the dilemmas of the Visio and arise from the narrator's efforts to get beyond, or around, them. The Visio itself assays a progressive series of approaches to the conflict of matter and spirit, of worldly materialism and moral idealism, of observable human behavior and the higher possibilities of human nature, of wicked desires and righteous ones. The specific terms of confrontation alter each time a new approach is tried, and the cast of characters alters as well. But the basic opposition remains constant. First, Theology confronts Falsehood; then Conscience, aided by Reason, confronts Lady Meed. Repentance confronts the Seven Deadly Sins, essentially sinners because, in contrast to Meed, they can repent and reform themselves.[22] Piers, an ideal of action in the workaday world, confronts this world's ordinary laborers, who more often than not are found to be ineffectual, shiftless, and sinful.

With each approach, the poem tries simultaneously to move toward a moral and spiritual ideal and toward the material, workaday world. After initial success, this movement bogs down in a seemingly endless cycle of want and waste, hunger and avarice, on both material and spiritual levels. It is at this point that Piers pulls the Pardon in two, "atweyne," and refuses to concern himself any longer with basic material wants—the sowing of wheat, the eating of bread, the need for sleep (VII.116–20)—the pillars of

man's life, as Spenser describes them just before Guyon faints. Piers tears the
terms of essential conflict apart and withdraws to a life of penance and prayer,
the inner life of the spirit. Shortly thereafter the Dreamer starts to follow suit,
leaving the Visio for the Life (Vita) in an effort to make more sense of
existence by finding Dowel. What Piers and the Dreamer do is analogous, at
times even verbally analogous, to Guyon's history.

Like Spenser's seventh canto, the Visio might be said to give Mammon, as
well as moral idealism, the voice he really possesses. Although Langland's
narrator is seldom as consistent even as Spenser's, he keeps a sufficient distance
from the immediate action of the Visio to give us the impression that he is
recording it objectively. Although he breaks into the action with an occasional warning and interrupts it with one lengthy tirade, on the whole he
lets worldly falsehood reveal its own face, by showing its painfully frustrating
but often grotesquely comic distortions of mankind's visage. His role as an
observer in this section allows Meed and Conscience to engage in a genuine
dispute, an argument which calls on reason and judgment far more than it
calls on faith.

Conscience's confrontation with Lady Meed is less autonomously dramatic
and still more speechlike than Guyon's confrontation with Mammon, perhaps because the stage of the former pair's argument remains the narrator's
dream and therefore, in a more direct sense, his own mind. Yet the
Conscience-Meed confrontation is also miles away from the transparent,
self-canceling argument of a morality play. In comparison with the Cave of
Mammon, Langland's hard-headed originality in the Visio is likely to be
diminished and some of his poetic importance for Spenser along with it.
Before looking closely at Langland's treatment of materialism in the Visio,
it will be useful to have in mind a more common, traditional presentation of
worldly wickedness, for instance, that in The Castle of Perseverance, a work
that draws on Piers Plowman but lacks its humane and realistic vision. One
example will serve this purpose.

In The Castle, a character called Mundus (World), whose treasurer is
Covetousness, occupies a raised scaffold opposite God's. As the medieval
diagram of staging for The Castle suggests, the fundamental opposition in
this play lies between God and the World, rather than between God and
Belial, who occupies another scaffold.[23] Mundus is the first speaker in the
play and the first patron of sin to whose scaffold Humanum Genus (Mankind)
mounts. Just before Mankind ascends, Mundus addresses him:

> Welcum, syr, semly in syth!
> Þou art welcum to worthy wede.

> For þou wylt be my serwaunt day and nyth,
>   Wyth my seruyse I schal þe foster and fede.
> Þi bak shal be betyn wyth besawntys bryth,
>   Þou schalt haue byggyngys be bankys brede,
> To þi cors schal knele kayser and knyth
>   Where þat þou walke, be sty or be strete,
>   And ladys louely on lere.
> But Goddys seruyse þou must forsake
> And holy to þe Werld þe take
> And þanne a man I shal þe make
>   Þat non schal be þi pere.
>
>   [584–96]

Mankind's reply, like Mundus's temptation, is characteristic of the treatment of conscious choice and motivation in this play:

> Ʒys, Werld, and þerto here myn honde
>   To forsake God and hys seruyse.
> To medys þou Ʒeue me howse and londe
>   Þat I regne rychely at myn enprise.
> So þat I fare wel be strete and stronde
>   Whyl I dwelle here in werldly wyse,
> I recke neuere of heuene wonde
>   Nor of Jhesu, þat jentyl justyse.
>   Of my sowle I haue non rewthe.
>   What schulde I recknen of domysday
>   So þat I be ryche and of gret aray?
>   I schal make mery whyl I may,
>   And þerto here my trewthe.
>
>   [597–609]

The exchange between Mundus and Mankind is a duet, not a debate. For all the verbal battles in *The Castle*, there never really seem to be two sides. Either the world or God is simply and deliberately abandoned. There is no middle ground of apparent or half-goods, confused motives, tangled needs and desires, strengths and weaknesses, such as we find in the poems of Spenser and Langland—and for that matter, in the world as we recognize it. Response to *The Castle* must be one of complicity rather than of engagement and earned assent.[24] It is as though we were watching the opposing pieces on a chess board as they move themselves according to a plan thought out by a mind never present.

The presentation of materialism in Langland's Visio is from the start more self-conscious and complex. As Lady Holy Church turns to leave the Dreamer, he implores her out of grace and for the love of heaven to show him "bi somme crafte to knowe the Fals" (II.4). The Lady's quick reply hardly seems gracious—"Loke vppon thi left half, and lo where he standeth" —for it reminds the Dreamer how very close to him Falsehood is found. Lady Holy Church does not reject the Dreamer's desire for this knowledge, however. Her behavior implies that, like Guyon, he needs it. When the Dreamer looks to his left, he sees a woman whose gorgeous attire ravishes him until Holy Church identifies her as Meed and decries her history of corruption. Commending the dreamer to Christ, Holy Church gives him one last loaded warning, "lat no conscience acombre the for coueitise of Mede" (50). Then she leaves him to observe in his sleep Lady Meed's marriage on the morrow "to a mansed schrewe, / To one Fals Fikel-tonge, a fendes biȝete" (39–40).

In *Piers Plowman,* as in Spenser's second Book and indeed throughout his poem, temporal and spatial movement has symbolic value. In the Visio, the ongoing process of life, activity in the world, energy itself, seem inevitably entangled in wickedness. As the Dreamer concentrates his attention on Meed's forthcoming marriage—in his own words, "how Mede was ymaried in meteles me thouȝte" (52)—he sees a scene crowded with "alle maner of men, the mene and the riche": knights, clerks, jurors, summoners, sheriffs, "Bedelles and bailliues and brokoures of chaffare, / Forgoeres and vitaillers and vokates of the arches" (55–60). Soon the verse quickens and comes alive with hectic activity, quite unlike the image we had in Passus I, a Lady in white standing still to address a single Dreamer:

> Thanne lepe Lyer forth and seide, "lo here! a chartre
> That Gyle with his gret othes gaf hem togidere,"
> And preide Cyuile to se and Symonye to rede it
> . . . .
> And thus bigynneth thes gomes to greden ful heiȝ—
>
> [II.68–73]

Physical energy seems possessed by the Vices.

The marriage charter itself abounds with unsavory vitality. It swiftly demonstrates the way Meed's link to Falsehood diffuses corruption, pervading every corner of life. There are first those areas in which we should expect to find Meed and Falsehood together "To be prynces in pryde and pouerte to dispise, / To bakbite and to bosten and bere fals witnesse" (79–80). Understandably, they are granted the earldom of envy and wrath, "The counte of coueitise and alle the costes aboute, / That is, vsure and auarice . . . In

bargaines and in brokages, with al the borghe of theft" (83–87). But some
of the other areas that belong to them are more surprising, for example,

> . . . al the lordeship of lecherye in lenthe and in brede,
> As in werkes and in wordes and waitynges with eies,
> And in wedes and in wisshynges and with ydel thou3tes
> There as wille wolde and werkmanship failleth.
>
> [II.88–91]

Theirs is the kingdom of all the remaining Deadly Sins as well:

> Glotonye . . . and grete othes togydere
> And alday to drynke at dyuerse tauernes,
> And there to iangle and to iape and iugge here euene cristene
> And in fastyng-dayes to frete ar ful tyme were
> And thanne to sitten and soupen til slepe hem assaille
> And breden as burgh-swyn and bedden hem esily
> Tyl sleuth and slepe slyken his sides
> And thanne wanhope to awake hym so with no wille to amende . . .
>
> [II.92–99]

Again, as in the Cave of Mammon, we start in Meed with what appears to
be a love of money but turns out to lead right into the heart of sin. At its
heart Lady Meed lies together with "False Fikel-tonge," more clearly a
breaker of words and promises than Meed is by herself. The abuse of man's
nature belongs to their union—everything from pride right down to sloth
and despair, the descent to the silver stool in the Cave of Mammon come
again (II.vii.63).[25] Meed's union with falsehood is obviously more than the
misuse of money, though it includes that. Together they unite the material
means and the falsifying reason, the human weakness and its exploitation.
They join to corrupt material good, thereby debasing life and destroying its
promise in the Word.

Meed's marriage charter is not only a vision of sin; it also belongs to a
larger process of thought. Right after the charter is read, Theology—a
figure never to reappear as an actual character in the poem—abruptly and
vigorously objects to a merely pejorative understanding of Meed's nature.
His sudden objection is one of the greatest surprises in a poem full of them.
"Tened," precisely as Piers will be when he tears the Pardon (VII.116) and
when he seizes a support from the Tree of Charity to strike out at the devil
(XVI.86), Theology redefines Meed. As Piers will do, though quite differently,
in the Pardon Scene and again in the Garden of Charity, Theology rejects
the complicity of falsehood with material good: "For Mede is moylere of
Amendes engendred, / And god graunteth to gyf Mede to Treuthe" (118–

19). He makes the telling point that the worker deserves, in fact needs, his hire and distinguishes carefully between "Fals [who] is faithlees and fikel in his werkes" and Meed, who is "a mayden of gode / And my3te kisse the kynge for cosyn, an she wolde" (129–32). Theology insists that Meed be taken to London, the center of the social order, to test whether her union with Falsehood is lawful, and after the forces of falsehood have distributed sufficient bribes to assure success in their view, they agree to his proposal.

The bustle of activity again crowds the poem. The procession of falsehood to London provides one of the most gargoylelike sequences in the whole poem. It bursts and tumbles with immoral, impetuous energy:

> Ac thanne cared thei for caplus to kairen hem thider,
> And Fauel fette forth thanne folus ynowe
> And sette Mede vpon a schyreue shodde al newe,
> And Fals sat on a sisoure that softlich trotted,
> And Fauel on a flaterere fetislich atired.
> Tho haued notaries none, annoyed thei were,
> For Symonye and Cyuile shulde on hire fete gange;
> Ac thanne swore Symonye and Cyuile bothe
> That sompnoures shulde be sadled and serue hem vchone . . .
>
> [II.161–69]

The procession is laughably grotesque, though as men turn into beasts, it is also debasing. The Devil of the old moral plays once again rides the sinner's soul to hell, though these devils are of man's making.

In the course of the journey to London, Meed is separated from falsehood, yet as soon as she gets there she starts, with the clergy's collusion, by corrupting the clergy. Although under arrest, Meed thus attracts falsehood again. Perhaps unaware of Meed's latest activities, the King pardons her association with falsehood and proposes that Conscience wed her. "I haue a kny3te, Conscience, cam late fro bi3unde," the King's proposal begins, and its phrasing leads us to anticipate the arrival of a moral faculty straight from the heavens. Lady Meed promptly accepts the proposal, and Conscience just as promptly rejects it. In the very real argument between Conscience and Meed which follows, we hear voices close at times to those of Guyon and Mammon.[26]

Conscience's horrified rejection is a generalized catalogue of Meed's misdeeds, the crimes money has fostered against the crown, the social order, the church, and the law. At one point, however, he becomes more specific, telling the King,

ȝowre fadre she felled thorw fals biheste
And hath apoysounde popis and peired holicherche;
Is nauȝt a better baude, bi hym that me made,
Bitwene heuene and helle in erthe though men souȝte!
For she is tikil of hire taile, talwis of hir tonge,
As comune as a cartwey to eche a knaue that walketh . . .

[III.126-31]

In rebuttal, Meed refers first to the utility of wealth. She presents herself as a force which can be used to good effect. With a disdain worthy of Mammon, she points out that Conscience himself has made use of her and might do so again. Impugning his "proude herte," she continues:

Wel thow wost, wernard, but ȝif thou wolt gabbe,
Thow hast hanged on myne half elleuene tymes
And also griped my golde, gyue it where the liked;
And whi thow wratthest the now wonder me thynketh.
ȝit I may as I myȝte menske the with ȝiftes
And mayntene thi manhode more than thow knoweste.

[III.179-84]

Taking the hint from Conscience, she turns next to specific events in the actual world. She ties him to history, as he has tied her. Flatly denying that meed has ever harmed any king, she reduces the "biȝunde" from which Conscience has come to Normandy:

In Normandye was he nouȝte noyed for my sake,
Ac thow thi-self sothely shamedest hym ofte,
Crope in-to a kaban for colde of thi nailles
. . . .
And hiedest homeward for hunger of thi wombe.[27]

[III.188-93]

Such is the historical role of Conscience in worldly affairs. From the viewpoint of Lady Meed, which includes honor and reward (194, 200-04), Conscience's role has been unknightly; his influence has made cowards of all: "Cowardliche thow, Conscience, conseiledest hym thennes / To leuen his lordeship for a litel siluer" (205-06). By merely looking at this world, Meed can impute hypocrisy and weakness to Conscience's proud heart. In a similar discussion, Mammon saw vainglory in Guyon. Like Book II, the Visio *is* a looking—a long, hard, probing one.

Meed aims next at the knight's common sense. She lectures on practical politics: "It bicometh to a kynge that kepeth a rewme / To ȝiue mede to

men that mekelich hym serueth" (208–09). She points out that meed makes
a ruler well-loved and considered great. Then she turns her attention to
economics:

> Men that teche chyldren craue of hem mede,
> Prestis that precheth the poeple to gode asken mede
>
> . . . .
>
> No wi3te, as I wene, with-oute mede may libbe.
>
> [III.221–26]

With increasing clarity, Meed's rebuttal uses a definition of herself different
from Conscience's. She identifies herself not with the misuse of wealth or
even simply with money, but with achievement, with efficacy, and, in these
last lines, with the material means of existence, the basic needs of life itself.
Her argument assumes that Conscience in condemning her has rejected these
means. She makes Conscience seem too unrealistic for the court of a king in
this world. Certainly the King in the poem, first convinced by Conscience's
argument, is now won over to Meed's, and he tells Conscience that "Mede
is well worthi the maistrye to haue" (228).

Conscience's second rejection of Meed is as uncompromising as Meed's
claim. This time he explicitly rejects her right even to exist on earth. He
explains that there are two kinds of meeds, one in heaven, the other on earth:
"one, god of his grace graunteth in his blisse / To tho that wel worchen whil
thei ben here"; the other is "mede mesurelees that maistres desireth; / To
meyntene mysdoers" (231–32, 245–46). One is unearthly and good; the
other earthly and evil. This distinction smacks of Manichaeism, but Conscience does not stop with it. He adds that earthly life's basic needs are satisfied
by what "laboreres and lowe folke taketh of her maistres"[28] and this "is no
manere mede but a mesurable hire" (253–54).

Stated without further glossing, as it is in the poem, Conscience's explanation is ambiguous. The distinction between what "maistres desireth" and
what laborers take from "her maistres" is not logically firm. At first sight
sin seems built into the system of things, and Conscience, like Guyon, seems
self-contradictory. One way out of this verbal impasse is to read morally,
taking "laboreres" to mean not just those who work but those who do
well and taking "lowe folke" to mean not simply poor people but people
who practice humility. Whether money is Meed or money is hire would
thus depend on the spirit of those accepting it. As stated, however, Conscience's distinctions do not require an exclusively moral reading. Without
the help of later portions of the poem—again, without reading backwards—
Conscience's statements here are likely to be as puzzling to us as they are to

the King and presumably to the Dreamer, and Conscience's position is compromised.[29]

Almost immediately after distinguishing between Meed and measurable hire, Conscience turns, much as Guyon does, from the present world to the lessons of the biblical past, and then to prophetic vision:[30]

> Shal na more Mede be maistre, as she is nouthe,
> Ac loue and lowenesse and lewte togederes,
> Thise shul be maistres on molde treuthe to saue.
>
> [III.288–90]

His words now acknowledge the present actuality of Meed's power, as his earlier definitions of meed did not, but his attention rivets on the future:

> Ac kynde loue shal come ȝit and conscience togideres
> And make of lawe a laborere; suche loue shal arise
> And such a pees amonge the peple and a perfit trewthe
> That Iewes shal wene in here witte and waxen wonder glade,
> That Moises or Messie be come in-to this erthe,
> And haue wonder in here hertis that men beth so trewe.
> . . . .
> Batailles shal non be, ne no man bere wepne,
> And what smyth that ony smytheth be smyte therwith to dethe, . . .
> And er this fortune falle fynde men shal the worste
> By syx sonnes and a schippe and half a shef of arwes . . .
>
> [III.297–324]

As Conscience and Lady Meed continue to argue, next about biblical quotations, the King makes a rather sensible suggestion, "Cesseth . . . I suffre ȝow no lengere" (IV.1). After all, he has the problem of governing this realm in the present, and six suns, a ship, and half a sheaf of arrows must strike him with doubtful relevance. The bickering of Conscience and Lady Meed— moral faculty and material means—only serves to convince the exasperated King that they should promptly be married.

For the third time Conscience refuses to comply, but he refuses for a reason the King can grasp. Reason himself is fetched, and Meed is caught trying to buy a pardon for Wrong by giving money to Peace, who has been wronged. She thus tries to substitute material comfort, material well-being, for justice. Though Peace accepts her solution, Reason does not, and Meed finally falls out of the King's favor. It is worth noting, however, that even as Meed is abandoned by the court, a juror and a summoner (IV.167) still cling to her. She is still becoming, by association, some of her bad social effects. Like so

many evil figures in *The Faerie Queene*—Archimago, Acrasia, Mammon himself—she is not destroyed, a fact which suggests both the poet's self-conscious
awareness of her as an image and his awareness of the reality she unhappily
represents.

With Lady Meed's fall from mastery in the poem, the King vows to live
with Reason and Conscience. Reason begins to preach to the realm until
Repentance takes over from him to hear the confessions of the Deadly Sins.
Then Piers Plowman suddenly appears to direct men on their pilgrimage to
Truth. When the road he describes sounds difficult and discouraging, he
offers himself as their guide, as long as they first help him to plow a half-acre.
Piers then organizes the pilgrims into a community, giving each an appro-
priate task. At first everything and everyone seem to work, but then,

> At heighe pryme Peres lete the plowe stonde
> To ouersen hem hym-self, and who-so best wrou3te
> He shulde be huyred ther-after whan heruest-tyme come.
> And thanne seten somme and songen atte nale
> And hulpen erie his half-acre with "how! trollilolli!"
>
> [vi.114–18]

Meed may have fallen from royal favor and may have been abandoned as
the material basis of society, but there has been no change in human nature.
The same impulses toward untruth and injustice, to broken words and
broken covenants, remain.

When Piers rebukes the "wastoures" of the world, they revert to fakery
and to force, begging or else threatening the Plowman for food. They seem
to multiply, occupying all Piers's attention and engulfing the stage of the
poem. Then Piers calls the vengeance of Hunger upon them. Wracked by
need, the wasters rush back to work, and Hunger affords Piers practical
moral lessons about alms and abstinence, about the proper distribution of
material good: feed the needy, especially those you know are unable to
work; avoid surfeit in your own diet and practice restraint—in short, be
temperate. Again men labor for a measurable hire, and so Piers bids farewell
to Hunger: "Wende now, Hunger, whan thow wolt that wel be thow
euere, / For this is a louely lessoun, lorde it the for-3elde."

Hunger's reply is startling: " 'By-hote god,' quod Hunger, 'hennes ne wil
I wende, / Til I haue dyned bi this day and ydronke bothe' " (vi.280–81).
Realizing the hunger of every man, Hunger himself becomes hungry, re-
quiring satisfaction not from the "lorde" but directly from Piers. Hunger's
effect is not, as Piers had hoped, truly to keep men from idleness but more

simply to make them hungry. Hunger breaks loose from a moral function in the poem:

Al Hunger eet in hast and axed after more.
Thanne pore folke for fere fedde Hunger ӡerne
With grene poret and pesen to poysoun Hunger thei thouӡte.
By that it neighed nere heruest, newe corne cam to chepynge;
Thanne was folke fayne and fedde Hunger with the best,
With good ale, as Glotoun tauӡte, and gerte Hunger go slepe.
And tho wolde Wastour nouӡt werche but wandren aboute . . .

[vi.298–304]

Hunger is not only a correction of sin, as we are first led to believe, but also a cause of gluttony. Its effects are shown to be merely natural, not moral, and once its appetite is stilled, other kinds of desires, then other greeds, take over. Now the laborer wants to be "heighlich huyred" (vi.314); in a word, he wants Meed, and "He greueth hym aӡeines god and gruccheth aӡeines resoun / And thanne curseth he the kynge and al his conseille after" (vi.317–18). Despite the best efforts in the world by Reason, in league with Conscience and the King, peace is wronged in the interest of profit and justice is undone. The seemingly natural cycle starts again.

Looking at the image of human nature the Visio presents, we might remember the needs and desires that repeatedly set upon Guyon: the unruly Pyrochles, the lustful Cymochles, Phaedria's idleness, Mammon's aggressive greed, hunger and exhaustion, then Pyrochles and Cymochles again (ii.iv–viii). Buried in this cycle we can already see Maleger—life badly diseased, the body of death—who, Antaeus-like, springs to life every time he falls to earth, every time he touches matter (ii.xi). Like Guyon, Piers is the human will at its very best, but the wasters are, as he tells Hunger, his "blody bretheren" (vi.210), related to him forever in Adam and in Christ.

In the plowing of the half-acre, the human spirit does well in the person of Piers, but the flesh proves too weak. After one more attempt to believe that the world can be saved through human effort, Piers tears the Pardon, whose terms mankind, as it actually and observably is in the Visio, will never fulfill. Piers faces the paradox of the Redemption and the observable lack of it in the world he knows. Now, as then, after Christ as before Him, mankind needs not a second coming but in the present to realize the first. It is the emphasis on realization, on the present actuality of the historical fact, which brings Langland's treatment of time and of the human will close to Spenser's and defies, in the interest of humanity, the historical differences we might expect to find between them.

Having seen the world which the Visio pictures, the Dreamer, whose name is Will, begins his search for Dowel. Like Piers Plowman himself, he turns from involvement in the world's endless cycle of corrupting materialism and tries to make more sense out of life. Questioning and questing, he passes from Thought to Wit to Study to Clergy to Scripture; frustrated by their answers, he rebels, embracing worldly Fortune and self-indulgence before he finds Imagination, a new understanding of Conscience, and Patience. Yet his questions in the first Vita have always behind them the quandaries he has observed, or formulated, in the Visio: is Dowel a man or no man; can Dowel be a man if no man can live without offending God; is every baptized person saved, whether or not he does well; can the unbaptized who do well be saved; in short, what relation has Dowel to faith and to the human will? These are certainly some of the fundamental dilemmas that bothered—and given the observable corruption of the Roman Church—obsessed the Reformers. It is easy to see what might initially have made sixteenth-century readers, and Spenser among them, interested in *Piers Plowman*.

The broader implications of Meed's debate with Conscience and of Piers's tearing the Pardon are, in fact, startling both with respect to developments in the Renaissance and to the commonplaces of late medieval thought. Consider this generalization about the two periods by Charles Trinkaus: "Whereas medieval thought attributed to man the rational capacity both to lead a moral life in the ordinary secular pursuits of this world and to achieve salvation, both the humanists and the reformers denied that man could do both." Trinkaus adds that the humanists—Pico, Ficino, Erasmus, Machiavelli —"took the first step and denied the possibility of subordinating economic to moral ends. . . . The reformers, particularly Luther, also denied that there was any possibility of morality in business or politics."[31]

We know that the positions of Humanists and Reformers did not emerge ex nihilo; nonetheless, by Trinkaus's definition, Langland wanted to be but had, if possible, to rediscover a way truly to be such a medieval thinker; and in his poem, as in a few—but only a few—other medieval works, we perceive something of the too often mysterious origins of sixteenth-century thought. And finally, we see as well a poetic source, presumably known to Spenser, which is close, perhaps closer than any other, to the essential meaning of the Cave of Mammon—closer to the whole of it, not merely to a few of its parts. In this profoundly original source we may also see something of Spenser's fundamental inspiration for his equally profound and equally original episode.

Part II

Growth and Expansion

Foreword to Part II

In individual Books of *The Faerie Queene,* we can speak of a growth of awareness perhaps most easily in terms of a central figure who occasions and embodies it, Redcrosse and Guyon in the first two Books, Britomart and Artegall in Books III to V, Calidore in Book VI. If we take several Books together, such growth is more complex than in any single Book. Understanding is continuing and accretive in the poem, but not simply accretive. Successive Books modify, as they expand, ideas and perceptions touched upon before. Although in one sense this expansion is the reader's, it predominantly belongs to the poem, being present in new themes and shifting emphases, in different relations among characters, in the narrator's changing role, in the use of poetic modes so significantly varied that they seem essentially new. In a real sense this expansion is the poet's.

There is likewise a genuine growth of awareness in *Piers Plowman,* though in view of Langland's more consistently obtrusive narrator, this growth is more easily described as that of a single mind. For this reason *Piers Plowman* invites comparison with a single Book of *The Faerie Queene,* Book I or II being obvious choices because of their decidedly religious concerns. Yet the juxtaposition of Langland's poem with a single Book of *The Faerie Queene* would never in itself be enough, and its results would be misleading if discussion were confined to one of the first two Books. If Spenser had written only these Books, *Piers Plowman* might well appear the more basically searching poem, more genuinely about life than about systems. Throughout *The Faerie Queene,* Spenser's artistry is richer and more controlled than Langland's, but in Book I, as in Book II, he seems to a greater extent working with, even if poetically working out, preconceived answers. Despite the impressive portrayals of a knight's developing awareness and the occasions of poetic self-awareness which these Books afford, taken alone or even together they do not demonstrate adequately the growth of awareness in the poem. For that we have to talk further about the poet, whose presence spans the poem, and in this chapter about Books III and IV, where a substantial change in the nature of his presence, vis-à-vis the first two Books, begins.

It is a larger growth in *The Faerie Queene,* including that in each Book but also that from opening to later Books, which makes this poem profoundly analogous to *Piers Plowman* and different from most Christian allegories. The difference might be clarified by reference to another context:

> with the increase in the number and variety of reactions in the higher forms of life, rote recapitulation and habit-behaviour are increasingly wasteful and it becomes more and more necessary to go direct to that portion of the organized setting of past responses most relevant to the needs of the moment. To do this the organism must acquire the capacity to turn round upon its own "schemata" and construct them anew. *This is where and why consciousness comes in.* It may be that what then emerges is an *attitude* towards the integrated effects of a series of past reactions.[1]

This statement describes an expanding awareness. With adjustment—the omission of "rote," the enlargement of the durational span of a moment, the substitution of "habitual" for "habit" and of "responses" for "reactions"— it also suggests a process which lies at the heart of both poems. In both, such expansion is early glimpsed, for example, in the evolution of the figure Piers Plowman in Langland's Visio, and in Spenser's evolving use of pastoral and approach to contemplative vision in his first Book; but it becomes far more remarkable, more extensive and self-conscious, about halfway through both poems, for Spenser in Books III and IV and for Langland in Passūs XI to XIV, which envisage Imaginative, Conscience, and Hawkin.[2]

Yet in some respects Spenser's third and fourth Books are farther removed from *Piers Plowman* than any of the others. Spenser's interest in human creativity, in the psychology of passion, and in the growth of human love appears in Books III and IV without primary reference to theological matters. As such, it has little in common with *Piers Plowman*. To be sure, there are elements in these Books not totally alien to Langland's thinking. Both Books are about the force that binds persons together in friendship, marriage, and society, the same force Langland calls charity. Although these Books express a concern with physical and emotional relationships which Langland, despite an occasional sensitive reference to them, does not share, charity and unity among persons, human and divine, are precisely what, as a Dreamer, he learns to seek. Books III and IV are also in a special way concerned with the mind, and a "Wonder it is to see, in diuerse minds, / How diuersly loue doth his pageants play" (III.v.1). These Books treat the mind, not in its dealings with specifically religious truths and methodically delimited experiences, but in a less-structured way with itself, with its own self-generated processes, the constant energies and impulses that feed it, in which these other truths and experiences must be embedded.

The central Books of *The Faerie Queene* have a less consistent and linear plot, a more flexible treatment of awareness, the preludes to relatively more extensive characterization in Books v and vi; and a more personal role for the narrator, a role which begins to be evident in Book iii and in Book iv becomes focal. The central Passūs of *Piers Plowman,* in which the Dreamer discovers Imagination, a new understanding of Conscience, and starts really to discover himself, are in an obvious sense close to Book i, to the history of the Redcrosse Knight in general, and particularly close to his expansion of awareness in canto x; but they are closer in a more fundamental, deeper sense to what begins to happen in Book iii of *The Faerie Queene* and what happens more explicitly, frequently, and purposefully in the Books that follow.

If Spenser leans toward personal restraint, distancing the realization of the poet's own personality in his first two Books, Langland positively lists toward personal chaos in Passūs x and xi. In Book iv or even Book iii of *The Faerie Queene,* some readers find Spenser's handling of his poetic material a little erratic; but Spenser can also be said to achieve a more flexible form without a conspicuous loss of control. Growth proves disorienting as well as reorienting in both poems, but it costs Langland's poem more than Spenser's. Parts of Langland's tenth and eleventh Passūs cross beyond process and search to confusion and poetic disorder. For over a hundred and fifty lines of Passus xi (148–310), speakers interrupt and succeed one another, arguing with vigor but without reasonable clarity: it is impossible to be sure whether Scripture, Trajan, Lewte, or Will the Dreamer, has the floor.[3] The situation is clearer at the end of Passus x, where the heated talker is presumably always Will, but given the jumble of good and bad views that well up in his talk, it is not entirely clear.

Whether or not these passages actually reflect the poet's personal condition, as R. W. Chambers suggests, they imitate confusion too directly.[4] Distanced by the reader and recalled as an imaginative whole, they are moving; but examined closely, their artistry is faulty, their disorder not quite subsumed into effective artistic expression. In revising the B-text of *Piers Plowman,* the poet himself appears to have reached a similar conclusion. He incorporates these passages more methodically into the C-text and creates a new character, Recklessness, who serves to clarify them. At one point in the C-text, the Dreamer's identity blends into Recklessness, thus illuminating the moral angle at which we should take remarks which most likely belonged to Will in the B-version (C, xii.254–276; cf. 199, 283; C, xiv.128–129). Langland's A- and C-texts make revision obvious, as is not the case with Spenser's poem. They underscore the validity of seeing *Piers Plowman* as a process of thought and enable us securely to speculate on the form it took.[5] Langland's revision suggests that a growth of awareness can be sought but obviously cannot be willed arbitrarily; it can be looked for, but it also has to be found. If it occurs and the poet is—or becomes—self-conscious about its occurrence, indeed, if the nature of his subject and vision invite its happening, he will not exclude it from his poem but will try to find the form adequate to its expression. Variously, in both *Piers Plowman* and *The Faerie Queene* we find such efforts.

4

Passūs XII to XIV:
Imaginative, Conscience, and Hawkin

In the tenth Passus of *Piers Plowman,* Dame Study interrupts her tirade about men's misuse of wit to remark, "Ymaginatyf her-afterward shal answere to 30wre purpos" (115). With no further pause she then catches her former train of thought and charges relentlessly onward. Her momentary interruption is cryptic, seemingly digressive, half overheard. It does not exist in the A-text, pretty clearly because the poet never wrote, and at this point had no intention of writing, Imaginative's answers in A. Study's seemingly chance remark is a telling instance of the poet's revision and the first specific indication in the B-text of the importance of the imaginative faculty as the poet came to see it in rewriting the poem.

After consulting Clergy and Scripture in Passus x at Dame Study's invitation, Will, the Dreamer, rebels in anger and frustration. Though already asleep, he goes to sleep again in Passus xi without first waking, and falls at once into a deeper, or inner, dream, a fantasy of wish-fulfillment in the Land of Longing. He dreams of a life of pleasure, into which he strays with lust of the flesh, lust of the eyes, and pride of life (xi.12–14), until he dreams that old age and poverty come upon him. Then he has second thoughts about greed, injustice, the words of Scripture (xi.103), and Dowel's relation to Clergy. In a moving passage "Kynde"—nature, kindness, the created expression of God's word, or God in His creative aspect—comes to him:

> And nempned me by my name and bad me nymen hede
> And thorw the wondres of this worlde wytte for to take.
> And on a mountaigne that Mydelerd hy3te, as me tho thou3te,
> I was fette forth by ensaumples to knowe
> Thorugh eche a creature and Kynde my creatoure to louye.
> I seigh the sonne and the see and the sonde after
> And where that bryddes and bestes by here makes thei 3eden,
> Wylde wormes in wodes and wonderful foules

With flekked fetheres and of fele coloures.
Man and his make I my3te bothe byholde . . .

[XI.313-22]

In a passage imaginatively reminiscent of Genesis, the Dreamer finds a new
beginning, the start of a renewed understanding. Before long, his observation
of the world leads him to rebuke reason for not pursuing "man and his make,"
alone of Kind's creatures (366). Briefly, his rebuke strikes the familiar key of
complaint which preceded his rebellion, but it also signals the return of his
wits to him. For the first time since that rebellion, characters who personify
his own mental functions reappear. Reason answers his rebuke directly, and
in fact tells him off in words that resound all the way back to the two friars'
parable: "*Nemo sine crimine viuit*" (XI.394). Ironically, the friars triggered the
Dreamer's active search through logical thought and reason alone. Now in
Passus XI, the Dreamer is shamed by a higher Reason: " 'Who suffreth more
than god?' quod he; 'no gome, as I leue' " (371).[1]

With Reason's rebuke of him, the Dreamer awakens, presumably from
the inner sleep, to see an unidentified figure looking at him, in whose presence
he formulates his first active, hence sound, understanding of Dowel: "To se
moche and suffre more" (402). The strange onlooker immediately turns the
Dreamer's insight back upon him: " 'Haddestow suffred,' he seyde, 'slepyng
tho thow were, / Thow sholdest haue knowen that Clergye can and con-
ceiued more thorugh Resoun' " (403-04). It takes poor Will another
twenty lines to assent to the truth of the onlooker's remarks, but when he
does, the latter begins to walk, to move or progress, and the Dreamer "aros
vp ri3t with that and folwed him after" (430), seeking his name—that is, to
know his own "Imaginatyf" power better.

Imaginative embodies a new kind of realization in the poem. He differs
from any of the characters found in it before. To an astounding extent he
recollects the Dreamer's earlier statements and conversations, for example,
about Aristotle and Solomon (XII.42-44, X.379-83), about Clergy (XII.156
ff., X.442), and about Reason (XII.217-18, XI.326 ff.). Imaginative is distinguished by his relation to the power of memory, but he is not a static
storehouse of ideas and past events. Without memory, which belongs to the
imagination, reason cannot function properly, indeed, imaginatively; with it,
Reason does not become imagination but can become Imaginative, as he
actually does at this point in the poem.[2] Imaginative is reason using the resources of the imagination in an imaginatively reasonable way. He might be
termed the proper perspective on experience, for he sees it in a special way.[3]
He makes meaningful connections among the Dreamer's earlier positions,

viewing them with a different attitude and in a new light. His recall is deliberate, thorough, and expansive, and it ought to be. As he himself points
out, he has been following the Dreamer for forty-five years (XII.3); he has
followed him "in feithe," in so far as Will had faith (or was faithful) and as
he had faith in Will. Now he leads, for Will "folwed him after."

Imaginative even sounds different from characters earlier encountered.
His positions are clearer, more sophisticated, more controlled:

> "Poule in his pistle," quod he, "preueth what is dowel:
> *Fides, spes, caritas; et maior horum . . .*
> Feith, hope, and charitee, and alle ben good
> And sauen men sundry tymes, ac none so sone as charite."
>
> [XII.30–32]

We all know Paul's words, as Langland did when he began the poem; but as
any reader also knows and as many pages of critical interpretation testify, the
Dreamer's efforts to define Dowel have been persuasively preoccupying and
maddeningly difficult to follow. Now the definition is brought to be recognizable, sensible, and simple. The same is true of Imaginative's explanation of
the functions of clergy and kind wit, once again terms which had earlier
driven the Dreamer near to distraction. Imaginative's positions are more
sophisticated because his relation to the Dreamer is more knowledgeable and
in this sense more intimate. His tone is more familiar and personal and less
sermonical than that of earlier instructors. Even his direct addresses are
specifically meant for the Dreamer, rather than only for "3ow riche," with
whom the poem was obsessively occupied before:

> For-thi I conseille the for Cristes sake Clergye that thow louye,
> For Kynde Witte is of his kyn and neighe cosynes bothe
> To owre lorde, leue me; for-thi loue hem, I rede . . .
>
> [XII.94–96]

The new attitude Imaginative expresses has room for wit and irony which
are not merely controlled but also constructive. It realizes an emotional
distance and control radically different from the jumble of accusations and
assertions that characterizes the Dreamer's confrontations with Scripture
(x, xi). A memorable instance occurs at the end of Imaginative's defense of
Clergy: "Wo was hym marked that wade mote with the lewed," Imaginative
exclaims, and then continues, "Wel may the barne blisse that hym to boke
sette, / That lyuynge after letterure saued hym lyf and soule" (XII.186–88).
These lines remind Imaginative of an even more practical use of clergy, for
with barely a pause for breath he adds:

Dominus pars hereditatis mee is a meri verset
That has take fro Tybourne twenti stronge theues
There lewed theues ben lolled vp; loke how thei be saued!

[XII.189–91]

Immediately after this outburst of ironic admiration, Imaginative refers to
the Dreamer's efforts to refute Scripture's emphasis on one's obligation to do
well. The Dreamer had asked Scripture who did worse than the Magdalen,
David, or Paul, and who did less to gain heaven than the good thief; yet
"On Gode Fridaye, I fynde, a feloun was ysaued / That had lyued al his lyf
with lesynges and with thefte" (X.414 ff.). Imaginative remembers the
Dreamer's words well:

The thef that had grace of god on Gode Fryday, as thow speke,
Was, for he 3elte hym creaunt to Cryst on the crosse and
    knewleched hym gulty
And grace axed of god that to graunten it is redy . . .

[XII.192–94]

Imaginative's movement from a defense of Clergy (learning and especially
religious learning) to Tyburn, to Calvary, is quick and compact but lucid. It
opposes dishonest evasion and the misuse of Clergy at Tyburn to sincere
contrition and the proper use of Clergy on Calvary.[4] Without entangling
himself in an unimaginative web of logical contradictions, Imaginative makes
both the point that learning is invaluable and the point that it has no value
unless it benefits a man's soul.

The figure Imaginative not only represents a synthesis of imagination and
reason and of observation and learning, but when he refers to Calvary and
Tyburn he also makes this synthesis real. He is actively Imaginative. Using
the resources of the imagination well, he does well and makes good use—
that is, imaginative use—of Clergy. In his references to Calvary and Tyburn
he aligns the spiritual "lyf" with the active "lyf" and brings the past to bear
on the present. He juxtaposes theory and practice, faith and works, spirit and
letter. The thief of Calvary and the thief of Tyburn meet without his begging
the reality of either one, and when they do, a moral world is made to seem
real despite the immoral reality of this one. Imaginative's Passus is a long
way from the welter of realities in the Prologue, from the Dreamer's obtuse
responses to Lady Holy Church's presentation of truths, and from the
rational impasses of Conscience's confrontation with Lady Meed.

Imaginative affords a new perspective on problems the Dreamer had
earlier found so insoluble that they had led him to abandon his search.

Probably the most important of these problems involves the relation of faith to works, or in terms the poem has used to this point, of Clergy (including faith, hence Baptism) to Dowel, or of bad priests and lazy Christians to righteous heathens. The passage about Tyburn and Calvary gives a fair sample of the way Imaginative settles the score with an unrighteous Clergy, but the problem of the righteous heathens gives even his use of learning, if not of theological wit, more trouble. Neither Imaginative nor the Dreamer can let go of this problem. The former alludes to it early in Passus XII (44 ff.), and by a natural process of association (262–67), finds it again at the end: "And where he [Aristotle] be sauf or nou3t sauf, the sothe wote no clergye, / Ne of Sortes ne of Salamon no scripture can telle" (268–69).

Continuing, Imaginative recommends faith and hope in God's fairness and mercy, but at this point, the Dreamer reverts to an earlier argument, in effect turning Imaginative's defense of Clergy back upon him: "Alle thise clerkes," he objects, preach that "no creature of Cristes lyknesse with-outen Crystendome worth saued" (275–77). Imaginative's reply to his objection suggests a crucial finality:

> "*Contra*," quod Ymagynatyf tho and comsed for to loure
> And seyde, "*saluabitur vix iustus in die iudicij*.[5]
> *Ergo saluabitur*," quod he and seyde namore Latyne.
>
> [XII.278–79]

Imaginative suddenly uses precisely the striking logical signals, *contra* and *ergo*, which the Dreamer earlier invoked to confute theological learning—first with the two friars (VIII.20–25) and later with Scripture (X.345). With these phrases, Imaginative lays claim to the tools of logic and uses them in an outrageously imaginative interpretation of Scripture. As the remainder of Passus XII makes clear, however, his interpretation is firmly based in an awareness of God and a patient trust in his works (280–93); we might say that he reads with the right spirit.

At the beginning of Passus XIII, the Dreamer wakens and reflects on the whole of the last two Passūs, on Imaginative's counsel but also on his own rebellion and on the behavior of covetous and ignorant churchmen. Initially, it is surprising to see that Will has not been totally convinced by Imaginative's insights, that his problems have not been resolved, and, in short, that the search is not nearly over. We realize here that Will's independence is real. He no longer is just the voice of confused or contentious responses but is instead more nearly a whole person. We do not find the same distance between narrator and Dreamer, satire and stupidity, as before. The awareness the Dreamer now embodies is double-sided, yet it is not committed to self-canceling contradictions. It touches the world, "And how this coueitise ouercome clerkes and prestes," but touches also the promise, for Kind "Leueth . . . no lyf, lasse ne more" (11, 17). The Dreamer ends his reflections with Imaginative's words on the righteous heathen and then remarks on "how sodeynelich he passed," feeling, perhaps, some emptiness at his passing.

Thus musing, Will goes again to sleep, dreaming that Conscience comes to comfort him and bids him to dine under Conscience's roof with Clergy. At the dinner which follows, the Dreamer finds Patience, with whom he sits; but besides Conscience and Clergy, he also finds in attendance a greedy, hypocritical friar. This setting recapitulates figures who had provoked the Dreamer's wrathful distrust earlier in the poem, namely, clerical learning and the false embodiment of it in a friar. The Dreamer's desire to meet Clergy again has been whetted by Imaginative's insights (xiii.24), and at first he does not recognize the friar's false nature: "what man he was I neste / That lowe louted and loueliche to Scripture" (25–26). All too soon, however, the friar's selfish greed makes recognition inescapable and brings vividly back to the Dreamer his former preoccupying awareness of Clergy's corruption by corrupt clergymen: "It is nou3t foure dayes that this freke bifor the den of Poules / Preched of penaunces" (65–66).

Instead of losing control entirely—indeed, losing himself—in the face of corruption, this time Will complains to Patience and, with the latter's reluctant permission, asks the fat friar to explain Dowel, particularly as it pertains to doing penance. Then, having exposed the friar's dishonesty, Will is silenced by Patience at Conscience's request. Thus, for once he justly and vigorously rebukes wrong, without being deflected from his own quest for something better. Conscience takes over the questioning from him and seeks knowledge of Dowel from the friar, from Clergy, and finally from Patience. Only Patience's explanation has love at its heart and sees love as the necessary fulfillment of learning. Imaginative's aid has led the Dreamer, "as Cryste wolde," to Conscience (xiii.22); and in Conscience's court, he has been introduced to Patience, an attitude toward experience equated by St. James the Apostle with living faith, and the first virtue Will finds which is impossible to attain without the supernatural assistance of grace.[6] Now, with Conscience's help, Will begins to discover what Patience can teach him.

Patience carries with him a box containing, in effect, the life of grace and charity—in a word, of love—which he recommends as the remedy for every kind of disorder, physical, demoniac, social, religious.[7] The friar, asked to judge whether Patience possesses Dowel, pronounces it "but a *Dido* . . . a dysoures tale," and, with unwitting irony, continues,

> Al the witt of this worlde and wiȝte mennes strengthe
> Can nouȝt confourmen a pees bytwene the pope and his enemys,
> Ne bitwene two Cristene kynges can no wiȝte pees make,
> Profitable to ayther peple . . .
>
> [XIII.173–76]

Impatiently, the friar pushes the table from him, telling Conscience and Clergy that Patience, doubtless a liar, should be made to pass on. Once again in the friar's words, a Christian remedy is contradicted by worldliness and is made to seem untrue by the observable realities of this world. With the friar's attitude, we are back again in the Visio, with the contradiction of spirit by flesh and, more specifically, of a holy pardon by a spokesman of the Church. We are back, in short, at the Pardon Scene (VII.112 ff.).

This time, however, an answer not so much new, given Piers's action in the Pardon Scene, but newly understood, is heard. Even though Imaginative's defense of Clergy was well-reasoned, Will's reservations at the outset of Passus XIII, intensified by the behavior of the fat friar, unexpectedly result in Conscience's taking leave of Clergy with quick but calm assurance, as soon as the friar has finished his dismissal of Patience:

> "Frendes, fareth wel," and faire [he] spake to Clergye,
> "For I wil go with this gome, if god wil ȝiue me grace,
> And be pilgryme with Pacience til I haue proued more."
>
> [XIII.180–82]

Conscience does not reject Clergy outright in these lines but only says that he must search further because he perceives the possibility of something better. The exchange between Conscience and Clergy that follows is, in its quiet way, moving. It expresses a radically new consciousness earlier sought and foreshadowed but never to this extent achieved.

Clergy's first, startled reply to Conscience's avowed intention to depart suggests a singular lack of awareness on his part:

> "What?" quod Clergye to Conscience, "ar ȝe coueitouse nouthe
> After ȝeresȝyues or ȝiftes or ȝernen to rede redeles?
> I shal brynge ȝow a bible, a boke of the olde lawe,
> And lere ȝow, if ȝow lyke, the leest poynte to knowe,
> That Pacience the pilgryme perfitly knewe neuere."
>
> [XIII.183–87][8]

Once more Passus XIII echoes the Pardon Scene, the priest's sarcasm, his insinuation that Piers's motivations spring from ignorance and pride, his derogation of riddling answers, no matter how partial or mystical they might be—in short, Clergy's failure to comprehend the need of an effort, and a will, to realize the import of any answer. Conscience's reply to Clergy sincerely emphasizes precisely the need to perfect the will.

> "Nay, bi Cryste," quod Conscience to Clergye, "god the forȝelde,
> For al that Pacience me profreth proude am I litel.
> Ac the wille of the wye and the wille of folke here
> Hath moeued my mode to mourne for my synnes."
>
> [XIII.188–91]

His next words interiorize the reason for his departure and hence the nature of his search itself:

> The good wille of a wiȝte was neure bouȝte to the fulle,
> For there nys no tresore therto, to a trewe wille.
> Haued nouȝt Magdeleigne more for a boxe of salue
> Than Zacheus for he seide, *"dimidium bonorum meorum do pauperibus?"*
>
> [XIII.192–95]

Conscience's choice involves a radical turning inward to the self.

Conscience's succeeding lines, whispered to Clergy, are mischievous— "Me were leuer, by owre lorde, and I lyue shulde, / Haue pacience perfitlich than half thy pakke of bokes!" (200–01). Clergy, responding appropriately to this engaging if unnecessary remark, changes his tune. He refuses to bid Conscience farewell and instead warns him "ful sobreliche, 'thow shalt se the tyme / Whan thow art wery for-walked, wilne me to consaille'" (203–04). The warning is one Conscience will have sad reason to recall near the end of the poem, and even now he recognizes its truth.[9] He suggests in his turn that if Clergy will also have patience, they can amend all the troubles in the world. When Clergy assents to the truth of this statement and prom- ises to continue to teach the unlearned, Conscience departs with the Dreamer (a will) and with Patience. Presumably, then, his final statement to Clergy cuts two ways, meaning that Clergy should teach the world about patience but also that clergymen should practice patience themselves. In other words, without rejecting Clergy's learning or social function, Conscience insists that the pilgrimage of every single man must be the one he now undertakes. The poem no longer tries to conceive of Conscience primarily in public terms—a Knight of the Realm in the Visio, the companion and means of access to Clergy at the beginning of Passus XIII. Conscience's role has been individualized and personalized.

When Conscience sets forth as a pilgrim in Passus XIII, he also turns from a figure expressed primarily in terms of intellect to one expressed primarily in the affective terms of the will, from expression through words alone to expression through action. Randolph Quirk has identified *inwit* as " 'intellect,' the *agens* aspect of *intellectus* in Thomist terms" and Conscience as "one aspect of inwit's activity; it is inwit's awareness of right and wrong brought to bear upon one's actions; it is inwit in action."[10] Yet it is not until this point in the poem that Conscience is truly brought to bear upon one's own actions, including, for the poet, the earlier actions of the poem; nor until this point that Conscience can truly be said to act. In Conscience's decision to part with Clergy lies a birth of conscious choice and a transformation from Conscience as a fixed concept, to a pilgrim, a figure who changes in and through time. In the Visio, Conscience stayed put in his position, and in a sense the pilgrimage did too, for it never went farther than the plowing of Piers's half-acre. We might say that Conscience's decision in Passus XIII interiorizes and explains Piers's similar movement in the Pardon Scene at the end of the Visio.

Conscience is not only the moral sense of right and wrong and the application of this sense to particular cases, but in usage now obsolete it is consciousness, internal knowledge, and conviction. When Wyclif writes, "The worschipers clensid oonys, hadden no conscience of synne ferthermore" (Heb. 10:2), he surely does not mean that they had lost the faculty which pronounces on the moral qualities of experience.[11] In Passus XIII the moving of Conscience to mourn for his sins involves not only his pronouncement about himself, a new self-awareness, but a realizing of this awareness in action. It is only as a pilgrim that he can benefit from his consciousness of sin and, as a figure in the poem, become his own decision. If he were to remain where he is, staying with Clergy, he would simply cease to be what he has become.

The first new character to appear after Conscience leaves Clergy is Hawkin, *Activa Vita,* minstrel and bread-supplier—analogously, therefore, poet and plowman. Like Piers in the Visio and like Langland himself, Hawkin hates idleness, "For alle trewe trauaillours and tilieres of the erthe, / Fro Mychel-messe to Mychelmesse I fynde hem with wafres" (XIII.238–40). In the remainder of Passus XIII Hawkin turns out to be an imagined composite of all the human activities with which the Visio dealt.[12] He wears a coat of Christendom stained by all the Deadly Sins. When Conscience and his two companions notice its filth, they stop him in his tracks for analysis, in the course of which he undergoes a transformation. He stops his unselfconscious complaining about lords, prelates, and his own hard life, to experience whole-hearted contrition and a will, with Patience, to do well. Hawkin's

figure gives form to repentance, in this sense embodying it. He completes
the stage of reform begun earlier in Passus XIII and brings the virtue of
Patience into relation with the workaday world.

Hawkin resembles other figures in the poem, the Seven Deadly Sins, Lady
Meed, or even Conscience and Piers in the Visio, but he is also in context
quite different from any figure encountered before. He is not met in a king's
court, in a plow-field, or in any other social context. He does not respond to
a knight, a plowman, or a preacher, but to Conscience and Patience. His
appearance is sudden, without a particular reason and without preparation
of plot or setting by the narrator.[13] To be sure, Piers's plow-field and the
King's court in the Visio are imagined landscapes, but they are also more
tangible than is Hawkin's in the poem, and they recognizably imitate the
landscape of this world. As a figure in the poem, Hawkin has no landscape
but the mind's, and his story, insofar as it exists, is the achievement of
a consciousness of self. Unlike Piers, Conscience, or Will, Hawkin exists
all at once in Passūs XIII to XIV and is found as a character nowhere else in the
poem.[14] He is not *in* a place but is *himself* the place where something happens.
He embodies a moment or act in which he participates but does not participate alone.

Hawkin's peculiar function in the poem is evident in the techniques of
analysis used with him. Noticing Hawkin's coat, the Dreamer begins to
describe the nature of its spots, some of which have notable pertinence to
his own failings as we have seen them earlier in the poem—for instance,
"Lakkyng lettred men and lewed men bothe ... And entermeten hym
ouer-al ther he hath nouȝt to done" (XIII.287–91). His description concludes
with a direct quotation, clearly introduced as Hawkin's own words:

> And of werkes that he wel dyd witnesse and seggen,
> "Lo, if ȝe leue me nouȝt or that I lye wenen,
> Axeth at hym or at hym, and he ȝow can telle
> What I suffred and seighe ..."
>
> [XIII.307–10]

Conscience speaks next and tells Hawkin that his coat must be washed.
Hawkin replies that the coat is even fouler than Conscience has noticed, and
with this admission, the Dreamer's description of the coat starts again, as he
remarks that "It was bidropped with Wratthe and wikked wille, / With
Enuye and yuel speche" (321–22). The Dreamer continues for several lines,
and then another quotation occurs, but this time the quotation is unqualified
direct discourse: "Auenge me fele tymes other frete my-selue / Wyth-inne."

There is no preparation for this sudden shift in persons and no narrative explanation for it after it has occurred (as there was in the previous quotation). When it occurs, we are left to wonder precisely who is talking. A pointed reference to Will introduced the confession of the Sins in the Visio, where Repentance "gert Wille to wepe water with his eyen," and a similar shift in person was noticeable at the end of Wrath's confession: Repentance "bad me wilne to wepe my wikkednesse to amende" (v.62, 187).[15] Now, in Hawkin's confession, it occurs a total of three times more: once just noticed, and the other times while the narrator is describing how Patience perceived Hawkin's coat (esp. 365 ff., 405 ff.). The third time is particularly interesting for its echoes of Hunger's effect on the Visio:

> [Hawkin] Swore there-by swithe ofte and al by-swatte his cote
> And more mete ete and dronke then kende miȝt defie
> And kauȝte seknesse sum-tyme for my sorfetes ofte,
> And thanne I dradde to deye in dedlich synne
> That in-to wanhope he worthe . . .
>
> [XIII.403–07]

In each instance the shift in person occurs, it becomes reasonably clear after a few lines that only Hawkin, the composite of all men—merchant, thief, wafer-seller, plowman, usurer, minstrel, fraud "Y-habited as an hermyte"— could be talking. The point is, however, that for a few lines in each instance we cannot be sure whether the direct discourse belongs to Hawkin, Conscience, or Will. This blending of identities appears to be intentional and certainly carries a perceptible significance.[16] The form works here, as it did not in the uncontrolled parts of Passūs x and xi, because it achieves meaning: in Passūs xiii to xiv, Hawkin's will is actively penitent, his consciousness enlarged, his realization of Patience started; and in him, Will, Conscience, and Patience make contact with workaday reality.

The final portion of Passūs XIII, roughly the last fifty lines (410 ff.), chiefly consists of direct discourse and includes the rhetorical questioning, answering, and direct address of exhortation: "Which ben the braunches that bryngeth a man to Sleuth?"; "Thise ben the braunches, beth war . . . ȝe lordes and ladyes and legates of holicherche"; in the form of direct address, it also includes a familiar warning, often delivered previously by the narrator himself: "For-thi I rede ȝow riche (410, 421–22, 442).[17] As before in this Passus, the speaker of this exhortation is not explicitly identified, a fact we are far less likely to be struck by than in the preceding instances: the shift in address is not so dramatically sudden; the context of the passage is timely, its treatment lucid. The speaker of the passage could be Patience, Conscience, or the Dreamer, but the distinctions among them are now unimportant, as well as elusive. The echoes of Will's earlier statements, the nature and tone of topics treated, and the explicit framing of the passage by Patience's and Conscience's presence, suggest that this exhortation should be seen as including all these speakers, because they are all in concord now—indeed, are at one (XIII.355, 459).

Passus XIV, which completes Hawkin's appearance, is full of the straightforward preaching of religious idealism; yet the poem has done a great deal to earn it and, with little touches in this Passus, still maintains contact with a reality less ideal. If this contact is now a defiant one, it is so through well-considered and self-knowledgeable conviction, not through naïveté. Hawkin hears Patience explain,

> . . . I shal purueye the paste . . . though no plow erie
> And floure to fede folke with as best be for the soule,
> Though neuere greyne growed ne grape vppon vyne.
>
> [XIV.28–30]

Hawkin just laughs, if only "a litel," at Patience's claims and "li3tly gan swerye, / 'Who so leueth 3ow, by owre lorde, I leue nou3te he be blissed' " (34–35). The inclusion of that hard-headed laughter makes Hawkin a little more convincing and his reform in this Passus a little more real. Patience patiently continues to teach him, however, nourishing him with virtue, treating directly the vexed problem of poverty and riches, and finally solving it, at least to the poem's present satisfaction. At the end of Passus XIV, Patience is said to be "payn," bread but also pain. This statement holds choice, in fact, radical commitment, but it at least acknowledges a realistic complexity as well. Convinced and contrite, Hawkin bursts into tears at the end of this Passus; and "there-with," the Dreamer tells us, "I awaked" (332). This statement carries a metaphorical weight greater than it ever has before. The Dreamer does not simply wake up or wake up to perplexity; he truly wakes up to a greater awareness.

Passūs XII to XIV, Imaginative through Hawkin, hold three reassessments of past action, each a further development of the one before. They provide the poem's own gloss on the partial answers of the Visio and first Vita, of which the Pardon Scene itself is a notable instance. Impressively dramatic—in some sense, perhaps, comparable to the first act of a play—the Pardon Scene is, in its immediacy and exteriorized symbolism, compressed, riddling, and not subject to incontrovertible or complete rationalization. Whether it was intended to be proleptic to such an extent or not when it was written, it turns out to be so. The Pardon Scene has to be regarded as the product of a habit of thought, an analogical habit of mind—perhaps an inspired one—on which the mind itself later doubles back to understand anew.[18] In the course of Passūs XII to XIV and as a result of them, the Dreamer wakes up to this new understanding, and after these Passūs he is nearly ready to catch up with Piers Plowman again, to enter the Garden of Charity which grows in the heart, and there to explore his own consciousness more deeply as he explores the expression of it in a more substantial landscape and more distinct form.

5

The Faerie Queene: Books III and IV

The development of awareness in Langland's and Spenser's poems has common features that affect the allegorical narratives of the two poems in analogous ways. These features are, perhaps, more generally common to the development of all human awareness, but their active, transforming presence in allegorical narrative is unusual. Like Langland's Passūs XII to XIV, Spenser's Books III and IV have a looseness of organization and narrative action (poet's and characters'); from an alternative view, they attest to a sense of personal freedom which permits growth and expansion and which, though earlier foreshadowed, is not previously realized so fully in *The Faerie Queene*. Before discussing Spenser's third and fourth Books, however, I must further summarize features of his first two Books which distinguish them from the two that follow.

The difference between Spenser's initial and central Books might simply amount to a change in subject matter and a corresponding change in the poet's role and relation to his fiction. We sense and respond to the nearness of realized human experience in Books I and II and sometimes encounter it directly, but it is characteristically distanced and qualified either by the poet's position—religious or narrative—or by the limited personalities of his agents. Perhaps it is best seen in the service—and in memorable instances *noticeably* in the service—of a principle or belief and perhaps, on the whole, best called self-effacing. The poet's position in the first two Books is a source of profound strength but also of weakness. We can recognize both facts without diminishing Spenser's marvelous achievements in these Books or forgetting that these particular achievements are also in large part the result of his taut control. Such recognition will greatly affect our reading of the rest of the poem and influence our judgment of it.[1]

Although narrative vision is wonderfully allied with the Knights' experience in Books I and II, there is also a sense in which it is confined by it and by them. The occasion is seldom or only distantly the poet's, and when the occasion is otherwise, as with passages treating despair and other powerfully affective experiences like contemplation, variously he pulls back from it or pushes it away. Poetic control—especially control through irony—can verge on emotional distance or suggest manipulation. The natural context of abstraction is the mind, and of an allegorical poem, the mind of a person. Such a mind in process is undogmatic and a little untidy. Settled intention and taut control can concentrate power but can also have a price:

> Gather therefore the Rose, whilest yet is prime,
> For soone comes age, that will her pride deflowre:
> Gather the Rose of loue, whilest yet is time,
> Whilest louing thou mayst loued be with equall crime.
>
> [II.xii.75]

Process trips over assertion. Here is at once the involved narrative consciousness and the narrator who not only has the answers already but is also prepared in a moral pinch to reveal this fact. In lines such as these the narrator's two voices coincide in an apparent contradiction which these Books, taken by themselves, do not resolve.[2]

Some other passages in which the narrator responds to the action of these Books sound overwrought and as a result puzzling, not to say unconvincing:

> Ah heauens, that do this hideous act behold,
> And heauenly virgin thus outraged see,
> How can ye vengeance iust so long withhold,
> And hurle not flashing flames vpon that Paynim bold?
>
> The pitteous maiden carefull comfortlesse,
> Does throw out thrilling shriekes, and shrieking cryes,
> The last vaine helpe of womens great distresse,
> And with loud plaints importuneth the skyes,
> That molten starres do drop like weeping eyes;
> And *Phoebus* flying so most shamefull sight,
> His blushing face in foggy cloud implyes,
> And hides for shame. What wit of mortall wight
> Can now deuise to quit a thrall from such a plight?
>
> Eternall prouidence exceeding thought,
> Where none appeares can make her selfe a way:
> A wondrous way it for this Lady wrought . . .
>
> [I.vi.5–7]

In this description of Una's distress, which I take to be seriously intended, one of Spenser's best readers has found "operatic parody" calculated to remind "us that in spite of all the fuss, everything is well under control.

... the final three lines serve mainly to alert the reader to Spenser's own inventiveness."[3] Spenser's lines are overdone, but they seem openly or inadvertently so. The initial Books of *The Faerie Queene* are often ironic and occasionally playful, but this passage is neither. The case might be different if the narrator expressed an ironic attitude toward the doctrine of grace elsewhere in Book I or, more crucially, if he had developed a sufficiently personal and dramatically autonomous voice in this Book either to express it suddenly here or to avoid the momentary impression that he might want to. Apart from the poet, the characters whose experiences are focal in Books I and II realize an understanding of principles intimately related to an awareness of the human self and doubtless posited on it; at the same time, these characters are too tidily exemplary, indeed too impersonal, to do more themselves than imply and only fleetingly realize the self-awareness that we have seen to underlie them and the Spenserian narrator as well.

With respect to both poet and characters, a sea-change materializes in Book III, and its effects are subtle and deliberate. There is nothing in Book III of the surprise, suddenness, and dramatic reassessment of Langland's central Passūs, but Spenser's more structured search also has its discoveries, a fact notwithstanding the possibility that Book III was written at least partially before Books I and II.[4] Insight once achieved and insight as finally presented are a continuing process that alters final effects. Through variety, invention, and considered change, Spenser's third Book realizes an enlarged personal awareness, with some ramifications for later Books which Spenser may or may not have foreseen at this point.

BOOK III.i–iv: THE VENERIAN FLOWER AND THE BOAR

At the opening of Book III, Britomart unseats Guyon, thereby proving that she possesses a superior power or virtue, although it is soon seen to be one also bound to temperance "with that golden chaine of concord" (i.12). Britomart's encounter with Guyon involves a far more emphatic qualification of his power than did Guyon's challenge to the Redcrosse Knight in the initial canto of Book II. At the end of Britomart's enchanted spear, the Knight of Temperance suffers a rude fall to earth and a fall into a broader context which includes the virtuous human love barely mentioned in Book II. Guyon's encounter and eventual accord with Britomart assert the connection of his virtue with her quest; but by her, his potentially fixating concentration on temperance is overthrown. In the context of Book III, Temperance by itself, burning "The verdant grasse" and "Full of disdainefull wrath," looks intemperate, though we might more kindly say that in the opening incident of Book III, Guyon shifts from the exemplar of human temperance to something more fully a man (i.5, 9).[5]

Values operate less absolutely (and abstractly) in Book III than in Books I and II. Arthur placates Guyon's wrath with tactful dishonesty (and for the reader of Book II, with double-entendre) when he tells him that the failings of his horse or page, rather than Britomart, must have caused his fall.[6] Later in canto i, the same two "gentle knights"—apparently *sans* Palmer—see the Forester's outrage on Florimell and spur after her "Full of great enuie and fell gealosy," if not of her pursuer then of themselves or each other (18). Britomart's armor is likewise quite different in value from Una's veil. It functions as a sign of her condition and as a means of protection, as did the veil, but also as a means of outright deception. When she deceives Redcrosse about her reasons for seeking Artegall, however, we are amused, not morally offended.[7] Her statement that Artegall has done "Late foule dishonour and reprochfull spight" to her has a sophistical relation to truth, but only if we read it as the projection of her love-pain onto the unwitting Artegall. The narrator takes the occasion of Britomart's statement to draw a distinction between the inner and outer realms, no longer so simply coterminous as they were in Books I and II: "The royall Mayd woxe inly wondrous glad, / To heare her Loue so highly magnifide," but she continues to speak in "strifull termes" to the Redcrosse Knight, blaming her Love (ii.11–12). A major problem in Book III and the following Books will be precisely the achieving of a genuine relation between the inner and outer realms which answers more immediately to the personal experience of life, as well as to principle and belief.

From its start Book III differs from the preceding Books in tone and context and in the behavior of narrator and characters.[8] The landscape is less overtly emblematic and more natural than before. In the first canto, Britomart, Guyon, and Arthur travel through a forest, seeing no creatures "Saue Beares, Lions, and Buls, which romed them around" (14). So very soon after the Bower of Bliss, the difference between these animals and Acrasia's immoral menagerie is not likely to pass unnoticed. Certainly these animals belong to the landscape of romance rather than that of the English countryside, but they are also more simply beastly, more themselves and less metaphors, than is Acrasia's hog Grille or the truth-loving lion of Book I. The narrator's tone is easier in Book III and his handling of the story both more direct and less tidy than it was formerly. With relative frequency, he talks over his character's shoulders, not blending his presence into theirs so much as adding a further or alternative dimension to it. The difference here is slight, far less obvious than it will become in Book IV, but it makes an early contribution to the distinctive quality of Book III.

Already in the seventh and eighth stanzas of canto i, for example, the narrator takes his unhurried time, while Guyon falls from his horse and has recourse to his sword, to explain not only the nature of Britomart's spear but also to sympathize with Guyon's wounded feelings: "Ah gentlest knight, that euer armour bore, / Let not thee grieue dismounted to haue beene" and again,

> But weenedst thou what wight thee ouerthrew,
> Much greater griefe and shamefuller regret
> For thy hard fortune then thou wouldst renew . . .

Had the narrator behaved this way with Una and Redcrosse in the Wandering Wood, the perceptual experience would have been lost. Now, overtly and deliberately, he produces the impression that he is creating his story, treating it more as fabrication than as revelation. At rather unpredictable moments he addresses his audience directly (i.49, v.53); he changes scenes or ends a canto for his own arbitrary reasons, often casually associative and, therefore, seemingly natural (v.12-13, viii.52). This narrative attitude of greater "dominion" over the poem lends the narrator a more distinct personality and, not so oddly, helps to lend Britomart one as well.[9] Despite the narrator's more straightforward display of special knowledge, we do not get the impression that he is controlling Britomart so directly as he did Redcrosse and Guyon. He reports, explains, and responds to her experiences, but without disappearing into them or into her; indeed, he devotes nearly half the Book to others' experiences, including some distinctly his own, like the Gardens of Adonis (vi.29). Although Britomart is a figure in an allegorical romance and clearly has metaphorical dimensions, she too is made to appear less simply a metaphor and more simply herself.

The fact that Britomart is a woman offered Spenser more than a chance to compliment the British Queen and to show his sensitivity to the female psyche. It is reasonable to assume that her womanhood had some influence in this Book on his narrative position and tone, poised in depicting Britomart between appreciative understanding and comic distance. Despite Britomart's metaphorical dimensions and the moderate proportion of episodes she dominates in Book III, her figure affords the poem some of the advantages which Shakespeare was to find in a character like Rosalind, another woman disguised as a man. Britomart is freed from her customary social role and womanly passivity by her disguise, and from the customary expectations and social commitments of a knight's role by her sex. Unlike Artegall's later appearance in woman's garb (v), her disguise is no sign of debasement. Doubly protected from limiting roles and predetermined commitments, she can engage in a quest that will bring an inner world of ideas and emotions into virtuous—true and powerful—relation with a more tangible, exterior one.

Spenser's presentation of Britomart's freedom, like Shakespeare's of Rosalind's, combines humor with human dignity. These characteristics are particularly memorable in the early cantos—the episode at Malecasta's castle, Britomart's revealing her love to Glauce and their visit to Merlin, Britomart's address to the sea—and these cantos largely account for our lasting impression of her. We need the first and last of their episodes to introduce our major concern in Book III, the poet's realization of a growth—an expansion—of awareness.

In the episode at Malecasta's castle, Britomart enters an experience that bears curious similarities to those in the earlier Books, but she is seen from a different point of view and as a different kind of figure. The presence of the Redcrosse Knight at Castle Joyous and the echoes in this episode of his experiences at the beginning of Book I suggest the connection of Britomart's experience with his, as before in this canto with Guyon's, but they also emphasize their diversity and the peculiar virtues of Britomart's role. This time Malecasta has the "falsed fancy" (47) that Redcrosse had in Book I (ii.30), but Britomart is otherwise in a situation and condition resembling his: "Who meanes no guile, beguiled soonest shall" (III.i.54; cf. I.i.53, ii.45). Like Redcrosse facing the apparition of a false Una and then Duessa, Britomart gives credence to Malecasta, for

> . . . the chaste damzell, that had neuer priefe
> Of such malengine and fine forgerie,
> Did easily beleeue her strong extremitie.
>
> [III.i.53]

The false Una and Duessa herald a weakness within Redcrosse, whereas Malecasta belongs to a more social and exteriorized condition. This difference is not so complete as it might first appear, however. Malecasta, falsity herself, sneaks up on Britomart "vnwares" (i.61), and unaware is precisely Britomart's state when she looks in the magic mirror and is wounded by love,

> . . . ne her vnguilty age
> Did weene, vnwares, that her vnlucky lot
> Lay hidden in the bottome of the pot;
>
> [III.ii.26]

and it is also her condition when Busirane's knife wounds her (xii.33).

Entering Malecasta's castle, Britomart passes into an inner room, a place

that will have a clear interior significance in canto xii (26), and before leaving
the castle she is wounded, as she will be once more in canto xii. She sees a
tapestry in Malecasta's inner room on which the story of Venus and Adonis
is depicted, a destructive combination of sensuality and brutality or, in symbolic terms, the Venerian flower and the boar. This tapestry pictures complementary forms of excess, or *acrasia,* which Britomart will meet again in
Busirane's tapestry depicting the loves of the gods. In Malecasta's tapestry,
Venus's attitude and behavior pointedly recall Acrasia's and, perhaps in
the fact that she leads Adonis into a shade away "from bright heauens vew"
(35), reach through the second Book to the Wandering Wood of the first
(II.vii.3, 19, 20; I.i.7). Malecasta does not result from a weakness within
Britomart, but she has special pertinence to her condition. Britomart is vulnerable to her approaches, yet she is wounded in Castle Joyous, not because
she has fallen like the Redcrosse Knight in Book I, but more simply because
she is human.

Figures as exemplary as Redcrosse or Guyon would have been hard-pressed
to survive credibly the experience that Britomart confronts in Castle Joyous, where Malecasta attempts to seduce her, mistaking her for a man.
(Coincidentally, it is noteworthy that Britomart's first action in Book II
is the unseating of Guyon, and her second, the rescuing of Redcrosse from
Malecasta's challengers.) The treatment of Malecasta's mistake, a passion
so shapeless that, panting and trembling, it pursues any attractive shape in
its path, hovers on the borders of farce. With a sensuality quivering so del-
icately as to pale that of any seductress of romance, Malecasta slips into
Britomart's bed, "And by her side her selfe she softly layd, / Of euery finest
fingers touch affrayd" (61). Wakened by Malecasta's presence, Britomart
leaps from her bed to get her sword, whereupon Malecasta, with somewhat
less delicacy, "Did shrieke alowd, that through the house it rong." When
Malecasta's household run to her aid, they find her laid "on the sencelesse
grownd"—the antithetical but complementary image of Guyon at the beginning of this canto. Above the swooning seductress and facing her household of perverse passions cloaked in social forms, Britomart stands in her
"snow-white smocke," her locks unbound, and brandishing the avenging
blade. In this image humor and human dignity triumph, and the conventional expectations of a romance seduction are laid on their heads. Britomart's youthful innocence, attractiveness, and strength could hardly have
been more victoriously, incongruously, credibly, and vulnerably presented
than in that smock, those locks unbound, and the dangerously pointed,
seemingly pointless, sword.[10]

"Ne euill thing she fear'd, ne euill thing she ment": this description of

Britomart's innocence precedes the tale of Malecasta. The same description might have been applied to Redcrosse at the beginning of Book I. His story would have been very different had he been viewed not only interiorly but, as Britomart is, also from his own point of view. Britomart's innocence is shown to matter despite the Fall of Man. Her conscious intention is the immediate and present concern. In Archimago's hermitage or even in the Cave of Mammon, a figure like Glauce is not there, as she is in Book III, to ask the hero, "why make ye such Monster of your mind?" (ii.40). The experiences of earlier Books have an inevitability about them. They hold something to be discovered about oneself and the world, to be faced, adjusted, or withstood. The emphasis in Book III is more positive. There are mistakes to be avoided, impulses to be controlled and directed, and values to be recovered, but there is also something to be created. While echoes in Book III lead us to recall earlier Books, they also emphasize a realm of the mind's dominion, the mind's active and creative part in achieving its own destiny. This dominion is not only Britomart's, as the central figure of Book III, but is, in the echoes themselves and in the sense of diversity and alteration they cause us to see, again the controlling narrator's. Echoes of earlier contexts, so persistently present in Book III, not only point to a different kind of awareness, but are themselves an integral part of it, as they were when Imaginative came to Langland's dreaming Will.

The fourth canto draws dominant strands of Book III together, accentuating its special qualities and concerns. At the beginning of this canto Britomart reaches the seaside and there complains of her love; at its end, Arthur, having lost Florimell in the darkness, complains bitterly of night. Between these two complaints, Britomart wounds Marinell, whose mother arrives at his side to complain of his passing but then, finding him still alive, takes him home to the sea to restore his vitality. Each of these incidents focuses attention on the imagination's power to project its own shapes on reality. First seen, Britomart feeds her love-wound with "selfe-pleasing thoughts"; she fashions a thousand of these in her mind and "in her feigning fancie" portrays Artegall "such, as fittest she for loue could find" (5–6). Dismounted, her helmet off, she sits by the sea and views

> . . . a while the surges hore,
> That gainst the craggy clifts did loudly rore,
> And in their raging surquedry disdaynd,
> That the fast earth affronted them so sore,
> And their deuouring couetize restraynd . . .
>
> [III.iv.7]

Then she begins to speak, finding in the sea an image of her passion:

> Huge sea of sorrow, and tempestuous griefe,
>   Wherein my feeble barke is tossed long,
>   Far from the hoped hauen of reliefe,
>   Why do thy cruell billowes beat so strong,
>   And thy moyst mountaines each on others throng,
>   Threatning to swallow vp my fearefull life?
>   O do thy cruell wrath and spightfull wrong
>   At length allay, and stint thy stormy strife,
> Which in these troubled bowels raignes, and rageth rife.

[III.iv.8]

The immediacy of Britomart's complaint and the self-conscious activity it expresses convey dramatically the autonomy of her figure. Her words, her action, create a metaphor and interiorize the sea. Referring to the making of metaphors and similes, Bruno Snell remarks that "man must listen to an echo of himself before he may hear or know himself." He must obviously listen self-consciously, must at least recognize in the echo what he will make of it or is already making of it. Britomart uses the sea to express her condition, instead of being sent by the poet to journey in a boat upon it, as Florimell will be later in Book III. It is Britomart who identifies herself with a sea of passion in this Book.[11]

Britomart's complaint continues for another two stanzas which include lines laden with memories of the earlier Books, especially of Guyon's journey by boat to the Bower of Bliss (II.xii; cf. vii.1; I.ii.1). She sees that love steers her vessel, while fortune rows it:

> Loue my lewd Pilot hath a restlesse mind
>   And fortune Boteswaine no assuraunce knowes,
>   But saile withouten starres, gainst tide and wind:
> How can they other do, sith both are bold and blind?

[III.iv.9]

The recall of Books I and II occurs with significance twice more in this canto. Here it accentuates what is new in Britomart's complaint and why her lines are poignantly striking. The action of her mind is not just a fact unknown to her, as it was to Redcrosse in Book I, or at one remove from her, as it was for Guyon in the Bower of Bliss, where Acrasia was not really his own; it is a process which as a character she initiates and controls in this passage, and one of which she is to grow increasingly aware in Book III. Interior action is hers in a way that it was not Redcrosse's or Guyon's because she uses it immediately and creatively. The act itself, not its consequences, first occupies our attention.

While Glauce is trying to comfort Britomart, the lady knight spies Marinell riding hastily toward her in the distance and within a few stanzas cuts him down, leaving him badly wounded on the shore. It is difficult to see anything morally positive on Britomart's side in this action. Marinell asks for what he gets, both literally in his challenge to Britomart and figuratively in the unnatural condition he seeks to defend, but before Marinell is even within earshot, Britomart is suddenly wrathful (12), on her own pendulum swing from "clowdy care" to "wrathfull stowre" and from grief to vengeance (13). Her courage is kindled by "Loue and despight," a combination of opposite, correlative impulses like those which characterize Malecasta's tapestry and also characterize so many paired marchers in the House of Busirane. Marinell is not an integral part of a psychic drama, as is Sans Joy, for example, in Book I. Britomart wounds him because he is a convenient object on which to vent her emotion; he is not part of her consciousness except in this sense. She never even knows Marinell's name, and neither do we, until the poet names the sorry figure left in her wake. Britomart projects her passion onto Marinell, as before onto the sea, and since he is human in form (though, ironically, a son of the sea), like the stormy sea itself she lashes out violently at him.[12]

The wound Marinell receives has its origin in nature more directly than in love. Britomart's aggressive behavior is humanly natural—but too natural, as yet too little shaped and fulfilled by forms and principles specifically human. The images associated with her in this canto are natural but no more. Her grief dissolves and pours into vengeance,

> As when a foggy mist hath ouercast
>   The face of heauen, and the cleare aire engrost,
>   The world in darkenesse dwels, till that at last
>   The watry Southwinde from the seabord cost
>   Vpblowing, doth disperse the vapour lo'st,
>   And poures it selfe forth in a stormy showre . . .
>
> [III.iv.13]

The wound she inflicts can be cured in the sea, in a merely natural place (if also under artificial conditions), and Marinell will remain confined to the sea until he is again wounded, this time emotionally rather than physically, and again cured, this time humanly rather than magically—both by Florimell's love in Book IV.[13]

Most readers of canto iv remark the change of tone that follows on Marinell's fall, and few fail to marvel at the loveliness of the pastoral stanzas which present the grieving of Cymoent, his sea-nymph mother. The delicacy and lyrical grace, the sensuousness and leisure of these stanzas are all the more remarkable after the summary harshness of the preceding battle—the indignity of Marinell's "sadly soucing on the sandie shore, / . . . tombled on an heape, and wallowd in his gore" and the insensitivity of Britomart's behavior: "The martiall Mayd stayd not him to lament, / But forward rode" (16, 18). With the sequence of wrath in the battle and grief in Cymoent's laments, we meet yet again in altered guise the paired opposites of Malecasta's tapestry—hostility or aggressive force and sensuous withdrawal or passive loveliness; beauty and brutality, the Venerian flower and the boar.

Nature and art, action and passion—in senses which include creativity, emotion, and reflection—touch with harmonious promise when, helmet significantly doffed at the beginning of canto iv, Britomart makes her lament by the sea; but they also touch briefly, incompletely, precariously. In its extremes and antitheses, the sequel to her address shows nature and art still to a harmful extent opposed and mutually exclusive. That sequel, first the battle with Marinell, then the story of Cymoent which grows out of it, too closely recalls the wounding of Adonis and his metamorphosis to "a daintie flowre" (III.i.38) to offer the reconciliation of opposites which Book III pursues.

The presentation of Cymoent is distinguished for its artificiality, both for its imaginative beauty and for its distance from an actual world of physical turbulence and emotional pain. Amazed by the sight of Cymoent and her mourning sisters, Neptune bids "the roaring billowes" to be still, while

> A teme of Dolphins raunged in aray,
>   Drew the smooth charet of sad *Cymoent;*
>   They were all taught by *Triton,* to obay
>   To the long raynes, at her commaundement:
>   As swift as swallowes, on the waues they went,
>   That their broad flaggie finnes no fome did reare,
>   Ne bubbling roundell they behind them sent;
>   The rest of other fishes drawen weare,
> Which with their finny oars the swelling sea did sheare.
>
> [III.iv.33]

Not only the violence of the sea, but that of Cymoent's emotion can be switched on and off with preternatural control. When she hears of Marinell's wound she flings away her flowers and garlands and throws

> ... her selfe downe on the Continent,
>   Ne word did speake, but lay as in a swowne,
>   Whiles all her sisters did for her lament,
>   With yelling outcries, and with shrieking sowne;
>   And euery one did teare her girlond from her crowne.
>
> Soone as she vp out of her deadly fit
>   Arose, she bad her charet to be brought,
>   And all her sisters, that with her did sit,
>   Bad eke attonce their charets to be sought . . .
>   [III.iv.30–31]

Cymoent's formal lament for Marinell, presumed by her to be final, occupies four stanzas and holds haunting memories of other addresses in the *ave-atque-vale* vein:

> Who dyes the vtmost dolour doth abye,
>   But who that liues, is left to waile his losse:
>   So life is losse, and death felicitie.
>   [III.iv.38]

Yet her emotion is strangely distanced, made to seem self-consciously ceremonial, leisurely, even self-indulgent, by the Chaucerian lines which immediately succeed it: "Thus when they all had sorrowed their fill, / They softly gan to search his griesly wound" (40). The next stanza reinforces this impression:

> Tho when the lilly handed *Liagore*,
>   (This *Liagore* whylome had learned skill
>   In leaches craft, by great *Appolloes* lore,
>   Sith her whylome vpon high *Pindus* hill,
>   He loued, and at last her wombe did fill
>   With heauenly seed, whereof wise *Paeon* sprong)
>   Did feele his pulse . . .
>   [III.iv.41]

Between the naming of the lily-handed Liagore and her feeling the desperately wounded knight's pulse, there is time for a five-line interlude to examine her medical and mythological credentials. By such touches the nymphs' emotion is consistently formalized, made to seem more decorative and noticeably less real.[14]

The portrayal of Cymoent's sorrow casts a new light on Britomart's complaint and her violent behavior right after it. Britomart identifies herself with the sea; Cymoent in effect identifies the sea with herself, or as Paul

Alpers has said, with her own idyllic wishes.[15] The sea nymph who addresses her son, "Deare image of my selfe," realizes too little outside herself. Britomart, on the other hand, cannot as yet see enough inside herself. The perceptions they embody are both essentially human, but either by itself is incompletely so—the knight's is too instinctual in its origins and too uncontrolled and impersonal in its effects, the nymph's too mind-made, too artificial, and too vulnerable, but also too lovely to be merely wrong. Britomart's sorrowful complaint and succeeding violence are psychologically realistic and powerfully natural, but the beauty and serenity of Cymoent's pastoral landscape have as undeniable an appeal: they tell us about a reality, even while their insulation from reality warns us away. Though artificial, the pastoral experience in canto iv is allowed, indeed made, to speak directly to us without the intrusion of a moral voice like the one the poet feels necessary in Acrasia's immoral Bower: "Whilest louing thou mayst loued be with equall crime."

In a special way canto iv shows itself to be a self-conscious imaginative act for the poet—as a poet and as a quester, names for much the same thing in a mode so heavily committed to conceptual content as the allegorical. In Britomart's complaint, and more remarkably in presenting Cymoent's experience, the poet has an eye on the creative act itself as much as on the ideas it serves and develops. We have a heightened sense of this presence, despite its being unobtrusive. The poetic role Britomart is given at the outset of canto iv and the underlying theme of this canto—the relation of the shaping imagination to external and instinctual nature, of the controlling mind to impersonal forces—play their part in creating this impression by providing the necessary context for it; but the story of Cymoent, occupying so generous a center in this canto, plays the decisive role.

Cymoent does not make a metaphor of the sea; she is one. Her watery, idealized nature, unlike Britomart's tempests, is all the being she has. Cymoent cannot be seen as the conscious shaper of her own perceptions to the extent that Britomart can. The nymph is in no way outside them. It is not simply that we know that sea nymphs belong to a landscape of fantasy, that they are creatures of the "feigning fancie" at its freest, but that Cymoent is treated and used in such a way as to make us continually aware of this fact. We have seen that she turns her emotions on and off with artificial control, but the control is not hers. In a word, she *is* turned; yet the control which informs her nature suggests not intrusive manipulation but artistic presence more simply.

In contrast to passages in earlier Books, such as canto x in Book I (Contemplation) or canto vii in Book II (Mammon), canto iv has a less linear, more episodic structure: Cymoent is not integral to Britomart's psyche or even a direct part of her experience. The nymph stands on her own and at length, yet she lacks the autonomy of a conscious, dramatic figure. Because of the artifice of the pastoral stanzas in canto iv, so fully and so long drawn out, we hear something besides an expression of Cymoent's nature. By first calling our attention to the dramatic process by which Britomart shapes the reality she presently finds in her quest, the poet ensures the likelihood of our becoming conscious of his voice, the voice which more directly shapes the wonderful art of these stanzas. These pastoral stanzas are, of course, no more Spenser's own than is Britomart herself and all that she utters, but his poetic presence is a more visible—indeed more audible—part of their meaning.[16] In the beautifully realized idyllic moments of canto iv, Cymoent is focus and occasion, but not to Britomart's extent, maker.

An arresting feature of the pastoral stanzas in canto iv is the manner in which they echo passages from earlier Books and evoke haunting, elusive memories for the reader, for example, of Night and of Despair in Book I. These echoes enhance a sense of the poet's presence and, perhaps because of that special presence, exist; for they do not serve the purpose of contrast or comparison so specifically as most earlier echoes do—indeed, it is not clear whether or not they are entirely conscious for the poet. (They are as close as numerous parallels in the *Variorum* suggesting Spenser's knowledge of others' works, however, and we can at least assume Spenser's acquaintance with his own.) They add another effect, a depth, to the pastoral scene, hardly heard, even doubtfully heard, until the poet signals that he has heard them himself.

Curious similarities of situation account for many of the echoes of Book I in canto iv. The poem tells us that Cymoent is in a state of despair when she utters her lament over the wounded Marinell, for learning that a little life flickers among "his feeble sprites ... despeire she from her flong" (iv.41). Her lament itself does not repeat the exact words of Despair in Book I (ix) but in tone and content is sufficiently close to them, that we might almost suppose they are meant by contrast to suggest that she operates in a lower, less serious key:

> O what auailes it of immortall seed
> To beene ybred and neuer borne to die?
> Farre better I it deeme to die with speed,
> Then waste in woe and wailefull miserie.
> Who dyes the vtmost dolour doth abye ...
>
> [III.iv.38]

We might also be reminded of Aesculapius here and of other interconnected passages on joylessness, the emotional threshold of despair, by the procession of Cymoent and her sister nymphs to Marinell's side. In Book I, Night travels to Sans Joy, drawn by "Her twyfold Teme" that "Did softly swim away, ne euer stampe, / Vnlesse she chaunst their stubborne mouths to twitch" and when she comes with Duessa to where Sans Joy lies,

> Deuoid of outward sense, and natiue strength,
> Couerd with charmed cloud from vew of day,
> And sight of men, since his late luckelesse fray.
> His cruell wounds with cruddy bloud congealed,
> They binden vp so wisely, as they may,
> And handle softly, till they can be healed:
> So lay him in her charet, close in night concealed.
>
> [I.v.29]

In Book III, Cymoent and the other nymphs do not take the "corse . . . To yawning gulfe of deepe *Auernus* hole" but take it "Deepe in the bottome of the sea" where Cymoent's bower "Is built of hollow billowes heaped hye" and "vauted all within" (I.v.31; III.iv.43). They take Marinell "in their tender hands" and "easily vnto her charet beare" him:

> Her teme at her commaundement quiet stands,
> Whiles they the corse into her wagon reare,
> And strow with flowres the lamentable beare:
> Then all the rest into their coches clim,
> And through the brackish waues their passage sheare;
> Vpon great *Neptunes* necke they softly swim,
> And to her watry chamber carry him.
>
> [III.iv.42]

If all the passages in Books I and III involved here were not markedly affective, the echoes in so long a poem would be lost. As it is, we hear an echo of a kind of despair in the third Book, a surrender to nature behind the artifice of Cymoent's world, as behind the passages about joylessness echoed from Book I. The touch once more is slight, not the sort of explicit criticism, the outright despair about time, that we find in Acrasia's Song of the Rose (II.xii.74–75); it is more fleeting—a sounding dimension, a depth. Whether these echoes exist as a slip of the pen, a habit of mind, or a distant memory, the poet overhears them himself, for in the final portion of canto iv, uncannily in view of these echoes, Arthur delivers his bitter complaint about Night.

The occasion of Arthur's complaint, his loss of Florimell, and the complaint itself afford a culminating variation on the central themes of canto iv. In her flight Florimell is controlled by blind instinct and emotional fantasies. Driven by fear, "vaine doubt, and needlesse dreed," she sees no

difference between the pursuing Prince Arthur and the vile Forester, a wild
beast, or even a "feend of hell" (47–51). When night falls, bringing both
"griesly shadowes" and many bright stars, and Arthur loses sight of her, he
curses night and fortune and wanders "Like as a ship, whose Lodestarre
suddenly / Couered with cloudes, her Pilot hath dismayd" (52–53). This
simile makes a connection between Arthur's experience and Britomart's
use of a strikingly similar image at the beginning of the canto, and this
connection is reinforced by the "thousand fancies," "sad sorrow, and disdaine" which occupy Arthur in the following lines (54) and take form in
his complaint about night.

Where Britomart identified herself with the nature of the sea and Cymoent
embodied an identification of nature with desire, Arthur might be said to do
both. He combines self-awareness with self-indulgence and at once identifies
himself with nature while defying the limits of this identification. His perceptions are more complex than either of the two which precede them in
canto iv. They are more fully human and potentially more distorting as well.
They summarize earlier actions in the canto and serve themselves as a step
forward and inward; but as the final, hardly edifying glimpse of Arthur in
this canto suggests, they too fail of a resolution: "So forth he went, / With
heauie looke and lumpish pace," signs of his "great grudge and maltalent" (61).
Arthur's nature in canto iv is morally exemplary, more nearly complete
than others', only if we take "moral" to mean both merely and more fully
human. In Arthur's complaint against night, even more than in Britomart's
address to the sea, it is the imaginative process, the imaginative act itself,
which occupies our attention. Though Arthur feels that he is blindly wandering, as to some extent he is—starless, like Britomart—that act is yet more
personal, more immediate, and more humane than hers.

The voice we hear in Arthur's complaint might have belonged to the
relatively dramatic speaker of an Elizabethan sonnet sequence, Sidney's,
Shakespeare's, or Spenser's own. He berates Night, the "foule Mother of
annoyance sad, / Sister of heauie death, and nourse of woe," and then he
elaborates on Night's horrors:

> Thou art the root and nurse of bitter cares,
> Breeder of new, renewer of old smarts:
> In stead of rest thou lendest rayling teares,
> In stead of sleepe thou sendest troublous feares,
> And dreadfull visions, in the which aliue
> The drearie image of sad death appeares . . .
>
> [III.iv.57][17]

It would be hard to imagine how complaints about the creation could have come in an earlier Book from this, the best of knights:

> What had th'eternall Maker need of thee,
>   The world in his continuall course to keepe,
>   That doest all things deface, ne lettest see
>   The beautie of his worke?

[III.iv.56]

These surprising words would seem ungraciously Manichaean if they were not modified by the personal immediacy of Arthur's voice and situation and by some awareness on his part of the role played by his own anguished vision: "But well I wote, that to an heauy hart," he adds, the darkness of Night is evil (57).

The content of Arthur's complaint is not so easily dismissed, however; there is more going on in it. Once we have recognized his words as the outpouring of a heavy heart—a form of verbal violence analogous to Britomart's more physical dissipation of tempestuous grief on Marinell—and once we have seen them to have more purely personal and emotional than abstract intellectual significance, they take a startling shift into a more mature and more philosophically minded key. His attention turns to the antithesis of Night, and he progressively hypostatizes Day, thus bringing it into a context of human relevance and control:

> For day discouers all dishonest wayes,
>   And sheweth each thing, as it is indeed:
>   The prayses of high God he faire displayes,
>   And his large bountie rightly doth areed.
>   Dayes dearest children be the blessed seed,
>   Which darknesse shall subdew, and heauen win:
>   Truth is his daughter; he her first did breed,
>   Most sacred virgin, without spot of sin.
> Our life is day, but death with darknesse doth begin.

[III.iv.59]

Unlike Britomart's, Arthur's days and nights, his personal heavens and hells, turn out to have universal dimensions. The images which his mythologizing imagination produces here recall Book I, explicitly alluding to the biblical children of day and of darkness (1 Thess. 5:5) and to the history of Redcrosse and Una. This last stanza clarifies and deepens the relation of Arthur's complaint to the rest of canto iv, Book III, and the poem.

The process we observe in Arthur's complaint is informed with passion's excesses but with penetrating insight as well. It involves Arthur's creation and metamorphosis of symbols whose roots we have seen to lie in his personal and emotional experience. The results of this metamorphosis are more (but not less) than Venus's flower, the form to which she changes the languishing Adonis and the culmination of her love for him as depicted in Malecasta's tapestry (III.i.38). Both the symbols and the process of Arthur's complaint are related to Redcrosse's experiences with night in Book I (i, v), when night is evil not in itself but as the inner darkness in which Redcrosse sleeps. Redcrosse's misguided passions grant this darkness its power. Arthur's complaint reflects and reflects on the sort of experience Redcrosse had in Book I. Arthur experiences as far more deliberately created and controlled meaning what Redcrosse experienced blindly as psychic and physical fact. Personifying Night and Day and thereby cloaking nature in the forms his mind creates, Arthur engages in an imaginative process which leads from a world of natural passion, like Britomart's; through a world of self-indulging art, like Cymoent's; to a world of Truth, like Una's, to be sure, though in the dilating process of this poem no longer exactly or simply like hers.

This mental process also has its attendant pains and dangers, present in Arthur's complaint and reemphasized in the "lumpish pace" of his departure. A similar imaginative act will account for the strange history of Malbecco, who turns himself into the monster Jealousy, which his mind has created, and thus actually becomes the metaphor he makes. Busirane, the culminating monster in Book III, will be an evil magician, invariably in Spenser's poem a figure who perversely expresses and perversely preys on the human imagination. In the first two lines following canto iv, lines separated by one stanza from Arthur's complaint about night, the poet comments on what a "Wonder it is to see, in diuerse minds, / How diuersly loue doth his pageants play" (v.1); his observation, reemphasizing once more Book III's concern with the mind, clearly looks both forward to the further expansion of a truly human awareness in the poem and backward to the expanding stage the third Book has already realized.

BOOK IV: "But antique age yet in the infancie / Of time . . ."

We have plausible speculations but virtually no certain knowledge about changes in Spenser's views or fortunes between the publication of the first three Books of *The Faerie Queene* in 1590 and the second three in 1596. Nor do we really know to what extent Book IV was composed between 1590 and 1596, to what extent it might have drawn upon earlier poetic fragments, or to what extent it might have been written at the same time Book III was. Approaching Book IV, we have, in short, the text, and it has proved at times a puzzling one. Surely there are numerous features of style and story in Book IV which further develop and substantially modify those of Book III. Many of these are among the signs of revision in Book IV, both of reconsideration and of rewriting, which should not be dismissed too quickly as clumsy patchwork. Such signs are generally interrelated: for example, the personal tone and references of the Proem and first canto, the nominal role played by the titular heroes, Cambel and Telamond;[18] the oscillating and often ambiguous alignment of narrative (dramatic) and mythic (symbolic) areas throughout the Book; perhaps even the curious, potentially ironic absence of Amoret from her reunion with Scudamour.

Whatever significance these signs have depends on others more obviously controlled, including recurrent disjunctions in the narrative, a thematic emphasis on masking, or the use of masks, in achieving social roles and forms;[19] and above all, the more insistently visible presence of the poet. Far more often and explicitly than in Book III, the poet speaks as the shaper of his poem rather than as its interpreter or observer.[20] He makes unqualified or barely qualified intrusions into the midst of the narrative and, in celebrating the Marriage of Thames and Medway, takes over an entire canto to create a mythic vision of harmonious natural forces that realizes his own role in this Book and almost totally excludes its actual (or actually by now, its other) dramatis personae.[21]

We can describe and characterize the nature of the poet's presence in Book IV but cannot fully rationalize it because it is not given a fully rational context. Our explanations are speculative and perhaps always to some degree doubtful in view of the puzzles in structure, tone, and historical reference which exist in parts of this Book. These puzzles surely suggest meaning, but a meaning elusive and incompletely realized, as is more blatantly the case in Langland's Passūs X and XI.148–310. The poet's presence in Book IV is nonetheless clear and emphatic, its emphasis born of a new extension and intensity. His presence is too controlled and recurrent to be unintentional, too sudden and disruptive to have been fully deliberated; it is most safely, if ambiguously, termed "revisionary." It is decisively responsible for making Book IV a continuing and as yet imperfect process, a transformation and renewal of insight by, indeed in, a new way of seeing. This process is open to criticism for its messiness and is strangely moving for its openness. It commands our interest while it disappoints, even offends, our formal expectations, and in fact could hardly have been better made to do just that.

The poet's role in Book IV, like that of Conscience in the central Passūs of *Piers Plowman,* expresses a new self-awareness and involves a further personalization of the role he took on in Book III. It, too, might be seen as a turning inward which results in an assertion of self made in the face of a more public and intractable world. The poet's action exists as a statement in canto viii, but it is realized throughout the Book in an alteration of form. His role emerges progressively but with an irregular pace.

The Proem to Book IV speaks openly of tensions between love and affairs of state, between poetry and politics. Here the poet talks about his critics and to his readers, explaining that honor and virtue are inseparable from love; he addresses the Queen less directly than in earlier proems.[22] He speaks more directly to his audience and in a manner more knowing and familiar than before. The voice we hear is a new one, angry, indignant, contemporary, and for all its effort to sustain a noble fiction about Elizabeth, "that sacred Saint my soueraigne Queene," neither unambiguous in next referring to "The Queene of loue, and Prince of peace from heauen blest" nor entirely compromising: "Sprinckle her heart, and haughtie courage soften, / That she may hearke to loue, and read this lesson often" (Pro. iv, v).

When the poet turns from the Proem and the world to his story in canto i, his attitude becomes less polemical and sadder, seemingly unposed and more plain-spoken. For four introductory stanzas he talks about Amoret, revealing her history prior to the House of Busirane and lamenting her plight so sorely that "with teares full oft" he pities it "And oftentimes doe[s] wish it neuer had bene writ" (i.1). Already the outcome sounds settled: "Yet should it be a pleasant tale, to tell / The diuerse vsage and demeanure daint" which passed between Britomart and Amoret (i.5). The word *yet* ("still," "nevertheless") marks only a qualified shift from past to present, from peril to pleasantry, and it is on this note that the action of Book IV begins.

In the next twelve stanzas (i.6–17), the action moves from one minor incident to another: Amoret's worrying because she thinks that Britomart is a man, Britomart's defeat of an unnamed knight, her gracious effort to gain entrance to an unnamed castle for herself, Amoret, and the knight; then Amoret's discovery that Britomart is a woman, their departure from the castle, and their subsequently seeing in the distance two knights with two ladies, the latter hiding treason and falsehood "vnder maske of beautie and good grace" (i.17). The clearest thread of significance in these many occurrences connects Amoret's confusion about Britomart's sex, hidden from Amoret to "maske her wounded mind" (i.7), with Britomart's removing her disguise at the castle (i.13–14). We note themes, familiar figures, situations that distantly recall Malecasta's Castle in Book III, but we are kept from getting any settled or strong impressions; we do not seem to get *into* the story in any way.

It is not that the opening is totally flat—the brief descriptions of exchanges

between Britomart and Amoret are pleasant enough, and the description of
Britomart's unmasking is a momentary expansion of the surface, a sign that
poetic vitality is present and an omen of power to come. But for the most
part it is exactly on the surface that we remain. We just listen. In the midst of
all this anonymity and lack of identity, there is virtually no landscape, no
texture, no depth. Our questions are not invited: we are told what is going
on; we are not asked to discover it. At this point, in fact, we might start
asking about this poem itself.

Once Britomart and Amoret have left the castle in canto i and have spied
the two unidentified knights and two ladies (17), the poem, still showing
little interest in perceptual activity, swiftly identifies the ladies as false
Duessa and foul Ate, "mother of debate, / And all dissention" (i.19). Thus
begins the description of Ate, a forthright explanation not at all surprising
by this time in canto i, and the next stanza continues in a similar vein, telling
us about Ate's dwelling. Then stanza 21 opens,

> And all within the riuen walls were hung
>   With ragged monuments of times forepast,
>   All which the sad effects of discord sung:
>   There were rent robes, and broken scepters plast,
>   Altars defyl'd, and holy things defast,
>   Disshiuered speares, and shields ytorne in twaine,
>   Great cities ransackt . . .

Stanza 22 continues this description, "There was the signe of antique Baby-
lon, / Of fatall Thebes, of Rome that raigned long," and at length stanza
23: "And there the relicks of the drunken fray, / The which amongst the
Lapithees befell." The passage reads as if we—or a character in some way our
surrogate—were again at Error's den, in hell, or in the Cave of Mammon. But
not even Ate herself is presently "Hard by the gates of hell" (i.20), at least
not as a character. No character moves through this landscape, surveying
its relics and monuments. In fact, there is no forward action at all in the
story itself; Britomart, Amoret, the two knights, and Duessa have been left
behind on the surface of stanzas 17 and 18.

Yet with gradual insistence, stanzas 21 to 23 give us a sense of movement
and the feeling that we are actually looking at a landscape. We hear that
"There were rent robes . . . there some relicks . . . There was the signe . . . on
high there hong . . . There also . . . And there." The word *there* quietly
draws and deftly guides our attention. Gradually the landscape takes on a
kind of existence, a tangibility, right before us. We realize that we are in
some sense by the gates of hell, and when in stanza 24 we hear "eke of priuate
persons many moe, / That were too long a worke to count them all," we

have a pretty fair idea of whose action this is. Numbering "sworne friends," "borne brethren," and "deare louers" among such private persons, the poet invites us to "Witnesse their broken bandes there to be seene." His invitation, addressed directly to the reader, makes it perfectly clear that we travel only in his company. The force, the vitality, the reality of the poet's vision of discord has taken over completely the action of the poem. It is "Hard by the gates of hell" that we now find poetic life, and there also, perception.

The presentation of Ate's "house within" (i.25) is followed by a description of the grounds surrounding it and then, in stanzas 27 to 29, by a description of her person: her "squinted eyes" and "loathly mouth," "Her lying tongue . . . in two parts diuided," her unequal hands, odd feet, and contrary action. This progression from Ate's dwelling to her person marks a movement back to the character Ate and thus back toward the narrative surface. In seeing Ate's house and grounds we have seen both the "sad effects" and the source of discord, but we have also, and perhaps more importantly, seen the present source of the poet's vision and of his characterization. Depths have first opened behind the flat surface of the story, and now the movement of the poem from depths to surface brings these depths to focus in the character of Ate: in effect, we are present at the formation of an emblematic character in canto i.

In the stanzas devoted to Ate, the poet seems to have digressed from the ongoing narrative to his actual subject.[23] Ate serves to relate depths to surface in canto i but never does so very closely or fully. Unlike characters in the first two Books, she does not return from the depths to play an important role as a character in the story; in fact, we see very little of Ate as a character hereafter. The primary direction of movement in canto i is from name to image or from abstraction to landscape; in the first two Books the primary direction of movement is just the reverse. With a figure like Orgoglio in Book I, for example, we find numerous stanzas of experience— facts, descriptions, actions—before the character is known and named.[24] With Ate we get first the name, which then seems to generate a background and landscape. Instead of participating in important actions, Ate is primarily the occasion of activity. This activity is perceptual and poetic, and it is one consequence of the poet's altered role in Book IV—a Book which significantly lacks a single definite hero.

The end of canto i and the beginning of canto ii present series of couples, companions, true or false friends: Britomart and Amoret, Ate and Duessa, Blandamour and Paridell, Scudamour and Glauce, Ferraugh, false Florimell, the Squire of Dames, Cambel, Triamond, Canacee, Cambina. One after another they move across the screen, briefly coming into focus and then

veering aside or merging into a single group. It is a never-never land of
narrative and symbol: characters fight and change partners with frequency
but without much significance; they mix and move and mix some more,
and that in itself is their meaning. Even such figures as Paridell can be present
without the moral demarcations of Book III, let alone of Books I and II.
The various characters have no direction, no purposeful movement, and
their encounters take no organized form until Satyrane's tournament becomes
a goal, somewhere specific to go and something in particular to do.

Once the Squire of Dames tells Paridell and Blandamour about this
tournament, they decide to stop their pointless striving for false Florimell
and to attend it. On their way they meet Cambel and Triamond, who will
in due course join them, but not until the poet has spent nearly half of canto
ii and all of canto iii on a series of three digressions, first about "Dan *Chaucer*,"
then about Triamond's mother Agape and her trip to the Fates, and finally
about the actual battle between Cambel and Triamond. While all this
explaining proceeds, Cambel and Triamond remain motionless silhouettes
on the surface of the poem. Again the reel has stopped; the major characters
have frozen, and then the poet steps forward.

He first reminds us that Chaucer had written the tale of Cambel and
Canacee:

> But wicked Time that all good thoughts doth waste,
> And workes of noblest wits to nought out weare,
> That famous moniment hath quite defaste,
> And robd the world of threasure endlesse deare . . .
>
> [IV.ii.33]

The poet continues, cursing "Eld the cankerworme of writs," worrying
about the fate of his own rhymes, and then addressing Chaucer: "pardon, O
most sacred happie spirit, / That I thy labours lost may thus reuiue," and
once again, "Ne dare I like, but through infusion sweete / Of thine own
spirit, which doth in me suruiue" (ii.34). The references to time, poetry, and
the infusion of one spirit into another touch themes and patterns of movement
central to Book IV. In the larger context of this Book, infusion of one spirit
into another—whether Chaucer and Spenser or Priamond, Diamond, and
Triamond—is a necessary condition of renewal and endurance. If the names
and histories of the three "mond"-brothers (first, second, and third world)
are any indication, endurance implies expansion and complexity, or perhaps,
to use Spenser's word from the Mutability Cantos, "dilation."[25]

Although the poet's presence is more direct and explicit this time than in
canto i, it again serves to alter and to adjust values and modes of expression.

His presence serves as the fulcrum or, from another view, as the buffer, between the world of Paridell and the Squire of Dames and that of Agape and Cambina. The movement from one realm of being to another in this canto also suggests the kinds of characters which assist a transfer from surface to symbol, from Cambel and Triamond as narrative silhouettes, to the same knights as idealized images of friendship. Cambel and Triamond, not to mention Priamond and Diamond, are themselves merely symbolic characters. They exist with any degree of fullness chiefly insofar as they are found in cantos ii and iii. The nominal heroes of this Book *are* in this sense themselves digressions. The infusion of life from Priamond to Diamond to Triamond works symbolically because Triamond's elder brothers are barely more than names in the poem. The poet creates this myth about the three brothers, their sister Cambina, Cambel, and his sister Canacee to realize the fluidity that "infusion" implies.

With only an occasional warning strain—or shriek from the less fluid, less tractable reality of Cambina's trampled victims (iii.41)—the poem moves toward an ever-increasing harmony and complexity, until Belphoebe fails to cooperate with this movement in canto vii. There she and Timias find Amoret and then, with Timias in disgrace, abandon both the wounded Amoret and one another. Unfortunately, Belphoebe has a somewhat intractable past in the poem:

> Ne let his fairest *Cynthia* refuse,
> In mirrours more then one her selfe to see,
> But either *Gloriana* let her chuse,
> Or in *Belphoebe* fashioned to bee:
> In th'one her rule, in th'other her rare chastitee.
>
> [III.Pro.v]

If Timias's figure alludes to Ralegh, as appears to be the case in Books III and IV, then he has a past in the poem and in the world as well. Although Belphoebe is reconciled to Timias in canto viii, their relationship, unlike Britomart's and Artegall's, makes no progress. We last see them exactly where they were in Book III.[26]

For whatever reasons—because Belphoebe embodies a historical allusion to Elizabeth, because of her rigid idealism, or both—her meeting with her complementary, completing twin sister Amoret fails of fulfillment. Injured because of Lust's action yet saved from him by Belphoebe, Amoret is then simply abandoned by her sister in the forest. There she remains with Aemylia until they are rescued by the panaceaic Arthur in canto viii.

At this point, in the middle of canto viii, the poet's voice suddenly intrudes.

Dropping a narrative role, he speaks in the first person and talks about his poem as a poem, as "these rimes" which others will read and some will probably misinterpret. First Amoret, Aemylia, and Arthur endure the railings of Slander, "Regardlesse of that queane so base and vilde, / To be vniustly blamd" (28); then the poet enters:

> Here well I weene, when as these rimes be red
>   With misregard, that some rash witted wight,
>   Whose looser thought will lightly be misled,
>   These gentle Ladies will misdeeme too light,
>   For thus conuersing with this noble Knight;
>   Sith now of dayes such temperance is rare
>   And hard to finde . . .
>
>   [IV.viii.29]

As surprising as the poet's intrusion is his sharp readjustment of our temporal viewpoint, a sharpness suggesting the difficulty of his own situation, at once in the poem ("*Here* . . . I weene") and in the world ("Sith *now* of dayes"), at once in time and, in a sense, outside it. For another four stanzas the poet reflects on the contrast between the present age and an "antique age yet in the infancie / Of time," an age "voide of vile and treacherous intent," holding "vertue for it selfe in soueraine awe" (viii.30). It is a mythic age, very like the one Guyon invoked to counter Mammon's claims; now in the poet's own voice, brooking no counterclaims, the assertion of its reality seems both less fragile and more personal, less limited and more. At the end of stanza 33 the poet's digression ceases, and he returns without transition to the thread of his story. This return, as abrupt as the initial intrusion, makes no attempt to smooth over or to minimize the effect of his presence.

In earlier Books, notably in Book III, the poet has often expressed interest, enthusiasm, or concern, but his comments have been neither so arbitrary nor so digressive in timing and content.[27] They have been primarily directed toward the story, underlining or expanding its significance; they have not called attention to themselves abruptly and at length in the center of a canto. Earlier comments have likewise dealt with the poet's situation as it pertains to the immediate needs of his narrative. Even Book III has maintained a more objective, impersonal dimension by not explicitly identifying the poet's creative role with the dreams and ideals to which that role can give life. Such dreams, defiled by Slander in canto viii, are in danger of slipping from sight, and at this point the poet intrudes, recalling a paradisal age in the infancy of time when the "Lyon . . . with the Lambe" consorted (viii.31).

Pressures and appeals from outside the poem and from beyond the poet himself—time, politics, slanderers, friendships—have evidently borne on the content of canto viii until the narrative, with its discrepancies in tone and its unfulfilled expectations, has fallen so short of the poet's dreams and ideals that he has broken from this narrative to recall and, at least in this limited way, to recreate them.[28]

The suddenness of the poet's presence in canto viii dramatizes the force of his indignation, but the length and content of his digression convey as strong suggestions of pattern and intention as of impulse. In his voice we hear possibilities excluded from the narrative given form in the poem. That voice embodies the alternative, the balancing corrective, to the rest of canto viii. It is a voice which no longer indicates but *is* the alternative.

The poet's voice in this canto has some resemblance to the one we heard in the Proem to Book IV, at the threshold of the fiction but not quite in it. What the poet progressively discovers in Book IV, and what this Book progressively dramatizes, concerns his own role in a world less deliberately evil than discordant, a world less clearly irrational than disappointing, a world at its best mixed rather than ever ideal; of necessity the poet's own role becomes a more exclusively personal one, and, paradoxically, his voice, a more complex whole. In the strength, the indignation, and the assurance of the poet's reflections in canto viii, we hear, not that modern discovery of a self essentially without a role, but the discovery of a role that is, in a sense that Langland—and later Milton—would have recognized, decidedly more personal than before.

At the beginning of the last canto in Book IV, the poet comments on his own role in the Marriage of Rivers, which occupies the preceding canto:

> O what an endlesse worke haue I in hand,
>   To count the seas abundant progeny,
> . . . .
>   So fertile be the flouds in generation,
> So huge their numbers, and so numberlesse their nation.
>
> Therefore the antique wisards well inuented,
>   That *Venus* of the fomy sea was bred . . .
>
> [IV.xii.1–2]

His comment testifies to the self-conscious nature of his task and particularly of his myth-making in canto xi, where, like the antique wizards, he shapes meaningful form out of the fertile shapelessness of the seas. The voice which makes an image of the natural world and celebrates its immense fertility is intensely creative and, as an ode might be, lyrical. The Marriage of Rivers is no character's dream unless, in a figurative sense of the word *dream,* it is the poet's own.

Again and again in canto xi the poet speaks in his own voice; his voice is nonetheless nearly indistinguishable from his communal and ritual celebration of the rivers:

> The first, the gentle Shure that making way
>   By sweet Clonmell, adornes rich Waterford;
> The nexte, the stubborne Newre, whose waters gray
>   By faire Kilkenny and Rosseponte boord,
> The third, the goodly Barow, which doth hoord
> Great heapes of Salmons in his deepe bosome:
> All which long sundred, doe at last accord
> To ioyne in one, ere to the sea they come,
> So flowing all from one, all one at last become.

> [IV.xi.43]

Canto xi is a moving triumph but not a final realization of the poet's role. The celebration of natural harmony which the poet makes and his own voice joins, or is in a sense swept into, is also the one-sided triumph of fluidity and blending: "So flowing all from one, all one at last become." Like Britomart's lament in Book III, it is beautiful, natural, mind-made; unlike her lament, it is the result of a specifically poetic self-consciousness; yet it is also the result of an imagination centered on a purely and merely natural world—the elemental world underlying all human artifacts.

In the closing lines of Book IV, the poet says of Florimell's love for Marinell:

> Ne lesse was she in secret hart affected,
> But that she masked it with modestie,
> For feare she should of lightnesse be detected:
> Which to another place I leaue to be perfected.

The final line, once again underlining the poet's dominion, resembles the end of nearly every canto in Book IV. These lines serve as a comment on the whole of this Book—on the shaping poet and on a form which he perceives to be still imperfectly realized.

We can suspect the direct influence of *Piers Plowman* on Books I and II of *The Faerie Queene.* But for understanding Books III and IV, Langland's poem is primarily a heuristic device that greatly illuminates the poet's role as a quester and a questioner, a role which progressively emerges in *The Faerie Queene*. To see these Books against a different yet comparable context, in many fundamental ways more comparable than Ariosto's, makes them look far more thoughtful and explorative than they have before and increases the likelihood that, indeed, they are so. In both the central Passūs of *Piers Plowman* and the central Books of *The Faerie Queene*, we respond to what happens in an allegory when that mode turns in on, back on, itself and does so self-consciously. The poet becomes aware—or at least displays his aware-ness—of his own imaginative role in the poem as shaper and actor, as creator and participant (Langland's Imaginative), and this action makes the form of the poem self-consciousness. Here we are talking about the pressures of personality on an allegorical form, pressures which must enlarge, transform, and perhaps finally subvert the authority of allegory. Paradoxically, we can see the subversiveness of this process at once in the assertive realism and the conceptual rigidity of *The Pilgrim's Progress,* or we can see it with less sense of loss in the fully and wonderfully realized symbolic forms of *Paradise Lost.* In comparison with these works, *Piers Plowman* belongs to an early stage in the process; *The Faerie Queene* belongs to a decisive middle one. We have already seen something of these stages; they take firmer form in later sections of both poems, to which succeeding chapters turn.

Part III

A Personal Voice

Foreword to Part III

From Passus xv to the end of *Piers Plowman,* the poet shows a quickening interest in what we might most simply call "personality," for it involves in the broadest sense the reality—metaphysical, psychological, verbal and actual—that a person might have. In the thought of the thirteenth and fourteenth centuries, personality emerges as the final human perfection, the one most godlike. A striking reference to it is present in the statement by Langland's Holy Church that a person true of tongue, works, and will "is a god, by the gospel, agrounde and aloft" (1.88–90). If we take the words of an influential and representative Franciscan theologian of these centuries, Duns Scotus, whose tradition, with its emphasis on psychology, experience, will, and love, is close to Langland's poem, personality is the *ultima realitas entis,* the *ultima solitudo.*[1] In the course of *Piers Plowman,* personality leads to the discovery of reality, simultaneously as meaning and as the means to actualize it; indeed, personality achieved becomes reality possessed. Passūs xv to xviii touch the heart of this ultimate reality and imaginatively grasp its implications. The two final Passūs of the poem, xix and xx, touch even more its *ultima solitudo,* its solitude both as affirmation and loss, as triumph and loneliness.

What we can see by juxtaposing Passūs xv to xx with the last two Books of *The Faerie Queene* and the Mutability Cantos is a reflection in terms of personal awareness of the larger cultural and historical movement from the Middle Ages to the Renaissance. In the latter portions of *The Faerie Queene* there is something of the same solitude realized in *Piers Plowman,* now recapitulated but also transformed. In comparison to Langland's, we might picture this solitude as the distant revolution of a widening—from another view, a narrowing—spiral. Medieval philosophy's interest in personality had its origin primarily in theological questions, the soul as the image of God, the relation of human being to Christ both in the Hypostatic Union and in the life of a man himself—in short, the relation of a human personality to the supreme personality of God. These questions and others like them nourished an interest in psychology and in one's own being, a self-consciousness, and they provided traditional vehicles for its exploration, forms which shaped consciousness but which it could shape in turn, as it did in *Piers Plowman.*[2]

The medieval interest in personality contributed ideas and observations that both reflected and produced a heightened sense of person, an awareness succeeding centuries developed. That interest also illuminates some strangely abstract and spiritual backgrounds behind such a heightening of awareness. The same might be said of *Piers Plowman* in relation to *The Faerie Queene*. Langland, giving the interest in personality truly literary and therefore more personal expression, produces a form which Spenser—by the same coincidental and empirical logic—develops and which illuminates some of the forces behind the most poignant moments of *The Faerie Queene*.

*

6

Passūs XV to XX: Long Will

In Passus VIII, near the beginning of the Vita de Dowel, the character Thought explains to Wit that Will would like to know "Where Dowel, Dobet, and Dobest ben in londe," and he continues, "whether he be man or no man, this man fayne wolde aspye" (123–25).[1] Like Dame Study's remark about Imaginative or Lady Holy Church's perplexing truths, Thought's statement is another cryptic foretaste of ideas later pursued and developed. In retrospect its childlike profundity, its simplicity, is almost amusing. Thought's three terms, *man, no man,* and *this man* look ahead to those well-known knots of Passus XV:

> "With-outen helpe of Piers Plowman," quod he, "his persone
> seestow neuere." . . .
> ". . . knowe shaltow hym neuere,
> Noyther thorw wordes ne werkes but thorw wille one,
> And that knoweth no clerke ne creature in erthe
> But Piers the Plowman—*Petrus id est Christus.*"
> [XV.190, 203–06]

Will, Piers, Christ—this man, man, and something more than man: the actual Will, the poet's encompassing symbol, and God's Incarnate Word. In XV and the following Passūs, these three terms (and their variants) are used to realize personality in as ultimate and self-conscious a form as this poem, and perhaps this age, conceived it. We shall return to these lines from Passus XV in their context. Here they serve at least to suggest the verbal complexity which is inseparable from imaginative fullness in these Passūs. In them abstract thought seems to wed existence; the perceptual act and the reality perceived, the will and the word, are one. Passūs XV to XX involve a further journey inward but outward, too; they involve freedom from space and time and a return to history, the triumphant achievement of personality and the full impact of its isolation.

At the beginning of Passus XV Will, once again dreaming, meets Anima, an embodiment of the unified powers of the human soul. Although Anima is capable of voicing one of the two lengthiest Passūs in the poem, he is described as lacking "tonge and teeth" (xv.13) and is pointedly conceived in terms more incorporeal than any earlier figure. The appearance of Anima suggests a more profoundly interiorized conception of and communing with the self. From the time that the Dreamer sees Anima, he is more intensively and directly engaged in a search for unity—the unity of his interior powers, of the whole man, of society, of past and present, of being and Being. It is in Passūs xv to xviii that the word, as Lady Holy Church used it in Passus I, is further realized as a continuous act and recalled not as cryptic, half-heard instruction but grasped as a more fully imagined, hence understood, event which the Dreamer himself might be said to realize—"thorw wille one," through will alone.

In Passus xv Anima begins Will's more explicit instruction in charity. Allowing for Langland's characteristic emphasis on the will and for the fact that the Dreamer now faces his soul, which includes both rational and volitional powers, we can borrow the words of a modern theologian to gloss Anima's action: "it was necessary for her [reason's] attention to be attracted by faith towards charity, in order that she might concern herself with what she already knew implicitly, that God is a person."[2] The beginning of Passus xv, like earlier new beginnings, is at first puzzling because it seems repetitious, distressingly like old times for the Dreamer. Once again Will wants knowledge, indeed to know "Alle the sciences vnder sonne and alle the sotyle craftes" (48). This is evidently the wrong kind of knowledge for Will because Anima rebukes his imperfection, echoing advice heard earlier in the poem but realized, we might have thought, by Conscience's action in leaving Clergy (xiii): "non plus sapere quam oportet sapere," and again, "ʒe aren enblaunched with bele paroles and with clothes also, / Ac ʒowre werkes and ʒowre wordes there-vnder aren ful vnlouelich" (67, 113–14). Anima's opening accusations strike so many familiar notes that we are likely to wonder whether Will has backslid or the poet is nodding, until we read enough of the Passus to see that this repetition, too, is functional and deliberate. Anima's central insistence in Passus xv is the need for knowledge to turn into actions, words into will: " 'Beatus est,' seith seynt Bernard, 'qui scripturas legit, / Et verba vertit in opera' " (59–60). Will, after all, has not as yet adequately done so, a point made dramatically by Anima's rebuke and likely at first to catch even a regenerate reader nodding.

Hearing Anima mention perfect charity, the Dreamer interrupts his rebuke to ask, quite out of the blue, "What is Charite?" (145). Significantly, this is Will's inquiry; he initiates Anima's active instruction about the life of love. The passages about Will, Piers, and Christ cited earlier in this chapter come in the sixty lines that follow Will's question. They define his quest, much as Holy Church's speech about love did in Passus I; but now, using the symbol Piers Plowman, they indicate it more clearly and in decidedly more personal terms.

Anima defines charity as a "fre liberal wille" (146), and the dreaming Will replies, "I haue lyued in londe . . . my name is Longe Wille, / And fonde I neuere ful charite bifore ne bihynde" (148–49).[3] We might recall Thought's earlier expression of Will's desire to know whether Dowel, Dobet, and Dobest "ben in londe . . . And whether he be man or no man" (VIII.123–25). If the dramatic situation, a dialogue between the soul and a figure—for the first time clearly a real man—called Will, were not already specific and self-referential enough, Will continues:

Ac charite that Poule preyseth best and most plesaunte to owre saueoure,
As, *non inflatur, non est ambiciosa, non querit que sua sunt,*
I seigh neuere such a man, so me god helpe,
That he ne wolde aske after his and otherwhile coueyte
Thinge that neded him nou3t and nyme it if he my3te.

[XV.152–55]

The Dreamer's next lines are rather surprising, for without further prompting from Anima, in fact without any further ado, he identifies Charity with Christ. Far from being untutored or simply dull, Will might be said to have not only the answers but also the Word:

Clerkis kenne me that Cryst is in alle places,
Ac I seygh hym neuere sothly but as my-self in a miroure,
Ita in enigmate, tunc facie ad faciem.

[XV.156–57]

Will's statement is itself enigmatic, full of wit and irony he does not quite control. It is a strange mixture of words and unrealized meanings, of knowledge and its lack. He quotes directly from an epistle in which St. Paul writes of the realization of charity: "Videmus nunc per speculum in aenigmate; tunc autem facie ad faciem" (1 Cor. 13:12). Doctrinally there is nothing wrong with Will's statement; it implies that Christ is found within. Yet the whole intention of his assertion is wrong. First, it is an objection—Clerks tell me . . . but I never saw him—and second, it opposes "alle places" and "sothly" to "my-self." Too quickly, perfunctorily in fact, Will recognizes and assents to the theoretical relevance of Christ to himself but undermines the actuality of that relevance. Thus Christ is real and the world is real but

Christ is not really present in it. He is *just* the Word in reality and just a word (or a neck verse) to the world. For Will at this point, He is little better than an abstraction.

The C-text retains the quotation from Paul in the passage parallel here to B, but in the line preceding it reads "bote figuratifliche" instead of "as my-self in a miroure." This change underlines the slighting quality of Will's phrase in the B-text and reinforces another suspicion this phrase invites: even in context Paul's statement does not account for the emphatic self-reference of the phrase "myself in a mirror." In B, Will's lines conflate Paul's statement with one from St. James, another of Langland's favorite authors. James's statement is equally relevant to Passus xv and more relevant than Paul's to Will's state of having and not having the word: "Quia si quis auditor est verbi, et non factor, hic comparabitur viro consideranti vultum nativitatis suae in speculo: consideravit enim se, et abiit, et statim oblitus est qualis fuerit" (1:23–24).[4] Hearing the word, a man can behold himself and his true nature, but he loses both if he does not turn the word to action.

Anima pointedly ignores Will's naming of Christ and again shifts the subject back to the abstraction Charity, endeavoring to show how love actually works in the world. Anima's description leads to Will's exclamation, "I wolde that I knewe hym," and to Anima's first enigmatic reply, "Withouten helpe of Piers Plowman . . . his persone seestow neuere" (189–90). In another two lines comes the second reply, equally enigmatic:

> "Clerkes haue no knowyng," quod he, "but by werkes and bi
>   wordes.
> Ac Piers the Plowman parceyueth more depper
> What is the wille and wherfore that many wy3te suffreth,
>   *Et vidit deus cogitaciones eorum.*"

Then Will hears that he can never know Charity by virtue of appearance or of theological competence,

> Noyther thorw wordes ne werkes but thorw wille one,
> And that knoweth no clerke ne creature in erthe
> But Piers the Plowman—*Petrus id est Christus.*

> [xv.204–06]

Anima's first reply identifies Piers as the means of seeing Charity, and hence with Charity's visibility, presumably both the understanding and the tangibility of Charity. His second reply imputes to Piers the interior perception of the will. Piers is not said to be the *"deus"* who saw men's *"cogitaciones"* (that which is in men's minds, thoughts, dispositions—even purposes), although he is certainly to be intimately associated in his power of perception and in the juxtaposition of these lines with God, and more specifically with Christ.[5] In the third quotation from Anima's replies, the will, like Piers in Anima's first reply, is identified as the means to know Charity but also as that which no one on earth knows "But Piers." This last phrase again reinforces the intimacy of Piers with Christ without simply equating them. The word *but* must be taken in both its senses: no creature except the creature Piers and no "creature in erthe" whatever, but rather Piers, who is Christ.

Never without some qualification or double entendre is Piers simply said to be Christ. Even the final phrase in Anima's statement, "Peter, that is, Christ," has a qualifying verbal form and a qualifying context which the Latin phrasing invokes. The word *id* is, after all, a demonstrative pronoun that illustrates, demonstrates, makes explicit. The phrase *id est* need not indicate identity in every respect between terms not in every respect identical, for example, terms less and more specific, parts and wholes, symbols and their meanings, natures and persons. Anima's phrase is characteristic of arguments found everywhere in medieval theology about the mode of the Hypostatic Union and the nature of the exchange between the attributes of divinity and humanity in the God-man. Two are worth citing for the richly suggestive, imaginative possibilities their wording implies. William of Auxerre brings a speculative question to this solution:[6]

> Dicimus quod Filius Dei secundum praecedentem positionem est plures homines. Tamen concedimus hanc: "Jesus est Petrus," quoniam est idem identitate personali; tamen est alius ali-/etate naturali. Non igitur valet haec argumentatio: "Est idem cum Petro; ergo non est alius a Petro.[7]

Discussing the validity of the statements "Deus est homo" and "Verbum est homo," Duns Scotus concludes:

> suppositum enim subsistens in aliqua natura, ut suppositum naturae, dicit tale formaliter secundum illam naturam; creditum est autem talem esse istam unionem, quod per eam Verbum subsistit in natura humana, ut suppositum in natura; ergo per eam Verbum formaliter est homo. Major hujus probatur per Damascenum *lib.* 3, *c.* 11. Deus autem et commune nomen significat, et in unaquaque hypostasi, id est, persona, ordinatur *denominative* quemadmodum et homo. Deus enim est qui habet naturam divinam, et homo qui humanam. Minor probatur per Augustinum I *de Trinit. c.* 13. *Talis fuit ista assumptio, ut Deum hominem faceret, et hominem Deum.*[8]

Then God could be designated man in some way denominatively—by *denominatio,* defined as "the substitution of the name of an object for that of another to which it has some relation, as the name of the cause for that of the effect, [or] of the property for that of the substance [as in] a metonymy."[9] Jesus, though human in nature, might also be denominated the Word God: "circa actum voluntatis creatae [of Christ], denominatur tamen Verbum."[10] In the freedom of poetic perception and association, if the symbol Piers, or Peter, could be seen as some aspect of Jesus and, perhaps denominatively, as Jesus Himself, he might similarly be identified as the Christ, as he is in Langland's phrase, "*Petrus id est Christus.*"

In Anima's third statement all possible meanings are connected: "wille one," is at once the power of willing, the individual will of Will the Dreamer, the will of Piers, Christ, God. In his statement Piers is first seen, though still somewhat darkly, as the humanity of Christ, and more specifically as His human will—both identical with Him but not in every respect. It is not surprising that anyone true of tongue, works, and will should be called "a god" in *Piers Plowman,* or that Passus xv, immediately preceding a Passus in which the Incarnation takes place, should envisage a continuity between Will and Piers and Christ. Anima's replies express the continuity of the "fre liberal wille," that is, of Charity, or Love as a continuous act.

From the fragmented experience, indeed the fragmented personality and persona, of the Prologue to *Piers Plowman,* through the tearing of the Pardon and Conscience's departure from Clergy, to the last words of the poem, the Dreamer's essential problem is one of unity. In Passūs xv to xx, this problem finally centers on the nature of the relationship of God's world to man's: "Et iam non sum in mundo, et hi in mundo sunt"; yet Christ asks, "ut omnes unum sint, sicut tu Pater in me, et ego in te, ut et ipsi in nobis unum sint . . . Ego in eis, et tu in me: ut sint consummati in unum" (John 17:11, 21, 23). This is the center of Christianity for Langland, the problem of incarnation, then and now, as an objective phenomenon and as a subjective one; it is the realization of a person in every sense.

In the remainder of Passus xv, Anima talks about living. He enumerates saints' lives and charitable actions, presenting and to an extent creating an antique ideal to enliven an abstract idea. His descriptions have coherence and vitality, especially when measured by those of earlier characters. Often anecdotes or vignettes, they have substance and constant movement:

> For I haue seyn hym in sylke and somme tyme in russet,
> Both in grey and in grys and in gulte herneys,
> And as gladlich he it gaf to gomes that it neded.

Edmonde and Edwarde, eyther were kynges
And seyntes ysette, tyl charite hem folwed.[11]
I haue seyne Charite also syngen and reden,
Ryden and rennen in ragged wedes,
Ac biddyng as beggeres bihelde I hym neuere.
Ac in riche robes rathest he walketh,
Ycalled and ycrimiled and his crowne shaue
[And clenlich yclothed in cipres and in Tartaryne.][12]
And in a freres frokke he was yfounde ones,
Ac it is ferre agoo in seynt Fraunceys tyme . . .

[xv.214–26][13]

In such descriptions, Charity might be said to begin to acquire a more realistic
flavor, to take on a more substantial form which prepares the way for a fuller
understanding and embodiment of the personality of Charity, Christ, and
Will in Passus XVI.

In gratitude for Anima's showing him the life of charity, Will exclaims
at the outset of Passus XVI that he will always love Anima on account of
"Haukynnes loue the actyf man." His remark underscores the relation of
charity to the actual world and recalls Will's connection with Hawkin, the
exemplar of that world a few Passūs before. But the Dreamer adds that,
despite Anima's fine exhibition of charity, he still does not fully grasp what
charity means. Rather than cite other concrete examples, Anima makes a
more direct appeal to the Dreamer's imagination. He tells about a tree—like
a plant of peace growing naturally upward—whose fruits are charity. This
tree grows in the garden of the heart, where free will ("*Liberum-Arbitrium*,"
16) cultivates it "under" Piers Plowman, hence in a subordinate role, neither
specified as a formal relationship, like that of a freeholder to his lord, nor
defined less formally as tutelage, guidance, or imitation. At Anima's mere
mention of Piers, the Dreamer swoons, falling into an inner dream, a pro-
founder, if also a more passive, level of consciousness.

It is important to remember that Will has been talking to the soul and
that as a result he now not only perceives but even enters the garden of his
heart, in short, an entirely interiorized landscape.[14] Here Piers acts for the
first time since Passus VII. He shows Will the tree on which "the frute
Charite" grows supported by three piles, the Trinity. Will sees an image of
the Trinity within his heart (or soul), a presentation of the common medieval
notion that the soul reflects the creative action, the life, of the triune God, and
there he finds that the Trinity upholds charity:[15]

Just as the Father engenders the eternal knowledge of the Word Who expresses Him, and as the Word is in turn united with the Father by the Holy Spirit, so memory or thought, big with the ideas which it encloses, engenders knowledge of the intellect or word, and love is born from both as the bond which unites them. It is no accidental correspondence that is here described; the structure of the creative Trinity conditions and therefore explains the structure of the human soul.[16]

After Piers explains the three piles as power, knowledge, and will, and describes the fruits as morally symbolic states of life, the Dreamer asks to taste the savor of a fruit, now not just charity, a state, or a state of life, but suddenly understood by him to be an apple (XVI.73). Will's sudden intuition —perhaps consciousness—of Original Sin is unerring. It gives startling, dramatic expression to a moment of insight and recognition.[17] As soon as Piers shakes down some fruit, next identified as "Adam and Abraham and Ysay the prophete, / Sampson and Samuel and seynt Iohan the baptiste" (81–82), the devil gathers them up and lays them "in *lymbo inferni.*" This interior garden, imprinted with an image of the triune God, is also the garden of a lost paradise into which Satan, sin, and death have broken (cf. "Elde"; C, XIX.68–105; B, XVIII.284, 356–57). Following the devil's intrusion, Piers seizes the second pile—earlier perceived as *sapiencia-Dei-patris* and now as *Filius,* the Son—and by the power of the Father's will and the special liberality ("frenesse") of the Holy Spirit, strikes out at the devil. After the speed and compression, the intensity of the intuitive grasping which this passage dramatizes, the Annunciation is made to Mary that Jesus is to be born in the fullness of time, when Piers's fruit, Charity, has flowered and ripened.

Imaginative compression, least of all Langland's abstractly verbal form of it, may be quickly grasped but not easily disassembled for annotation. This difficulty pertains with special force to Passus XVI, where unified power is lost in the retelling. What Passus XVI presents is the Incarnation of the Word, in time and in the person, both then in the man Christ and now in the Dreamer, or sleeping Will, and both within Christ and within this Dreamer: Will conceives the conception—and the conceiving—of Christ.

Several difficulties in the B-text to this point need additional explanation. If Piers is to be identified in these Passūs with Christ's humanity, his grasping the second pile, or Son, has to be in some sense a reaching up to God. This symbolic action could, but need not, be seen as heretical by Langland's contemporaries, and certainly should not be seen so by us. It could look like a form of the Nestorian heresy and, more exactly, of the Assumptus Theory —namely, that Christ assumed a human person—with the likely implication that a human being somehow earned, or initiated, the Hypostatic Union.[18] Although these difficulties of interpretation very probably accounted for Langland's modifications of Passus XVI in the C-text, the B-text properly understood is not in the least heretical by the standards of the fourteenth century.

Repeatedly, Passus XVI, like earlier sections of the poem yet more clearly than they, stresses a united power, a community, between God and man. At the threshold of this Passus, Anima concludes, "And so thorw god and thorw good men groweth the frute Charite." In the B-text free will, or *Liberum Arbitrium,* cultivates the tree of Charity under Piers and is said to seize the third pile supporting the tree through grace and the Holy Spirit's help, even as Piers seizes the second pile through the Father's will and the Spirit's liberality. This continuity between the will of God and man is further rationalized by changes in the C-text: the Anima of B, XVI, becomes free will, *Liberum Arbitrium,* and so does Piers, except in one instance where he also becomes the free will of God, *Libera-Voluntas-Dei* (C, XIX.119). Generally speaking, these changes in the C-text simply clarify the notion that the Holy Spirit and man's power of willing are united in charitable action.[19] In time, B will explicitly identify the Spirit with Grace (XIX.202–03) and will put grace and human love on a continuum, as they are, for example, in the theology of the Franciscan Duns Scotus.[20] In the B-text, Charity is "a fre liberal wille" and the Holy Spirit is Grace, the will of God understood in its freest and most liberal, most merciful and charitable expression.

I shall have occasion to examine two of the C-text alterations more closely, but even in summary, Langland's association of man's power of freely willing, his power of love, with God's, suggests the emphasis on Will's freedom which produced one of the most imaginatively provocative formulations of these centuries about the nearness of God and man—in a psychological rather than in a metaphysical sense: namely, that the Incarnation, essentially an expression of love, was destined to have occurred even without Adam's fall (lest God's free will be compromised by human willfulness).[21] Such a view might even be taken to suggest that, in terms of the absolute personal perfection of human being, it was, if not necessary, then ideally desirable and, in Langland's richly ambiguous sense, "Kindly," that such being should be united with the Word.[22] In Piers's reaching out for the second Person of the Trinity, we perhaps see a reflection of this paradox as well.

Piers's reaching for the second pile acts out the Incarnation as well as the Dreamer's understanding of it. In the interior landscape of the Garden, there is movement from the presence of the triune God through the heart, mind, or soul, to history, the birth of Christ. There is a continuity of act, perceptual and historical, from *Sapientia,* the Old Testament term peculiar to the Word in His providential and creative aspects; through the manifestation of the Person of the Word to human will and intellect; to the human actuality of Jesus.[23] These parallels strongly suggest that in Piers's reaching for the second pile we are to see an imaginative evocation of the psychology or inner order of the Incarnation. In clarifying this suggestion, I shall rely here, as elsewhere, chiefly on the works of Duns Scotus, which are representative of doctrines commonly held and nonheretical but which also have a decided voluntarist bias. My point is not that Langland knew Scotus's writings but that he could have known them, or others like them, and that his poem makes more sense in their light than in others.

We might begin with Piers's first act of reaching upward in Passus xvi, that puzzling moment in which, at Will's desire to taste an apple, he "caste to the croppe" for the fruit. It is worth noting that Will the Dreamer initiates this action rather than Piers, and that in the C-text Piers's role is given to *Liberum Arbitrium,* a free will no further specified, and to "Elde," a mere fact of life and fallen human nature. For Scotus and his followers, Jesus possessed the capability of sinning—as He did not for the Thomists— because He possessed human nature: "natura, quam assumpsit, erat de se possibilis peccare, quia non erat beata ex vi unionis, et habuit liberum arbitrium, et ita vertibile ad utrumlibet."[24] Granted the fact that Piers's implication in Will's desire for the apple is only formal, it looks as though Langland's passage is an imaginative rendering of this Scotistic position.

To this position, Scotus adds, thereby avoiding heresy, that Christ, in the first instant of His union with God—which has not, of course, occurred in Langland's poem when Will wants the apple—knew beatitude (*fuit beatus*), and that "beatitudo abstulit sibi omnem peccabilitatem vel possibilitatem peccandi, quae potest auferri per beatitudinem, licet cum hoc dispensative staret potestas merendi; plenitudo enim gloriae, qua ipse fuit conjunctus fini, non minus quam alius beatus, licet potuit mereri, aeque excludit omnem potestatem in eo avertendi a fine, sicut in aliis."[25] Granted that the ability to merit is consonant with this dispensation, granted that He could merit— the insistence of these qualifying phrases derives from other Scotistic views which emphasize repeatedly and uncompromisingly the reality, hence the uncompromised freedom, of Christ's human will. These views pertain closely to Piers's reaching, indeed seizing, the second pile. Holding with Peter Lombard that Christ merited not only on the cross but also "ab ipsa conceptione, ex quo [*sic*] homo factus est, per charitatem et justitiam et alias virtutes," Scotus has to explain how this can be the case.[26] Eventually his reasoning leads him to conclude that Christ could merit in the first instant of his creation and conception because his soul had in it everything needed to love God in or on account of Himself (*propter se*), namely "potentia, perfecta gratia, objectum praesens per intellectum, scilicet tota Trinitas, cui poterat velle bonum propter se, et non impediebatur."[27] Scotus's position is orthodox, but his statement of it is distinguished once again by those qualifications which, it turns out, protect the freedom of the will: "et non impediebatur," "si non impeditur."

If Piers's reaching for the second pile symbolizes the sort of meritorious, hence free, action of Christ's impersonated humanity which Scotus describes, then it is not at all heretical. Further, it is an act which, according to a voluntarist psychology, is wisely imagined to protect the freedom of Christ's human will and the continuity of its powers with ours—in other words, to protect the reality of the Redemption. One of the most fundamental dicta of Christology states that only what is assumed is redeemed: "quod est inassumptible est incurabile"[28]—incurable, not subject to "lechecrafte." If Langland's poem is voluntaristic—a point which hardly seems in serious question—then he is likely to have made special room for the human will in this assumption, not only in the humanistic notion that Christ merits in us as members of Him ("in membris autem, quae nos sumus, quotidie proficit")[29] and therefore in the Dreamer's vision of the Incarnation in Passus XVI, but also, and actually, in Himself. We might say that Piers's action is conception in two senses—a birth both spiritual and physical.

Christ's human will is like ours: "Voluntas autem humana assumpta a Verbo est voluntas naturae humanae univoce cum nostra; igitur ipsa non potest frui sine charitate."[30] This will needs created charity for fruition, or beatitude, and it does not of necessity find fruition in the presence of the object—the Trinity—to the intellect.[31] Christ's human will remains sinless (*impeccabilis*) not formally but virtually—in effect, then, through "the Fader wille and frenesse of *Spiritus Sancti*" (XVI.88), through a factor in some way external or remote, and through the "*summam charitatem*," the highest charity or grace.[32] Even so, the fruition of Christ's human will "non est necessitas, sive perpetuitas necessaria ex habitibus determinantibus potentias ad actus, sed tantummodo ex habitu gloriae est necessitas secundum *quid*, quia habitus est naturaliter inclinativus; nec ex charitate talis necessitas est in voluntate, quia talis libere potest uti charitate, vel non uti."[33] In reaching for the second pile, Piers grasps the Word, the vision of the Logos;[34] as Christ's humanity, more specifically as His human will, he is free, through God's power—His will and grace—to choose freely to love God for Himself. Through God's power alone he merits, but he nonetheless has to act meritoriously.[35]

In view of this, it is possible to see how easily Langland might have attributed Piers's seizing the second pile to *Libera-Voluntas-Dei* in the C-text to avoid hostile or unimaginative misinterpretations of the symbolic action in B. Three further points are worth remarking in the C-version's treatment of the Incarnation. First, that this is the only line in the C-Passus (XIX.119) in which Piers becomes a force other than *Liberum Arbitrium,* an unspecified power of freely willing, a power which must have some connection with the meaning of Piers in B; and second, that when his place is taken by a specifically divine will in C, this special will is not called *Liberum Arbitrium Dei* but is given a different name. Matters pertaining to the person of Christ were hot issues in Langland's time, and it is tempting to see them behind Langland's very un-Langlandian care to separate the powers of God and man here. The third point relates to this same passage and mediates between the first two. In the line preceding the seizure of the second pile by *Libera-Voluntas-Dei* in the C-text, we read, "Thenne meuede hym mod *in maiestate dei*" (C, XIX.118)—"mind moved him in the majesty of God, with the result that the free will of God seized the second pile." Here we have not only the pronoun *hym,* referring to *Liberum Arbitrium,* but also in the word *mod* the emphasis on something internal, in the mind and affective, both of which are appropriate to my reading of the parallel text in B and appear to have been derived from B. In a word, Langland's separation of the powers of God and man is by no means complete; nor is it so very un-Langlandian.[36]

Part of the problem in interpreting the image of Incarnation in Passus XVI arises from the mysteriousness of the subject itself and from the difficulty of portraying instantaneity (*in primo instanti conceptionis*) in the necessarily sequential lines of a poem.[37] In this respect, the Annunciation to Mary, some four lines after Piers's grasping the second pile, might seem troublesome:

> And thanne spakke *Spiritus Sanctus* in Gabrieles mouthe
> To a mayde that hiȝte Marye, a meke thinge with-alle,
> That one Iesus, a Iustice sone, moste Iouke in her chambre . . .
> [XVI.90–92]

The poet seems to emphasize not only the drama of this event but the fact that it is posterior in some sense to the creation and conception of Christ— "And thanne"—as indeed one would logically expect it to be. The problem here, if one exists at all, is minor. The God of a will-based theology, whose will cannot even be circumscribed by Adam's fall and who must as a result be held to have intended the Incarnation before that fall, hardly needs Mary's consent to proceed with it. Perhaps we need worry this matter no further than an *Ave* to a maid "full of grace"—that is, of the Spirit,—the fruit of whose womb is "blessed." The issue sounds already settled. Mary's assent, of course, is needed and is meritorious, but formally so: there is no more possibility of her refusing than there is of her son's sinning.

After the birth of Jesus in Passus xvi, we learn that He could

... haue y-fou3te with the fende ar ful tyme come;
And Pieres the Plowman parceyued plenere tyme,
And lered hym lechecrafte his lyf for to saue
That, thowgh he were wounded with his enemye, to warisshe
   hym-self ... [38]

[xvi.102–05]

Once again the C-text replaces this reference to Piers with *Liberum Arbitrium*. The reference to Piers's "lechecrafte" is the culminating and clearest portrayal of Piers as a symbol for Christ's human will. In retrospect at least, its clarity is not surprising in a Passus of progressive realization—understanding and embodiment—and all the less so because Piers in this last passage represents the action of that will not in the invulnerability of its beatitude but at its most merely human. Scotus's writing again provides an appropriate context for Langland's poem:

fuerunt in Christo ad minus tres voluntates vel appetitus, scilicet intellectualis increatus, rationalis creatus, et irrationalis, scilicet sensitivus; sed quia voluntas addit super appetitum, quia est appetitus cum ratione liber, sic stricte loquendo, fuerunt in Christo tantum duae voluntates.[39]

There were two wills, though only one with the power to will, one person. Scotus's assertion helps to clarify what Piers Plowman might be doing in teaching Christ "lechecrafte," or how to cure. Jesus Christ's mission gradually becomes clearer to Him, and He gradually accomplishes it. He is human as well as divine, committed to time and to experience as well as to eternity and to immediate and total apprehension. Only insofar as He is human can His divinity redeem humanity. Having merited in His conception, He merits more, according to Scotus, in the supreme obedience of His human nature, now specifically including the inferior aspect of the human will, to God:

Sed Christus secundum aliquid fuit viator, et passibilis secundum partem sensitivam et portionem inferiorem voluntatis, ideo multa habuit objecta praesentia sensibus et portioni inferiori, circa quae potuit libere velle contra affectionem commodi, quae semper est ad conveniens illi, cujus est; ideo jejunando, vigilando, orando, et multis aliis talibus potuit mereri.[40]

Langland's text actually speaks for itself. Christ, through the "lechecrafte" of His free human will, taught Him by Piers, becomes the "leche of lyf" (118). Piers "lered hym lechecrafte" is conceivably a reflexive construction because, in a denominative sense at least, Piers is himself Christ.[41] As so often in *Piers Plowman,* the word *lyf* has here both a bodily and a spiritual connotation and very likely a stronger sense of physicality in the phrase "leche of lyf," with its bloodletting connotation, than in such another phrase as "lorde of lyf." Perhaps the C-text offers the best gloss on this point: "be-leyue leelly vpon that litel baby, / That his likame schal lechen atte laste ous alle" (xx.92-93)—"likame," that is, body or flesh.[42] Only what is assumed by the Word is *curabile;* it is necessary that Christ should assume the whole human nature and, in Langland's poem, specifically the whole will. The fact that Piers's "lechecrafte" saves Jesus' "lyf" and teaches Him to cure Himself even if wounded by His enemy establishes the fact that Piers's power pertains to areas in which Christ is vulnerable, to His emotions and appetites, to the reality of feeling human. Here Piers's power is that will's power over its own inferior aspects, a power still essentially human.[43]

The remainder of the Dreamer's swoon in Passus xvi, the inner dream or state of vision which began with Anima's mention of Piers Plowman, occupies itself with a résumé of Jesus' life, in the midst of which Jesus begins to speak (121). We might think of his speaking as a fourth dimension in the poem. Prior to it the dimensions of utterance are those of the wakened Dreamer, of the sleeping Dreamer and his faculties, and of the external, public world in the dream (kings, friars, and the like); now a public world again reappears, but since it belongs to the distant past, its present existence depends in a special way on the Dreamer's consciousness, the surface in which it can now find a direct reflection. This surface is the mirror in which the Dreamer truly begins to recognize himself and another, like images superimposed.

While Jesus is speaking in this Passus, He refers to Judas as a false mirror, a mirror false because it reflects "vnkynde wille" and, a few lines before, "enuye and yuel wille" (149, 136). These phrases echoed through Hawkin's confession and the Dreamer's earlier experiences, too. In this inverted mirror we finally see that what lies behind Fals Fikel-tonge, the fiancé of Meed, behind the essential greed and hypocrisy which suffocate charity, is the distorted personality of a Judas, false in his "faire speche," guileful in his glad face, and rancorous in his laughter (154-55). In Judas we see the image of a man who has looked at *"vultum nativitatis suae,"* at what Langland calls man's "kynde," but has then gone away to obliterate what he was: "consideravit enim se, et abiit, et statim oblitus est qualis fuerit" (James 1:24).

Turning from man's true nature, Judas reflects his false one, a self-willed image of darkness and denial—unkyndenesse. In the definitive wording of these Passūs, it is he who becomes no man, because there is none so wretched "That he ne may louye, and hym lyke, and lene of his herte / Good wille and good worde" (XVII.345–46).

The Dreamer, having now surprised the mirror of truth in his own soul, by which falsehood's measure is taken, is at pains in the rest of the poem to give its meaning an even more fully self-conscious, more expansive and active, form. He pursues in effect what he might and will be, and as before, his figure invites us to follow him. Not surprisingly, the subject of "kynde" and images of light become focal in Passūs XVI to XVIII. While remaining an inner event, the poem also becomes increasingly historical and dramatic. The imagery, word-play, and heightened actuality of the form are themselves conscious parts of a process of possession—perception, verbalization, actualization. Though all three of these terms apply to Passūs XVI to XVIII, "verbalization" is perhaps the most useful in describing Langland's characteristic practice in them, for their action is primarily a process of realizing through the word.

When Jesus speaks in Passūs XVI, actually voicing the word for the first time in the poem, the Dreamer is still in his swoon, which ends with a reference to the Redemption. As it ends, Jesus is no longer speaking, and the speaker is not specifically identified, as he has not been since Piers seized the second pile, *Filius:*

> On crosse vpon Caluarye Cryst toke the bataille
> A3eines deth and the deuel, destruyed her botheres my3tes,
> Deyde, and deth fordid, and daye of ny3te made.
>
> [XVI.164–66]

This narrative anonymity is appropriate to the Dreamer's swoon and to the initial presentation of Jesus' life and work, recalled here in its least interpretive, most directly and compositely biblical form. Once again Langland uses a verbal form to parallel a stage in the process of comprehension. The swooning Dreamer's recollection of Christ's redemptive work is received more passively, less consciously or actively willed, in this Passūs than will be the case in Passūs XVIII, where the Dreamer's presence at the Redemption is dramatic and immediate and where he is explicitly identified with its narrator (XVIII.18 ff., 110–12).

We are more apt to notice the narrative anonymity at the end of the Dreamer's swoon because of the sharp shift in the dramatic situation of the next few lines, in which the Dreamer's presence is reasserted:

And I awaked there-with and wyped myne eyghen
And after Piers the Plowman pryed and stared.
Estwarde and westwarde I awayted after faste
And 3ede forth as an ydiote in contre to aspye
After Pieres the Plowman . . .

[XVI.167–71]

It is striking that Will looks anxiously here for Piers rather than for Christ.[44]
His action underlines all the more clearly his need to find a figure immediately available and experiential, one with meaning for him because he belongs to the poet-Dreamer's own process of discovering and recovering
truth.[45] As if intuitively, indeed by a kind of reflex action, Will pursues the
figure who bridges the distance between him and Christ, embodying at
once their likeness and the way to make it real. Piers, after all, is the figure
whose power of love belongs to the will.[46]

Searching for Piers, Will successively finds characters identified as Faith
or Abraham, *Spes* or Moses, and the Samaritan or Charity. These three figures, all types of Christ, embody a historical progression which leads in Passus
XVIII to Christ's Passion and descent into hell and then to the triumph of
Easter. As the three theological virtues, they also present the Dreamer's inner or moral progression. In numerous ways, Abraham, Moses, and the Samaritan continue the Dreamer's realization of unity both in interior and
exterior senses, a unity of understanding with temporal action. Each of these
characters, representatives of the mind and of history, of the present and the
past, of God's work and man's, progressively illuminates the nearness of the
human personality to God. What they are and what they say—their presence as such and their words—not only instruct Will but are in themselves
already an achievement for him, simultaneously a greater possession of reality and of himself, of his own reality as a person.[47]

The poem devotes over 450 lines to Abraham, Moses, and the Samaritan,
enough space to suggest that their instruction is important. Its amplitude,
the result of expansion rather than of simple repetition, suggests an import
that is psychological to a considerable extent. It suggests an intensity of attention and understanding,—verbalization, to use my earlier term. Their
instruction doubtless has its tedious moments; yet when the verse quickens,
when characters appear with sudden, dramatic spontaneity, when their statements become verbally dense, we recognize the excitement of discovery
which helps to make the subsequent developments in Passus XVIII emotionally credible and humanly comprehensible.

Abraham tells the Dreamer about the Trinity and in effect offers him a further gloss on the Tree of Charity which enforces its relationship to the exterior world, to human history and institutions. He uses the generation of the human family as an analogy for the relationship of the three divine Persons and thereby associates their procession with men's, as a historical race and as a moral and spiritual community (XVI.196–224). His comparisons suggest the penetration of the forms of this life by the Spirit at the same time that their fertile ingenuity accentuates the role of the human intellect in perceiving it.

Abraham might be said to start with God, with origins and the order of knowing; Moses starts with God's law, but he concentrates on man's behavior. His teaching, "*Dilige deum et proximum tuum,*" is simpler and shorter, a direct command to love which requires a heavier commitment of the will. The Samaritan, who literally heals a wounded man through the "lechecrafte" love has taught him, brings the Trinity and love, or the emphases of Abraham and Moses, inseparably together in a new realization. He joins the concerns of the mind and the heart and of knowledge and action. The gist of his teaching can be seen in his likening the Trinity to a candle, an analogy which illuminates still further the ties, in fact the continuity of love, between God and good men.

This analogy is remarkable for its affirmation of a genuine reciprocity between God and man and its balance of man's radically free will with God's power.[48] It offers the fullest gloss on the poem's earlier statement that a true man "is a god, bi the gospel, agrounde and aloft" (I.90), for it associates the Holy Ghost's action intimately with human love and even identifies the grace of the Holy Ghost with a loving nature, God's but also man's. As the Samaritan explains to Will, the Trinity is likened to a taper—wax, wick, and fire—sending forth flame and light and in like manner fostering the flame of love and belief in men. If fostered by the Trinity's action in and for itself, man's love is therefore an extension of it, an idea the Samaritan develops.

He first describes human life and love, actually identifying the two as natural for man and their destruction as "vnkynde," a denial of nature. Then he emphasizes the activity of man's role in setting the Spirit in motion, an emphasis which suggestively recalls Piers's reaching up for the second pile in Passus XVI: "So that the holygoste gloweth but as a glede / Tyl that lele loue ligge on hym and blowe" (XVII.223–24).[49] This surprising reciprocity— "mercy to mercyable and to non other"—is next seen to involve a more passive or receptive role for man, though still a responsible one. Now a good man is seen as the "towe"—tinder or other inflammable material—without which the Spirit will not flame into mercy and grace. Perhaps the most astonishing statement comes in the Samaritan's continuation of this idea:

> Thus is vnkyndenesse the contrarie that quencheth, as it
>   were,
> The grace of the holy gooste, goddes owne kynde,
> For that kynde dothe, vnkynde fordoth . . .

[XVII.269–71]

A denial of one's nature quenches grace or the Holy Ghost's love. This grace is God's own nature, a fact reaffirmed at length in Passus XIX, where the Holy Ghost's name is said to be Grace (203). But it is obviously only in a qualified sense—"as it were," therefore in some but not in every sense—that man can quench "goddes owne kynde"; as the line that follows this last phrase forcefully suggests, God's "kynde" here is also God's nature in man, His love or grace. This is the identification of grace and human love shadowed more enigmatically in the Garden of Charity and the continuum between God and man aligned earlier in this chapter with Scotistic positions. The Samaritan's concluding simile seems inevitable:

> For euery manere good man may be likned to a torche
> Or elles to a tapre to reuerence the trinitee;
> And who morthereth a good man, me thynketh by myn inwyt,
> He fordoth the leuest ly3te that owre lorde loueth.

[XVII.276–79]

We often tend to think of abstractions and symbols as being opposed. Here, through the poetic alchemy of ontological puns, the abstract word *kynde* is transformed into a dynamic symbol of relationship. Though abstract, the Samaritan's word-play vibrates with poetic and perceptual life—perhaps to its author, with a life more simply real.

It is a short step from the Samaritan's concluding simile to Christ's stating to Lucifer in Passus XVIII, "I were an vnkynde kynge but I my kynde holpe" (396); but it is also an important one. In the Samaritan's punning, an abstraction becomes a symbol; in the next Passus symbols such as "kynde" and "ly3te" become dramatic acts, words fully realized in the historical past and, now, in the poem's dreamworld. When Christ descends into hell, "the li3te bad vnlouke, and Lucifer answered, / 'What lorde artow?' " Then "Lucyfer loke ne my3te so ly3te hym ableynte; / And tho that owre lorde loued in-to his li3te he lau3te" (XVIII.313–14, 323–24). The simple, dramatic form of Passus XVIII attests to life ("lyf") and vision truly grasped. It is at the end of this Passus that for the first time Will acts decisively immediately on waking from a dream in which the Daughters of God—Mercy,

Truth, Justice, and Peace—take forms real and personal enough to merge with his waking reality. There, too, for the first time the Dreamer appears to act with positive virtue (to do better) in terms of the world in which he really exists; that is, he acts with his wife and daughter:

> Tyl the daye dawed this damaiseles daunced
> That men rongen to the resurexioun, and ri3t with that I
>   waked
> And called Kitte, my wyf, and Kalote, my dou3ter—
> "Ariseth and reuerenceth goddes resurrexioun
> And crepeth to the crosse on knees and kisseth it for a
>   Iuwel."

[XVIII.424–28]

Easter's rebirth exists in his waking present.

The Dreamer has finally achieved some unity between his personal vision and the actual world. At the outset of Passus XIX he speaks confidently of writing his poem, and he goes to Holy Church, the "Unity" in this Passus where two worlds meet (XIX.1–2, 325). This time he writes not with a nightmarish awareness of impinging realities, a parody of wholeness as in the Prologue, but with felt wholeness and joy. But the movement into history, action, personal wholeness, which began with Passus XVI, also has its price. The Dreamer soon finds that he has wakened to the world he left behind him, which his personal vision has changed, if not at all, at least not in all the ways he expects. This world remains his own, as it must, and not just somebody else's. Even to readers willing to grant to the fourteenth century an acute awareness of one's own existence, Passūs XIX and XX are unexpected and moving.

Sleeping once again in Passus XIX, Will sees the Paraclete come to the Apostles "In lyknesse of a li3tnynge" (197). Urged by his Conscience, a faculty not specifically utilized since Passus XIV, he raises his voice to welcome the Spirit's coming and thus participates in its meaning (204–06). Here the poem identifies the Apostle Peter with Piers and in the following scenes pictures Piers as the type of the Christian leader, tilling truth with the aid of the four Evangelists and the Fathers, planting the cardinal virtues in men's souls, and establishing "Vnite, holicherche on Englisshe" (325).[50] Gradually the poem moves further in time toward the present. While Piers plows "As wyde as the worlde is," Pride gathers his forces to destroy Piers's crops (330–32); this is the last time that Piers is seen as an actor in the poem. Hereafter Unity is threatened, assaulted from without and undermined from within; Piers becomes exclusively a symbol, while receding to a possibility. Again as in the Visio, Conscience begins to play a more public, collective role as the representative of the Christian community and becomes the dominant spokesman in the poem, as it returns to the observable facts of human behavior in the late Middle Ages and to the practical judgments of an actual life.

At Conscience's advice, Pride's first efforts are repulsed. All "kinde" Christians repent and withdraw into Unity, "saue comune wommen . . . saue they one";

> And fals men, flatereres, vsureres and theues,
> Lyeres and questmongeres, that were forsworen ofte,
> Wytynge and willefully with the false helden
> And for syluer were forswore . . .
>
> [xix.364–69]

Like wishful thinking, the phrase "saue they one" softens an ominous shadow cast by the next lines all the way back to Passus II of the Visio, which introduced Meed, "Fals," "Fauel," "Fals Fikel-tonge," and their fellows. In short space this shadow darkens. Pride's next attack defies the ameliorating narrator, breaking into the poem with dramatic realism: " 'ӡe, bawe!' quod a brewere, 'I wil nouӡt be reuled, / Bi Iesu, for al ӡowre Ianglynge with *spiritus iusticie*' " (394–95). He adds that he will not follow Conscience so long as he can gainfully adulterate good ale with bad, "for that is my kynde" (398). As used here, the word *kynde* is an uncompromised denial of everything Passūs xvi to xviii have established. Before this Passus ends, the brewer's denial is twice reinforced by other representatives of the social order, first a lord and then a king. The latter announces that he can take what he needs where he can soonest find it, "for I borwe neuere / Ne craue of my comune but as my kynde asketh" (472–73). In these lines the word *kynde* takes on the sort of ambiguity we might associate with the word *nature* in *King Lear*. Given the self-seeking company the king's words keep at the end of this Passus, the force of their ambiguity is largely negative.

The more puzzling, perhaps more disconcerting, voice of a vicar also intervenes between brewer and king. His words even more clearly echo early sections of the poem, especially the Prologue. His entrance into the narrative, a direct reply to Conscience, is also sudden and dramatic:

> "Thanne is many man ylost," quod a lewed vycory;
> "I am a curatour of holykyrke, and come neure in my tyme
> Man to me that me couth telle of cardinale vertues
> Or that acounted Conscience at a cokkes fether or an hennes.

I knewe neure cardynal that he ne came fro the pope,
And we clerkes, whan they come, for her comunes payeth,
For her pelure and her palfreyes mete and piloures that hem folweth.
The comune *clamat cotidie* eche a man to other,
'The contre is the curseder that cardynales come inne' . . ."

[XIX.407–15][51]

The description of the vicar as "lewed" could be ironic. The vicar is a
sharp observer and an honest critic of his world, one well aware of the ideals it
betrays. But in any event, the vicar is not now the poet's unqualified spokesman. In his figure the more oblique satire of the Prologue is clarified. His
appearance is a necessary reunion with present worldly realities and therefore
a reunion for poet (and Dreamer) with a part of himself, including the
views of his own past. These views are still valid, even enforced by their
frank recurrence, but the Dreamer does not endorse them; he listens to
them. They do not as yet engulf his present.

The vicar is throughout his appearance a consistently dramatized speaker.
His utterance is longer, less cryptic, more controlled and autonomous than
is the case with similar speeches in the Prologue. His denunciations are
straightforward: "god amende the pope that pileth holykirke" (439). The
vicar is angry but rational, and he sees the perversion of values and powers as
no puzzle but as definite, damning facts: "For *spiritus prudencie* amonge the
peple is gyle," and again, "Eche man sotileth a sleight synne forto hyde"
(452, 454). When the vicar speaks, it is as if parts of the Prologue had become
more lucid and certain for the poet, as for us, because they have become more
dramatically real for the Dreamer.

After hearing the vicar and king, the Dreamer wakens: "Heuy-chered I
3ede and elynge in herte; / I ne wiste where to ete ne at what place" (XX.2–3).
Where we should have expected him to feel wretched after what he has
just heard, his misery results from hunger and homelessness. Both these
causes could have been made metaphorical here, but they have not been.
That other world of physical needs and material realities is reasserting itself.
As if by subliminal influence or by a kind of psychic contagion, the Dreamer
begins to reflect the dislocations of value he has heard in the final stages of
Passus XIX.

Now, at the beginning of Passus XX, while still awake, he meets a figure
named Need, who is related to Hunger in the Visio.[52] This slippery figure is
whatever need the Dreamer feels—real need but no further specified—and
an embodiment of his reasoning under need's influence. Need first berates
Will, sarcastically asking him why he does not twist morality to his own

convenience, as have the lord and king. Seeming more serious, Need then expounds the traditional view that need is a law unto itself, but he begins to lose sight of any higher laws at all: "So Nede, at grete nede, may nymen as for his owne / Wyth-oute conseille of Conscience or cardynale vertues" (20–21). Posturing self-importantly, he derogates virtue itself—"And *spiritus iusticie* shal iuggen, wolhe, nolhe, / After the kynges conseille and the comune lyke"—and strikes the cynical notes of worldly wisdom: "And *spiritus prudencie* in many a poynte shal faille / Of that he weneth wolde falle, if his wytte ne were" (29–32). Need, in short, "sotileth a sleight" to hide sin, and from it proceeds next to blasphemy and self-contradiction:

> *Homo proponit et deus disponit* and [God] gouerneth alle good vertues,
> Ac Nede is next hym, for anon he meketh
> And as low as a lombe for lakkyng of that hym nedeth.
>
> [xx.34–36]

The last time we met this Latin quotation it was spoken by Recklessness during Will's first inner dream, his rebellious sojourn in the Land of Longing: " '*Homo proponit* . . . And *deus disponit*,' quod he, 'lat god done his wille' " (xi.36–37). Under the pressure of need, the Dreamer seems about to give up again, this time with waking awareness and waking will. But in the last line quoted—"as low as a lombe"—something else happens. Need seems to overhear himself, to become aware of another side of his nature, another kind of need. The image of a meek lamb looses associations at some remove from lamb dinners. The rest of Need's words are about voluntary poverty, the willing need of Christ on the cross, the bitter sorrows "that shal to Ioye tourne" (46):

> For-thi be nou3te abasshed to bydde and to be nedy,
> Syth he that wrou3te al the worlde was wilfullich nedy,
> Ne neuer none so nedy ne pouerere deyde.
>
> [xx.47–49]

Need sounds in the end just like Patience. Now more responsive to a spiritual need than to a material one, he calls back to mind the redemptive action of Passūs xvi to xviii.

Need's final expressions offer an alternative to his earlier ones, but they do not cancel them. Both exist side by side, joined by an association. Need is a figure arising directly from experience, not from doctrine. A speaker of half-truths and wisdom, he reflects the Dreamer's uncertain state, which is poised between opposite values and courses of action. He serves to bring the unworldly counsel of Patience to the surface of the Dreamer's wakened awareness, open to all realities and still trying to see himself as he really is.[53]

Need introduces Will to his final dream, a vision of Antichrist who comes "in mannes forme" to spread falsehood and to "spede mennes nedes" (xx.51–54). In this last dark vision, the nightmare of the Prologue returns more powerfully because it returns in a more certain, more deliberative form. Ironically, this form is more rational; its evil purer and more abstract. This last dream is full of historical suggestion and is punctuated by grimly realistic detail—"Rewmes and radegoundes and roynouse scalles, / Byles and bocches and brennyng agues" (82–83)—yet most of its characters loom larger and starker than life. They are huge, impersonal, and dehumanized, and it is with a start that we see them reach out to the poet's own person, implicating him in their action (182 ff.). This dream has a dense population of barely elaborated abstractions, who do not give long speeches or engage in debates but use words briefly, if at all, before rushing or being rushed by others from one bad event to one worse. Their life consists in their activity, in their crowding, in the details that give realistic force to their movements, and most of all in the disturbing context of allusion and recognition they bring with them; the Dreamer has seen something very like all of them before. Without elaboration, their abstract outlines are charged with meaning the poem has already created, and largely for this reason Passūs xx achieves an overwhelming impact of speed and compression.

Will's last dream encapsulates the corruption of Unity, or Holy Church, in the late Middle Ages and ends in the poet's present. In this dream we meet, one after another, inverted mirror images of the action of Passūs XVI to XIX. "Kynde," formerly God in His creative aspect or the created expression of God's Word, becomes an avenger on unkind men, their destroyer rather than their healer, a dispenser of pain and plague. "Lyf," formerly a name for Christ and love, now takes Fortune as his mistress, and together they beget Sloth, who marries Wanhope, "a wenche of the stuwes" (159). This family circle and Life's subsequent history strongly recall the Dreamer's rebellion in Passūs XI. At Conscience's request, Life is beset by Old Age and so flees to Physic, a parody of Christ's "lechecrafte," for "Lyf leued that lechecrafte lette shulde Elde / And dryuen awey Deth with dyas and dragges" (172–73). Age promptly fells a physician, and Life, reckless now, rushes into revelry:

> And Elde anone after me and ouer myne heed 3ede
> And made me balled bifore and bare on the croune,
> So harde he 3ede ouer myn hed it wil be seen eure.
> "Sire euel-ytau3te Elde," quod I, "vnhende go with the!"
>
> [xx.182–85]

"Elde" suddenly and rudely gets personal, and for the second time in the poem the Dreamer grows old. In this passage we recognize that the world in Passus xx is his, its experience also his own. The bond is a real one, never in life to be really broken. Faced with an impasse once more resembling Piers's experience with Hunger in the Visio, and also faced with gout, impotence, and a frustrated wife, the Dreamer does what comes naturally to him. He calls out to Kind for help, who crisply tells him to get himself into Unity and to "Lerne to loue" (207). Then he travels swiftly through repentance to Unity, only to find Unity besieged and fast disuniting.

At this point, fulfilling Clergy's warning in Passus xiii, Conscience, the keeper of Unity, cries out for Clergy's aid, and a plague of friars come running to offer assistance. The voice of Need now speaks for the spiritual need Conscience feels and vehemently rejects the friars as hypocrites, men whose felt need, if real at all, is material.[54] Heedless of Need's stern warning, however, a practical and hopeful Conscience welcomes the friars, assuming, as Piers did many Passūs before, that the cessation of hunger will cure their envy and greed and thus satisfy the spiritual needs of conscience. The friars prove incurable, in fact, prove themselves to be agents of disunity, fragmented persons actively defying Conscience's counsel; and so Conscience retreats once again behind the gates of Unity, it would seem to an ever-receding domain, a region increasingly private and symbolic.

Through a lack of commitment to repentance, a will weakened by sin, one Friar Flatterer then gets back again "in-to Conscience" (353). He is the walking fulfillment of Pride's earliest threats to Piers Plowman:

> . . . ȝowre carte the Byleue
> Shal be coloured so queyntly and keuered vnder owre sophistrie
> That Conscience shal nouȝte knowe by contricioun
> Ne by confessioun who is Cristene or hethen . . .
>
> [xix.342–45]

He brings the whole history of Lady Meed back to Conscience (xx.361–66). As Sloth and Pride now advance with "kene wille" against Conscience, he cries out once again for Clergy and Contrition; Will then dreams the answer received: "He lith and dremeth . . . and so do many other; / The frere with his phisik this folke hath enchaunted" (375–76). The only "lechecrafte" left seems to be a friar's falsehood, until Conscience, in the most surprising of the many surprising twists in this poem, suddenly relives an earlier decision:

> "Bi Cryste," quod Conscience tho, "I wil bicome a pilgryme
> And walken as wyde as al the worlde lasteth
> To seke Piers the Plowman that Pryde may destruye . . ."
>
> [xx.378–80]

If Clergy is false, then the parting with it must come, even though the parting is not, in principle, real because the symbol Piers Plowman includes it. Conscience seems about to embark on exactly the same journey begun in Passus XIII, which after all led to Passus XX. This would be recommitment but not progress, an act of admirable futility, even escape, commitment finally to a circle. Conscience continues, however, asking Kind for helpe, " 'til I haue Piers the Plowman'; / And sitthe he gradde after grace til I gan awake" (383–84).

Like Conscience, the poem ends on a personal note. With these last two lines, Will the Dreamer finally wakes to reality and finds it to be himself, what with God's grace he *will* be. Given this world, Piers Plowman will never be more than a symbol unless realized in wakened activity, unless truly realized in himself, "wille one," and Piers will never be a public or communal reality unless realized by the "many other[s]" who dream as well. At the end of the poem Will has no face to look at but his own. His last two lines hold the simple strength and the simple loneliness of self-realization—*solitudo*. Given grace, the shield of belief, it is not quite the sharp crack of one's own voice, one's own words, that we hear in this stillness, but it is like, very like it.

7

Books V and VI: Justice and Courtesy

Like the first two and the central Books of *The Faerie Queene*, Books V and VI are complementary pieces, related by theme, direction, and parallel incidents. Both move toward the poet's own world, toward a more specifically contemporary and immediately human context. Personality becomes a more explicit, self-conscious concern in these Books insofar as its presence becomes more real. Unity of experience and wholeness of being also become more problematical. All these developments occur likewise at the end of *Piers Plowman*. The thoroughly Langlandian subjects Spenser chose to treat in his last two Books imply these developments. Justice and Courtesy suggest meanings ranging from precise observances to cosmic movements and from realistic detail to visionary perfection. As Spenser fashions them, these virtues have breadth and reality, on the one hand inviting the image of a golden world, and on the other, the image of a world which is lifelike. Justice and courtesy are more expansive, more social, than a virtue like temperance, and although perhaps more limited, specific, and earthly than one like holiness (wholeness), they are also more actively concerned with this world, with the mundane affairs of everyday life.

By the standards of traditional morality, justice is the most inclusive and exalted of the natural moral virtues in *The Faerie Queene*: "Most sacred vertue she of all the rest" (V.Pro.x).[1] Justice is also the most objective and impersonal virtue, a fact which gives it a godlike quality of transcendence but also makes it elusive in human terms. According to Aristotle and Aquinas, whose views on justice are essentially those of the Renaissance, justice is "distinguished among the virtues by the fact that it governs relations among men."[2] It is the most socially oriented of the traditional moral virtues, and "alone of the virtues, is thought to be 'another's good,' because it is related to our neighbour; for it does what is advantageous to another."[3] The quest for justice lies outside the self: "It is no longer a question . . . of *someone who keeps himself in the just mean* but of *keeping the just mean of some thing*."[4] Justice therefore implies a landscape of quest which is objectively realistic, and if the criterion of objectivity is seriously pursued, then a landscape which points to actual history. The ideal of justice is peculiarly liable to attack, even to disfigurement, by the unyielding facts of wordly injustice, as proves the case in the last two cantos of Book v, precisely as it had in the final Passūs of *Piers Plowman*.

The objectivity of justice presents one difficulty, its impersonality another. Justice as such is external to men and indifferent to persons; yet it assumes as its agent the just man, a virtuous and whole man who operates in a human world, not merely a world of beasts, myths, and abstractions. Justice is impersonal but cannot be dissociated from human (or divine) personality. In actual fact its inclusiveness can make the Justicer peculiarly vulnerable to the conflicting claims of his own being, his personal nature and needs, and those of his ideal, which exists at one more remove from his self than a personal virtue like temperance. If the conflict comes, as it does in Spenser's fifth Book, it draws attention to the strain, perhaps the fissure, between a private world, whether of selves or symbols, and a public and impersonal one. This strain serves to define both worlds, sharpening their outlines, finding their limits but also suggesting their powers. If the claims of an exterior world gradually become more real in Book v, so do those of the person.

Courtesy, as Spenser conceives of this virtue in Book vi, seems the appropriate, in fact the right, successor to justice. Courtesy, too, has a social orientation, but it operates in a more personal way than justice; it implies direct continuity less between the self and the objective world than between the self and other selves. As the poet describes courtesy at the end of the Proem to Book vi, it is a virtue of reciprocity, essentially personal but implicitly natural and communal as well:

> Then pardon me, most dreaded Soueraine,
>   That from your selfe I doe this vertue bring,
>   And to your selfe doe it returne againe:
>   So from the Ocean all riuers spring,
>   And tribute backe repay as to their King.
>   Right so from you all goodly vertues well
>   Into the rest, which round about you ring,
>   Faire Lords and Ladies, which about you dwell . . .

Contrastingly, at the end of the Proem to Book v, Artegall is described as the "instrument" of Justice, a word well suited to the impersonality of his virtuous role. It is noteworthy that this knight knows his "selfe from perill free" only in Book vi, where he is entitled to disavow his personal guilt and to assert his own self-knowledge (vi.i.9). As his action suggests, justice and courtesy pertain to different kinds of questions. The unjust man essentially denies a principle; the discourteous man may act unjustly, but essentially he denies himself.

Of course the personalizing of a social virtue, of a redemptive force in society, can also operate as a limitation, as it does in Spenser's Legend of Courtesy and as Langland's Clergy warns his Conscience it will when the latter takes leave of him to explore an inner landscape. Emphasis on the self can become a withdrawal from a larger world, from objectivity and real diversity. It can see the affairs of this world shrink to personal needs and desires, as happens in Calidore's sojourn among the shepherds; and if it makes the state of an ideal society subject to exclusively personal gifts, whether the endowments of inherited nobility or of divine election, then it assumes a society limited to certain kinds of men, not the real society in which Spenser locates himself and his poem at the end of Book VI. We might say that the claims of courtesy cannot exclude those of justice, just as well as we can say the reverse, and that as personality becomes more immediate and determinant, it also becomes more specific, exclusive, and isolating.

Artegall's meeting with Calidore at the beginning of Book VI pointedly indicates the complementary relationship between justice and courtesy. Their meeting is a recognition scene: "whenas each of other had a sight, / They knew them selues, and both their persons rad" (i.4). On Artegall's part, however, the scene is muted and reserved until, with evident feeling, he describes the assault of the Blatant Beast, whose "thousand tongues" still seem to roar in his ears (i.9). On sight, Calidore hails Artegall as the "noblest Knight / Of all this day on ground" (i.4); in effect, he then picks up a torch which Artegall was not meant to handle. He pursues the Beast, the vocal witness to Artegall's vulnerability, the force before which the virtue of justice proved inoperable, still righteous but powerless. As the passing of power from Artegall to Calidore suggests, courtesy, which might seem merely human or even superficial, is a virtue as ennobling as justice and, perhaps given human nature, even more so.[5]

The early episodes of Book VI recall those of Book V: a wronged squire, an iniquitous price for passage, a lustful knight who mistreats a lady. But the emphasis in these episodes, unlike those in Book V, is on human feeling, identity, and dignity. This emphasis helps to explain the otherwise puzzling deadliness, the spreading pain and debilitating weakness, of the Blatant Beast's bite. The Beast serves Envy and Detraction. His ancestry associates him with hell and with the profound corruption of anything natural (or kindly).[6] His bite is venomous; yet as he appears in Book VI, barking and baying, he seems an anomaly, an animated gargoyle, incongruous in so human a context. His conception involves a total lack of human dignity, a monstrous denial of human nature, yet with his many tongues, implying speech, an ugly human denial. The recurrent linking of misused words with the destruction of humanity in Langland's poem elucidates this denial. When Langland's Samaritan likens the Trinity to a candle, he explains that "Vnkynde cristene men for coueityse and enuye / Sleeth a man for his moebles wyth mouth or wyth handes"; thereby they extinguish life and love, the flame of man's body, at once denying their own "kind" and denying another man's to him (xvii.272–75). Such a connection between unkind words and a man's very being, his life and love, invests the Beast's spite and malice with a specifically inhuman poison. When he inflicts the wound of infamy on Timias's and Serena's names, his mouth destroys something of their personal being. Worse than the biting of any sword, this wound can be cured "by no art, nor any leaches might,"

> Ne all the skill, which that immortall spright
> Of *Podalyrius* did in it retaine,
> Can remedy such hurts; such hurts are hellish paine.[7]
>
> [vi.vi.1]

Spenser's conception of courtesy has the weight of a long medieval tradition behind it. *Piers Plowman* is not the only medieval work which could have influenced his conception, but it offers an especially pertinent matrix of the meanings and associations evoked by this virtue.[8] This matrix includes polite and gracious manners, associated particularly with knights and their king; the weakness of courteous behavior in the face of wickedness; and the usurpation of courteous forms by falsehood and flattery.[9] In *Piers Plowman* courtesy has a particular association with speech and a "trewe tonge," and discourtesy has a corresponding association with a mean spirit and a vicious mouth: every word that Envy speaks comes "of an addres tonge . . . bakbitynge and bismer and beryng of fals witnesse; / This was al his curteisye" (v.87–90).[10] According to Conscience, true courtesy is an expression of love, for "thauh the kyng of hys cortesye" might choose to give land, lordship, or other large gifts, "loue ys the cause" (C, iv.317–19). Then courtesy is an expression of divine love, for Kind, the Creator and Preserver, is "curteise" to the nature he has made (xiii.15, 1.20, xx.105), and it is likewise an expression of the mercy and grace of the Redemption: so "cryste of his curteisye" saves the woman taken in adultery, and "So wil Cryst of his curteisye, and men crye hym mercy, / Both for3iue and for3ete" (xii.79, xvii.241).

As these examples suggest—the last taken again from the Samaritan's image of a candle—courtesy becomes a virtual synonym for "kindness," invoking the perfection, and conversely the denial, of a truly human nature, hence a nature which images God's. In the C-text, Imaginative goes even further to associate courtesy not only with love and with God's graciousness but with the new dispensation of love, and indeed with God's will. Here he asserts that all true men will be saved if the Lord be true "And cortesie more than couenant was, what so clerkes carpen, / For al worth as god wole" (xv.215–17). His assertion has exactly the rich ambiguity that we have already remarked in Christ's statement to Lucifer: "I were an vnkynde kynge but I my kynde holpe"—"vnkynde," then, unnatural, ungracious, unloving, and since a king, uncourtly (xviii.396).

Repeatedly in Book vi, Spenser associates courtesy with nature and with a graciousness which is naturally and therefore somewhat ambiguously and mysteriously attained. Nobility and gentleness of spirit are birthrights in the poem, but neither the word *noble* nor the word *gentle,* as Spenser inherits and uses them, need imply exclusively aristocratic meanings.[11] Both these qualities and the notion of a birthright itself slide into inclusive metaphors for true humanity, even while they also include, and are often weighted toward, aristocratic or otherwise exclusive assumptions. When we balance the hypocritical courtesy of Blandina and the self-canceling knighthood of Turpine against the generous nature of the Salvage Man, whose "gentle blood" then turns out to spring from "noble" birth (v.2), the issue of aristocracy is far from clear; and when we add the insensitive cruelty of the flesh-eating Cannibals and Calepine's foundling—"spotlesse" in spirit and fit to embrace "What euer formes ye list thereto apply" (iv.35)—the issue of origins, of nature and nurture, seems equally open.

What is clear, however, is that everyone ought to possess courtesy, that some do and some do not, and that those who lack it are themselves blameworthy, while those who have it have gentle or noble blood. Courtesy was first "Planted in earth" by the gods and "deriu'd at furst / From heauenly seedes of bounty soueraine" (Pro.iii); its origins are as mysterious as those of divine election itself—a birthright for all through the Redemption, in reality available only to some through God's inward enlightenment yet lost to others through their own inexcusable "blindness" and, in the final analysis, just an explanation "of *why* some refuse and others accept."[12] Perhaps in view of the religiously oriented medieval tradition which informs the virtue of courtesy, it is not surprising to find questions of birthright and origin in Book vi noticeably coincident with others about fate and free will and blindness and vision.

Spenser's Books of Justice and Courtesy are not specifically theological, but they are impregnated with spiritual meanings.[13] A human principle of justice is rescued by love in Book v and seemingly rescued a second time in

Book vi by courtesy, itself an expression of love. These Books secularize the first two Books of the poem, to which they frequently refer, and might equally be said to spiritualize life, a fuller life in a realer world. They distance God and bring Him closer. In this sense they suggest one of the old cruxes of Reformed theology, its paradoxical tension between sacramentalizing everyday life and distancing heaven, between the withdrawal from one kind of vision and the more powerful assertion of another, between a tendency to depersonalize God and to personalize further man's vision—in short, a shift in the approach to a person.[14]

This shift resembles the evolving realization of personal being and awareness already evident in *Piers Plowman,* even while it develops and profoundly transforms such realization. Spenser, giving realization a more deliberative and artificial form, still treats it less often as immediate discovery than Langland; and yet in the process of treating it, he discovers more and more fully what it actually is and means. The Mutability Cantos might be seen as the climax of this process, and though Spenser pursues a peculiarly Renaissance route to them, one different from Langland's, his vision there touches *Piers Plowman* at its core. In humanistic terms, inseparably in the terms of literature and history, the relation between the two poems remains revealing throughout their evolving courses.

PRINCE ARTHUR: I, II, V, VI, CANTO viii

Simply as an important, evolving figure throughout *The Faerie Queene* and as a complex symbol with theological dimensions, Prince Arthur has some relation to the figure Piers Plowman. His presence in the first and last two Books can serve to clarify the evolution of Spenser's concerns, insights, and methods, and thus its relation to Langland's. My intention here is not to discuss every appearance of Arthur in these four Books but merely to use his presence in the eighth canto of each as a touchstone which the poem conveniently provides. Both in general and particular ways, Arthur's experiences in canto viii of Books v and vi—his meeting with Artegall, battle with the Souldan, and aborted rescue of Mirabella—recall the parallel cantos of Books i and ii, his rescues of Redcrosse and Guyon, with which we must briefly begin.

In Book i, Arthur's significance is conspicuously theological. His action in canto viii represents the Redemption in a pointed way, and he is never closer to a representation of Christ than here, where he fights the Giant Orgoglio, who has materialized out of Redcrosse's affair with Duessa. Orgoglio is a complacently arrogant pride of the flesh, who, in sharp contrast to Lucifera's lineal pretensions, actually boasts of his descent from Earth and Aeolus, in fact a more elemental parentage than Lucifera's (vii.9–10, iv.11).[15] Associated with earthquake and tempest, the giant embodies the most basic disturbance of nature. Arthur's battle with him, his ensuing victory, and his final rescue of Redcrosse allude repeatedly to the presence of Christ throughout biblical time. These allusions are familiar to readers, but for the sake of future argument several examples will bear remarking.

Arthur's wounding of Orgoglio is compared to the streaming of "fresh water . . . from riuen rocke," and the beast which Orgoglio has given Duessa receives a gaping wound from the Prince which gushes a red "sea of bloud" (10, 16). Both instances recall events in Moses' life that show the Word's presence in history and prefigure Christ himself.[16] Other images, particularly those associated with Duessa's beast, draw heavily on Revelation; the description of the blood which defiles Orgoglio's castle combines the martyrs of Revelation (6:9–10) with more specific references to "guiltlesse babes" and "innocents . . . out of the fold," perhaps the victims of Herod, and to true Christian martyrs (35–36).[17] In brief, the allusive context of canto viii includes Old Testament images which traditionally prefigure the coming of Christ, images which belong to the time since Christ's birth, and images which point to an Apocalypse yet to come; but the symbolic action of this canto centers specifically on the *accomplishment* of the Redemption itself, the death of the giant and the freeing of his captive from "a deepe descent, as darke as hell" (39).

Still less than Piers, however, *Arthurus est Christus*. The association of Arthur with Christ is never so close as is Piers's when he teaches Christ "lechecrafte," when he functions in the poem as a synonym for Jesus and as the historical, humanly real aspect of Christ. Arthur is at once more autonomously himself and less abstractly symbolic in canto viii than is Piers in Passus xvi, but it does not make sense to stop with this statement, implying as it does that the difference between Piers and Arthur is simply the result of poetic naïveté or primitivism on Langland's part. By Passus xvi the mere mention of Piers invokes everything he has already been in the poem, including that complexly symbolic figure whose tearing of the Pardon simultaneously suggests so many meanings, and in a sense it prefigures as well everything he will become. The difference between Piers and Arthur in the redemption passages concerned involves method, but it is essentially a difference of meaning, a sophisticated meaning in both instances. Appropriately Protestant, Arthur's redemptive act has in it much more of imitation than of near identity; it is more exclusively a question of spirit than of flesh.

It is certainly right to see Arthur as human and to avoid the simplistic equation of him with Christ, who is not, after all, full of passionate desire for the Faerie Queene.[18] But it is equally right to see him as an agent of grace and to recognize the depth and detail of the symbolic dimension in canto viii which associates him specifically with the historical Christ. This dimension is insistent, and although not the only one present, it is the crucial one here. In defeating Orgoglio, Arthur reenacts Christ's victory over the proud flesh, more generally the corruption of nature. He acts as if he were Christ's humanity and therefore actually represents it. By no stretch of the imagination, however, can Orgoglio be seen as the flesh—unviolated by sin, if not hypothetically inviolate—of the God-man.[19] The Giant is what threatens, attacks, and, if not prevented by the highest of powers, could hurt it. Insofar as he is human, a true Christian or Christ-like man, Arthur might be said to fight himself in fighting Orgoglio, but even this reading seems forced: Arthur is kept at one shielded remove from the vulnerability, the weakness, of even Timias's "weaker parts" (14) and, it would seem, more at a remove from himself, more in the service of something else, than at any other point in the poem.

Orgoglio's humanity is far more immediately Redcrosse's, born right out of his sinful experience. He is Redcrosse's body of sin, his fallen nature, and only in the most formal and distant of senses, Arthur's—in much the same way that of Will is Piers's in the Garden of Charity. The unveiling of Arthur's shield, so providential, seemingly fortuitous but necessary for his victory, suggests something possessed but also given. As a piece of armor and as Arthur's ultimate instrument of defense, the shield's lack of total identification with him is appropriate to his essential humanity, as symbolically to Christ's, and curiously appropriate to the notion—not new in Calvinist thought but newly emphasized—that Christ's godhead was in a state of repose, of concealment, whenever it was necessary to His redemptive office that His human nature should work according to its own character.[20]

In fact, Arthur's battle with Orgoglio looks very much like a reflection of Calvin's view of the Redemption as the sinless God-man's substitution of Himself for sinful humanity, rather than His compensation for it, as Catholic theology argued.[21] For Calvin the Redemption had historical and objective validity: in some sense all men were called in it to salvation. It was outside, before and beyond us, although in some symbolically real sense we were all there. In apparent paradox, while Redemption is real and total for Calvin, it is nonetheless not so until and unless individually realized. In other words, to a follower of Aquinas and his tradition, Calvin makes the historical Redemption, while real, become in present time an unrealized possibility. It becomes subjective and finally dependent on faith, on a kind of vision.

In this regard the fact that Arthur's action in the eighth canto of Book I takes place outside Redcrosse's consciousness, though in a sense the knight is there, is worth noting; the effect of Arthur's action on Guyon's consciousness, and implicitly its relation to Guyon, will be quite different in Book II. Arthur's victory over Orgoglio enables him to free Redcrosse, once he has displaced Ignaro, who presumably indicates an ignorance of the victory and its meaning. The freeing of Redcrosse brings him to an awareness of his shame but does not otherwise affect him. When Arthur finds him after defeating Orgoglio, the knight is weak, calling for death, woefully vulnerable. Having been freed, he proceeds, in fact, next to Despair (ix). Redcrosse's real awareness of his personal election does not come until he enters the House of Holiness, and it is not fulfilled until he meets and defeats his own dragon, in canto xi, in a battle which interiorizes Arthur's for him and completes the real possibility of salvation which Arthur's releases.

Books I and II are frequently associated with the Reformers' ideas of justification and sanctification, respectively. These ideas are perhaps more useful to emphasize the relation rather than the distinction between these Books. It would be difficult at best to separate the destined St. George's richly symbolic and ritualistically timeless battle with the dragon from sanctification, a "continuing and deepening union with Christ," a "continual unfolding and maintaining of our justification." The terms *justification* and *sanctification* imply overlapping: "Sanctification is not a response of man that must be added to justification, but the continual renewing and re-enacting in the believer of a justification that is made once and for all."[22]

The eighth canto of Book II reenacts that of Book I, bringing its action to bear specifically on the problems and areas of experience to which temperance pertains. It unfolds and deepens the earlier canto's redemptive significance. Perhaps inevitably, it presents that significance in more exclusively human forms and in a more interiorized light. In Book II the historical Redemption exists simultaneously with its present realization, not before or apart from the titular hero's realization, but in it. Although this development merely heightens the Calvinist emphasis we have already observed in Book I, it also suggests an inward direction of movement in the poem.[23]

In Book II, Arthur enters the eighth canto soon after Cymochles and Pyrochles, usurpers of the concupiscible and irascible powers, reappear to despoil the swooning Guyon of his armor. Guyon's reasoning Palmer, physically weak and helpless against the two pagan knights, invokes and receives Arthur's aid. Guyon's faint, ironically caused by the denial of human nature and ultimately of himself in resisting Mammon, has produced a vacuum in the world of heroic action, but it has more obviously dramatized a vacuum in Guyon's consciousness: the knight is described as "slumbring," as being in a "senselesse dreame," in a "deadly fit," and in a "traunce" (viii.4, 7, 53). While Guyon is an image of mortality in canto viii, Arthur is an image of "Life." The prince obviously fills—or fights with Pyrochles and Cymochles to fill—the vacuum caused by Guyon's faint. He stands in for Guyon, externally fulfilling Guyon's role but also inwardly perfecting him (viii.51–53). Arthur fights both as an external form, an idealized expression and exemplar, in an active and heroic world, and as an interior force to fill Guyon's consciousness. It is only after this battle that Guyon can proceed to the Castle of Alma and to the awareness of an interior harmony of forces.

Arthur's defense of the Knight of Temperance constitutes an assertion of wholeness lacking in the poem since canto i of Book II. Arthur combines physical with verbal power and honor with reason (26); in his actions and person he unites figures and forces continually and deleteriously sundered in Book II, Guyon and his Palmer not least among them. In fighting Pyrochles and Cymochles, Arthur has need of Guyon's sword, which the Palmer gives to him. This gesture establishes the necessity of a relation from Guyon, through the Palmer, to Arthur—from the "good" but sleeping and ineffectual natural man (4), through enlightened reason, to active heroism; from the image of mortality, through virtue (prudent Palmer—sword of Temperance), to the image of Life. The Prince uses Guyon's sword against Guyon's shield, which Pyrochles has stolen. In a general sense, he therefore fights against the abuse and perversion of ideals such as love and honor. In a particular sense, Arthur this time fights himself, for the shield has a picture of his beloved, the Faerie Queene, upon it (43). When Arthur begins to "adore" this image, for example, the concupiscible Cymochles slashes his armor and sends him reeling; whereupon Arthur kills Cymochles with Guyon's sword of Temperance. Arthur clearly fights for the sleeping Guyon in more than one way.

The complexity of Arthur's relationship to Guyon is evident when Guyon regains his senses after the battle. First Arthur offers "Life" to Pyrochles. "Wilfully" refusing this "grace," the pagan "in despight of life [calls] for death" (51–52), and so Arthur, with appropriate symbolism, beheads him. Without any transition we next read: "By this Sir *Guyon* from his traunce awakt, / Life hauing maistered her sencelesse foe" (53). "Life" is what fled from Guyon at the end of his ordeal in the Cave of Mammon: "The life did flit away out of her nest, / And all his senses were with deadly fit opprest" (66); but in context "Life" is just as clearly a reference to Arthur, who has just mastered the senseless, or "all desperate," Pyrochles (46–47).[24] Before fighting Pyrochles and Cymochles, Arthur has delivered, in effect, a brief lecture on Original Sin (29); during the battle he has sustained a wound in his right side and has heard his desperate adversary cry, "Harrow

and well away," thus borrowing the devil's best-known line from the
morality plays (38, 46).[25] While Arthur remains more fully the British
Prince here than in the parallel canto of Book I, his figure very clearly alludes
to the "Lord of life," or simply "Life," as Spenser and Langland both call
Christ (cf. II.vii.62). Guyon's senseless trance suggests the totally God-given
nature of faith, of the inward enlightenment which opens the eyes of the
blind. As Guyon wakens from this trance, Arthur might be said to touch the
knight's life, to be one with it. In this moment of unity, the heroic and
the redemptive, the natural and the spiritual, the external form and the inner
consciousness of it touch one another as well. It is no accident that Archimago, that "demon of perverted reason,"[26] and Atin, that agent of discordant affections, should flee "apace" in the last line of canto viii, to be succeeded
in canto ix by the Castle of Alma.

Between Arthur's rescue of Guyon and his appearance in Book v, we see
him as the prince and patron of British history; as the exhausted victor over
Maleger, fainting "in his infirmity" (II.xi.48–49); as the disgruntled pursuer
of Florimell; and as the man who rescues but then seems to lose Amoret.
Dimensions of Arthur's humanity beside the historically Christ-like or explicitly Christian ones are developed, so that our sense of his being is enlarged
and modified. By Book v we are prepared to see him in any virtuous role,
including one that is wholly secular. It is in the eighth canto of Book v,
however, that Arthur again uses the diamond shield, as he has memorably
before in Book I.[27] This time the unveiling of the shield is not the direct
result of a providential accident but of his own deliberate decision.

If in some sense Arthur is a redeemer in Book v, that sense is quite different
from what it has been before. When he comes on the scene in canto viii, the
rescue of Artegall, the titular hero, is already over. We might look first at
that rescue because it provides the necessary context for Arthur's arrival.
Britomart is the agent who effects Artegall's rescue, and it is their reunion
in canto vii which recalls an earlier scene, the reunion of Redcrosse with
Una. Like Redcrosse's intimacy with Duessa just prior to Orgoglio's attack,
Artegall's experiences at Radigund's hands might be said to leave him
"Disarmd, disgrast" and at a crucial moment "dismayde" (I.vii.11, cf.
v.v.12–13). When Britomart frees him from Radigund's prison, he has been
humiliated. Like Redcrosse he remains conspicuously silent. Britomart,
almost dismayed herself by the sight of him, vents her feelings:

> Ah my deare Lord, what sight is this (quoth she)
> What May-game hath misfortune made of you?
> Where is that dreadfull manly looke? . . .
> . . . .

> Could ought on earth so wondrous change haue wrought,
> As to haue robde you of that manly hew?
> Could so great courage stouped haue to ought?
> Then farewell fleshly force; I see thy pride is nought.
>
> [v.vii.40]

Her words have in them memories of Una's response to Redcrosse when he emerges from Orgoglio's dungeon:

> . . . Ah dearest Lord, what euill starre
> On you hath frownd, and pourd his influence bad,
> That of your selfe ye thus berobbed arre,
> And this misseeming hew your manly looks doth marre?
>
> [I.viii.42]

Britomart's conclusion—"Then farewell fleshly force"—shares also something of Arthur's chastened view when he finds in Redcrosse's imprisonment the lesson engraved now in his own heart "with yron pen, / That blisse may not abide in state of mortall men" (I.viii.44). Even without these similarities between Books I and V, Britomart's rescue of Artegall suggests a theological dimension. Artegall's imitation of Old Testament figures—Solomon in canto i, Samson in Radegone (viii.2)—and his enactment of an Old Law of Justice, unmitigated prior to Radegone, considerably strengthen this suggestion.

Artegall falls to Radigund "ouercome, not ouercome" but "yeelded of his owne accord" and "iustly damned by the doome / Of his owne mouth" (v.17).[28] Once imprisoned in Radegone, he can only wait "Vntill his owne true loue his freedome gayned" (v.57). Artegall needs both his own love and the person he loves, Britomart, to rescue him. Britomart embodies a force external to his assent—knowing, willing, and wrong—to the conditions of his own imprisonment, and she is therefore not bound by that assent. Her position is consonant with traditional views on the prisoner's obligation to his oath, though it is also curiously analogous to the one Christ traditionally takes when he painstakingly explains to Lucifer the justice of Adam's release from hell's dominion.[29] Throughout Artegall's imprisonment, it is noted that he saves his loyalty to his own love and that if he had not, what remains of his honor would have been blemished, perhaps irreparably (vi.2). Britomart is not love as such, but she is Artegall's love; love brings her to him and keeps him faithful to her, though fallen and otherwise helpless. In short, love is the principle that results in his rescue; an expression of love, mercy or clemency, enables him to return to his quest for a just society.

In Artegall's waiting for Britomart, we can also see Justice's waiting for

Mercy, and fallen man's waiting for Love. Yet the theological dimension
of her rescue is an undertone, unobtrusive, even inexplicit, a pervasive
rather than a decisive influence on the story. It is typical of the more inclusively (not exclusively) worldly context of this Book that Britomart,
who lacks Arthur's explicit associations with Christ in earlier Books and
therefore lacks his already established allusive potential, should effect this
rescue, and it is further typical of its personal context that she should rescue
her own lover. Both Artegall's fall and Britomart's rescue are striking for
their human, personal qualities. These are crucial and primary.

Artegall's fall at Radigund's hands is natural, human, and inevitable
(despite the fact that he has no one to blame for it but himself). Engaged in
furious combat with Radigund, he finally knocks her to the ground "In
sencelesse swoune." The moment Artegall sees her down, he leaps to her,
unlaces her helmet, and intends to cut off head and helmet in a single blow:

> But when as he discouered had her face,
>   He saw his senses straunge astonishment,
>   A miracle of natures goodly grace,
>   In her faire visage voide of ornament,
>   But bath'd in bloud and sweat together ment;
>   Which in the rudenesse of that euill plight,
>   Bewrayd the signes of feature excellent:
> . . . .
> At sight thereof his cruell minded hart
>   Empierced was with pittifull regard,
>   That his sharpe sword he threw from him apart,
>   Cursing his hand that had that visage mard:
>   No hand so cruell, nor no hart so hard,
>   But ruth of beautie will it mollifie.
>
> [v.v.12–13]

The vice corresponding to mercy is "vain" pity; hence Artegall has fallen
into sin. But the vice corresponding to justice is cruelty, and it is Artegall's
"cruell minded hart" which is pierced with "pittifull regard."[30]

This passage recounts Artegall's fall into a natural, human condition.
"Natures goodly grace" is embodied in a woman, and it is as a man that he
reacts. Once Artegall sees Radigund as a human being, a personal reality
instead of an abstracted Vice or objectified Tyrant, he becomes aware of
his own feelings and, at least to this degree, of himself. He *realizes* "his
senses straunge astonishment" because he sees Radigund. He does not simply
"feel" his "senses" astonishment; he becomes aware or conscious of it. Such

astonishment is "straunge" or new to him. Artegall has no choice; he is caught between cruelty and pity, between the inhumanity of a principle ruthlessly enforced and the humanity of a fallen world. The issue is not between principles but between human beings, and it is no longer external to the just man. Artegall moves from one extreme to another, from cruelty to pity, and he throws away the sword of Justice, the symbol of his quest. He retreats from a world of actions and things external to himself, into a world of selves and psychic experiences, an exclusively personal condition. By the end of this canto, he is involved with Radigund and her handmaid Clarinda in a typical romance situation, which, except for his personal loyalty to Britomart, would be a triangle of selfish love.

Britomart's rescue of Artegall, despite the many facets of its significance, preeminently belongs to an inner and personal world. Although Britomart has to learn how to use her power to free Artegall from the condition which Radegone is, she alone possesses this power because she is his own love. As she journeys toward her knight, she comes to embody the inner mean relevant to a psychic world. Artegall has been trapped between two extremes, sensuous pity and insensitive cruelty, and only a new habit of mind, such as mercy or clemency, can release him. In other words, he needs the inner mean between emotions which corresponds to the outer mean between things—namely, justice—and when Britomart finally reaches him, she represents it.

When Britomart defeats Radigund and reaches Artegall, she suddenly finds true what earlier her jealousy had untruly feared: "And then too well beleeu'd, that which tofore / Iealous suspect as true vntruely drad" (vii.38). Her realization complements Artegall's in his battle with Radigund. Unlike Artegall, however, she is astonished to discover, not the power and validity of her passions, but the limitations and deceptions of them. In recognizing the relation between Artegall's quest in an external world and his honor, she also becomes conscious of a relation between an impersonal and a personal world (vii.40–44). Thus Britomart deals "true Iustice"; she reforms Radegone, moderates her own smart, and tempers her passion. In short, she embodies the inner mean, and she becomes truly like Isis. Yet even in the culmination of her redemptive journey, we do not find the image of an all-inclusive Eden, only the world of inner and personal order to which Britomart belongs. Artegall is strangely passive and silent at the end of canto vii. His presence is itself a qualification.

At the end of canto vii, Artegall has no specific role, for his quest properly belongs to another kind of world. Like any other virtue, "justice must be interiorized if it is to become Christian. Before being just in the City, we

must be just in our own eyes in order to be just in the eyes of God." Nonetheless, justice does not pertain directly to the passions of the soul. Personal
virtues enable a man to keep the passions "in a just mean in relation to
himself." Justice seeks the just mean in a relationship between things external
to the virtuous man, to his acts, and to the person acted upon: "It is no longer
a question, therefore, of *someone who keeps himself in the just mean* but of
keeping the just mean of some thing."[31] It is at the point where the consciousness
of being himself justified and being a Justicer is continuous that Artegall
must leave Radegone—and Britomart as well—to reenter a social world, a
less exclusively subjective and personal condition. Potentially, Artegall now
embodies the relation between an impersonal and a personal world, but he
has to externalize and thus fulfill this wholeness. Appropriately, in the
remaining cantos of Book v topical allegory becomes increasingly inescapable
and finally transparent (Irena's island, Belge's seventeen sons, Burbon's
love for Fleurdelis).

In the first of these cantos, the eighth, immediately on Artegall's recommitment to the quest for justice, he finds Prince Arthur. Artegall joins in
the rescue of a lady whom Arthur is also rescuing from two pagan knights.
There is one pagan for Arthur to kill and one for Artegall. The lady's name
happens to be Samient ("sameness," "likeness," or "togetherness," from
Middle English *sam / samen*). If these coincidences were not sufficiently
obvious to underline a relation between Arthur and Artegall, we have in
addition Artegall's name—Art equal or Arthur's equal—and the fact that
they are related according to Merlin's prophecy in Book III, as well as to the
sources of British history which Spenser consulted.[32]

The two Christian knights' identities are at first unknown to them, and
they have no sooner killed their pagans than the Prince mistakes Artegall
for one of the pagan knights, that is, for one of the Prince's opponents.
The Prince and Artegall begin to fight, but sure enough, Samient stops
them. Then they

> . . . Ventailes reare, each other to behold.
> Tho when as *Artegall* did *Arthure* vew,
> So faire a creature, and so wondrous bold,
> He much admired both his heart and hew,
> And touched with intire affection, nigh him drew.
>
> Saying, Sir Knight, of pardon I you pray,
> That all vnweeting haue you wrong'd thus sore,
> Suffring my hand against my heart to stray:
> Which if ye please forgiue, I will therefore

> Yeeld for amends my selfe yours euermore,
> Or what so penaunce shall by you be red.
> To whom the Prince; Certes me needeth more
> To craue the same, whom errour so misled,
> As that I did mistake the liuing for the ded.
>
> [v.viii.12–13]

The meeting of Arthur with "Arthur's equal" is both recognition and reunion. Arthur sees Artegall in armor, presumably the armor of Justice, and mistakes him for the dead, for that which is not living.[33] More explicitly, he mistakes him for a pagan, for one who lacks "Life" in a theological sense and whose power, or indeed whose virtue, has not been transformed by love. Only when both knights lift their visors does each recognize in the other what is within, the true person and symbolically the inner self.

Their mutual recognition is imbued with a romantic and affective quality missing from Artegall's character before Radegone. This quality by itself is spontaneous enough to suggest reunion. It is especially evident in Artegall's response, in his "intire affection" and in the contrast between his hand and his heart, though it is implicit in Arthur's as well ("Certes me needeth more / To craue the same"); and it is capped by Artegall's yielding, or giving, himself to Arthur, as if he had indeed been rescued or else bested in battle. There has been neither conquest nor rescue; yet this scene is remarkable at once for its dramatic emphasis, present for no explicitly stated reason, and for its easy, natural humanity. If the scene has any meaning besides this humanity, it is a most unobtrusively symbolic one.

Arthur's rescue of Guyon—another scene in which two pagans lie dead on the ground—offers a contrasting and, perhaps, complementary point of reference. The earlier scene, with Guyon in a trance, has a dimension of abstraction, of verbal and allegorical complexity, which is lacking here. At the same time, it belongs to the only other Book in which Arthur and the titular hero conspicuously share the last cantos between them. It is no accident that Guyon is actually present in an early canto of Book v. No other virtue in The Faerie Queene is more directly and traditionally associated with a mean than are these two, temperance and justice. Guyon appears in Book v to reclaim the horse he lost at the outset of Book II, the symbol in that Book of his heroic passions and aspirations, a symbol associated also with the vessel which is his flesh.[34] In a real sense, Guyon appears in this, the appropriately social Book, to reclaim his personal wholeness, the symbol of a quest in the active world without which he is neither a real knight nor quite himself. Arthur's appearance in Book v has more than accidental significance, too. His figure, like those of the many other figures from earlier Books who enter Book v, is being further expanded and more nearly completed and brings to this Book a significance that expands and perfects Artegall's as well.

In the three exploits immediately following Artegall's meeting with Arthur, we see the Prince acting in conjunction with the Knight of Justice, who has previously refused any companionship (even Britomart's) but that of Talus. In the first exploit Arthur battles the Souldan, while Artegall, disguised as a pagan, confronts Adicia, the principle of wickedness the Souldan has wed and the wife who incites him to lawless acts (viii.20). In the second, Arthur bars the entrance to Malengin's cave, which extends into the earth "A dreadfull depth, how deepe no man can tell; / But some doe say, it goeth downe to hell" (ix.6); and Artegall dispatches the principle of Guyle which has assumed natural shapes—fox, bush, bird, hedgehog, and snake—the way Adicia did when she turned into a tiger.[35] In the third, Arthur, standing on one side of Mercilla, feels compassion for Duessa's "dreadfull fate" and for the "ruine of so high estate" (ix.46); he gives her the benefit of the purely personal doubt until Zeal accuses her of personal crimes, murder, incontinence, sedition, adultery, impiety. In the meantime, Artegall stands, ever impersonal, on Mercilla's other side and "with constant firme intent, / For zeale of Iustice was against her bent" (ix.49).

The precise significance of Arthur's presence in these exploits varies, although it has this constant at its core: the response of a *specifically Christian* knight to the perpetrators of injustice. In the same exploits Artegall, whose justice has been interiorized and personalized by Britomart's rescue, is nonetheless freed by Arthur's presence to take the part of a *purely natural* principle of justice—abstract, objective, impersonal. Prince Arthur's role thus balances, complements, and completes Artegall's, for it is associated with the spiritual and personal dimension of justice, which Artegall's history prior to canto viii has proved inescapably, if paradoxically, real.

The spiritual aspect of Arthur's role is most clearly established in their first exploit together, when Arthur deliberately unveils his shield in order to defeat the Souldan. Evidence for the commonly accepted view that this battle alludes to the defeat of the Spanish Armada is strong: the hooked wheels on the Souldan's chariot, the tyrannical, foreign power implied by his name; the comparisons of him to mythic figures who overreach, deny, or pervert the natural order; his parodic resemblance to Philip II's *impresa,* showing the sun god in his chariot; and the providential nature of his defeat.[36] The poem explicitly states that the Souldan is a political as well as a religious power who seeks to subvert another's crown (viii.18–20), and that he threatens both the life and sovereignty of Mercilla, who bears on her throne the lion and fleur-de-lis of the English royal arms and whose trial of Duessa alludes rather blatantly to Elizabeth's treatment of Mary Stuart.

In other words, it is quite clear that the Souldan embodies a public, institutional evil rather than merely a personal, interiorized vice or sin, and that the episode in which he appears alludes to contemporary history. In battling the Souldan, Arthur is wounded in the side, as he was in Book ii, and his shield when unveiled flashes with the same power it had in Book i: in the earlier instance, "As where th'Almighties lightning brond does light, / It dimmes the dazed eyen, and daunts the senses quight (viii.21); and now in Book v, "Like lightening flash, that hath the gazer burned, / So did the sight thereof their sense dismay" (viii.38). When the battle ends in Arthur's victory, men might finally see "How worthily, by heauens high decree, / Iustice that day of wrong her selfe had wroken" (viii.44). Arthur might choose the moment to unveil the shield and might therefore be seen as being in more active control of his own fate than in Book i, but the power of his shield still comes from another.[37]

As long as Arthur accompanies Artegall in Book v, there are no recriminations, no conflicting demands, no blunders. When they part company, Arthur goes off to campaign against injustice in Belge's land and achieves wholly idealized results. With never a snag he kills his tyrant and destroys his beast. His victory very closely recalls Redcrosse's entrance into Eden (i.xii.6–9):

> Then all the people, which beheld that day,
>> Gan shout aloud, that vnto heauen it rong;
>> And all the damzels of that towne in ray,
>> Came dauncing forth, and ioyous carrols song:
>> So him they led through all their streetes along,
>> Crowned with girlonds of immortall baies,
>> And all the vulgar did about them throng,
>> To see the man, whose euerlasting praise
> They all were bound to all posterities to raise.
>
> [v.xi.34]

Arthur, rather than Artegall, undergoes the kind of apotheosis Book v earlier described in connection with Osiris (vii.1–2); he becomes a myth. Artegall lacks Arthur's good fortune. Once on his own, he gets entangled first in Burbon's confusion and conflict of interests and then is subject to the biting abuse of Envy and Detraction—the accompaniment, and implicitly the cause, of his recall from Irena's land.

By first separating Arthur from the personal rescue, the interior justifying, of Artegall, then by having Arthur avail himself of the power invested in his shield and by associating his actions with an idealized and spiritualized treatment of political events, Spenser locates in Arthur's figure the further "unfolding and maintaining" of sanctification as it specifically pertains to contemporary history. Few beliefs are dearer to Reformation thought than the desire to see eschatology active in everyday history instead of removed to some realm beyond history, a removal conventionally associated with the Middle Ages—perhaps too conventionally in view of a poem like *Piers Plowman*. Calvinism gave this desire one of its more cogent expressions, holding that the society of the faithful "actually and continuously participates in the new humanity of the resurrection" and thus anticipates increasingly in this world a glory yet to come.[38]

A closely related, though not identical, desire informs even Hooker's less radical emphasis on temporal increase and growth, on change which is purposeful and providential. It would be difficult to find a more provocative gloss on the cantos in which Arthur and Artegall cooperate to embody complementary emphases on the spirit and nature of justice, than the following summary of Hooker's view by a modern writer: religion "must be rooted in natural law and must seek to consecrate not only the inward life of the spirit but the whole outward structure of social life lived in the body."[39] The consecration of society is for Hooker a historical process. The Protestantism of Luther, another formative influence in the Tudor Church, shared with Calvinism a belief that the end of the world pertained to the history of men and nations, but emphasized the decay and degeneration of a world working out its own judgment far more obviously than the growth and renewal of the resurrection.[40] Spenser's fifth Book may reflect both emphases, on the one hand in the Proem's pessimistic sense of decline and perhaps in the aborted success of Artegall's final mission, and on the other hand, in the scenes involving Arthur, whether with Artegall or alone.

The contemporary historical dimension in Book v is symbolically present in earlier Books, but here it is incorporated more fully. In earlier Books—for example, in the imagery of Orgoglio's castle or of Redcrosse's battle with the dragon—this dimension is assumed rather than examined; here it is directly faced and its nature explored, though never quite settled. It seems inevitable that in any poem which takes account of actual history, such a move toward the present and socially tangible should also be a move toward the controversial and problematical. In the face of contemporary historical fact, faith is seen to be more exclusively personal at the end of Book v; optimism is seen to be more a matter of interpretive choice, and political success to be more a matter of human choosing.

While together, Arthur and Artegall are an affirmation of renewal and of the essential unity of life. They promise a greater unity to come. Apart, their meaning alters. Their parting does not simply mean that spirit and nature have split, however. The emphases we have seen them enact in cantos viii and ix are complementary, not mutually exclusive. Either knight alone— Arthur, the best of princes; Artegall, the personally justified champion of Justice—embodies both emphases; they are, after all, equals. But it is precisely because of their equality that the contrasting outcomes of their last ventures, so clearly juxtaposed in the poem, are especially striking. Arthur basks at the end in the light of idealism, a light which transcends, or ignores, the messy inconveniences of worldly fact—and certainly of Elizabethan expeditions to the Netherlands.[41] Artegall withdraws at the end in the unflattering glare of realism, his quest for justice overwhelmed by disagreeable worldly facts. Arthur experiences no discontinuity between his personal righteousness and the establishment of righteousness in society. With Burbon and then with his recall from Irena's island, Artegall faces a discontinuity which is exacerbated by what the interiorization of justice, his personal justification as a result of the Radigund episode, implies in this Protestant poem.

The concluding adventures of Book v are not arbitrarily different but pointedly so. This end is neither affirmation nor denial, and it is both. In Arthur's last adventure we find an affirmation of God's special providence in a situation that alludes unmistakably to contemporary history and makes us aware of human interpretation—idealistic interpretation, though not invalid interpretation by Elizabethan lights. At the end of Artegall's adventures, we find an evident lack of divine purpose, whether through fate or through human fault, and a situation which seems more realistic and strikes most readers as reflecting more closely the actual facts of history.[42] The effect of the final adventures, Belge, Burbon, and Irena combined, is certainly to make us aware of the Spirit's relevance to human history but perhaps even more aware of the process of interpreting it. Whether political or poetic, the interpretive process is becoming more self-consciously personal at the end of Book v. Not surprisingly, it is a major theme in Book vi, and it is associated with Arthur's presence there.

Arthur's presence in Book vi lacks the dramatic emphasis it has in the other Books discussed in this chapter. It has neither the concentrated symbolism of Books i and ii nor the historical impact of Book v. In Book vi the significance of Arthur's presence is actually subsumed in a developing context. This difference is admittedly one of degree, not very great with respect to Book v, much more so with respect to the first two Books. In Book vi,

Arthur looks more like a character in a narrative and less like a dramatized symbol than he did in Books I and II. His actions are less autonomously remarkable, the significance of each is less full, than in these earlier Books. This fact suggests the conditions of meaning we find in Book VI, conditions as human and in every sense as self-defining as the virtue of courtesy itself.

Arthur's actions in Book VI are so simply natural for a true knight that, if they were taken in isolation, there would be nothing extraordinary about them. There are no lightning flashes from the diamond shield and no explicit references to divine intervention. This is not to say that Arthur's role is merely narrative or that it might equally well have been performed by an anonymous knight who lacks Arthur's background in the poem. Arthur comes with another dimension to canto viii, for when he fights there the Giant Disdain, Mirabella's tormentor, he fights the "sib to great *Orgolio*" (vii.41). Arthur's presence spans the central third of Book VI, starting in canto v and culminating in canto viii, his last appearance in *The Faerie Queene*. The cantos in which he participates lead into the symbolic core of this Book, the pastoral experience in which Melibee and Colin Clout figure. His effort to rescue Mirabella is a vital step in the development of a central theme, the relationship of fortune to human responsibility and to human freedom.

In a sense this theme begins with Artegall's presence in canto i and with the questions about God's role and man's, His purpose and human responsibility, which the braying of the Blatant Beast left unanswered at the end of Book V. References to chance and fortune, which traditionally have as ambiguous a relation to God as nature or courtesy itself, occur frequently in the first three cantos of Book VI. Here fortune looks primarily like an impersonal and arbitrary force: it is "by chaunce" that Calidore meets a young squire who has suffered "misfortune"; then he is "fortunate" in his battle with Crudor. We next learn that an unnamed, evil knight, whose blazon suggests Lady Fortune herself, has "chaunst" to meet Priscilla and Aladine, about whose "fortunes" we hear at length; then it is Calidore's "fortune, not his fault" to stumble upon the love-making of Calepine and Serena, and at the close of canto iii, a "wondrous chaunce" brings the Salvage Man to Calepine's aid.[43]

With this last incident, a new note is added. We become increasingly aware not only of fortune as a providential force in human affairs but also of the interpretive role of both the narrator and his characters. As fortune appears less blind, it is thus seen to be relative to human vision. In the center of canto iv, for example, Calepine kills a bear: "catching vp in hand a ragged stone, / Which lay thereby (so fortune him did ayde) / Vpon him [Calepine] ran" (21). The narrator's comment "(so fortune him did ayde)" is gratuitous and clearly interpretive. It draws attention to itself because it is parenthetical and noticeably interrupts the action, intervening between Calepine's grabbing the stone and his doing something to the bear with it.

In canto iv fortune is at various points also equated with natural necessity (15) and with pure chance (25). These aspects of fortune are not forgotten, but it is the providential aspect of fortune which receives more emphasis. We hear at the outset of the canto that "fortune, passing all foresight" provides help for Calepine, and at the end of the canto we see Sir Bruin's childless wife complaining "of fate, and fortune oft" defying (26), only to have "good fortune" in the person (and words) of Calepine present her with the baby whom he has saved from the bear.

Yet the complaints of Sir Bruin's wife dramatize the possibility of a gap between human foresight, or human interpretations of destiny, and the actual workings of providence. If the providential aspect of fortune is in some sense relative to human vision and interpretation, it can also be obscured by human blindness or distorted by passion. The cantos which succeed Calepine's fight with the bear and lead into Melibee's pastoral condition explore precisely these dangers; at the same time they stress increasingly the importance of the human will and of human vision. They indicate the very considerable extent to which fortune, whether for good or for ill, is subject to human control.

Arthur figures centrally in these same cantos, his experiences interlacing with those of Timias and Serena. After finding Serena in canto v, Arthur commits her, along with Timias, to the ministrations of a holy, aged hermit because they have both been so badly bitten by the Blatant Beast that they can travel no farther. Their wounds having festered inwardly, they learn from the hermit that their only help lies in their own wills:

> For in your selfe your onely helpe doth lie,
> To heale your selues, and must proceed alone
> From your owne will, to cure your maladie.
>
> [vi.vi.7]

His counsel is followed by episodes involving Arthur, in which failure to exercise a good will leads in the case of the cowardly, vicious Knight Turpine to utter ignominy (a form of self-destruction), and in the case of Mirabella leads to self-entrapment.

Mirabella's story radically emphasizes the role of the human will in personal salvation. After Prince Arthur fells Mirabella's Giant Disdain and the Salvage Man (pure nature) knocks down her Fool Scorn, the Prince first heeds her desperate pleas for their lives, but then, evidently not crediting her reasons, he tells her,

Now Lady sith your fortunes thus dispose,
That if ye list haue liberty, ye may,
Vnto your selfe I freely leaue to chose,
Whether I shall you leaue, or from these villaines lose.

[VI.viii.29]

Mirabella replies that her freedom from endless penance "may not be";
she simply turns away from the Prince, politely and with unwitting irony
thanking him for his "good will" (viii.30). Mirabella's Disdain, the giant
who leads her horse around the countryside and is sib to the Giant Pride
who imprisons Redcrosse in Book I, makes striking the contrast between
the concerns of Book I, in which "all the good is Gods, both power and eke
will" (x.1), and those of Book VI, in which the human will alone stands
between freedom and self-destruction.

Arthur's offer to free Mirabella is a knight's courtesy to a lady but suggests
a great deal more. The power of Disdain and Scorn, Mirabella's tormentors,
is essentially to degrade human beings. Timias is led "like a dog" when
captured by them (5). Scorn threatens "to yoke" Timias together with
Enias, who tries to rescue the Squire but lacks Arthur's special fortune and
power (11, 10, v. 1; 15, v. 5). Enias himself is pinned, then roped, by the two
tormentors as if he were only a "stubborne steare" (12). Their whole effort
is to destroy human dignity and to reduce men to the condition of trapped
and tortured beasts, helpless to help themselves. Mirabella's condition is
profoundly psychological. She has been self-loving, and now, with infinite
irony, love has sentenced her to herself (21–22). The disdain and scorn with
which she plagued others have turned in guilt and penance back upon
herself and now lash out at any who would save her. They are still her
masters and in a sense have become her gods.

Cupid's imposition of Mirabella's penance, wholly deserved but nonetheless self-destroying, is remarkable for its legality. A jury is "impaneld,"
an indictment made, a "*Capias*" willed, a "warrant" issued, and when
Mirabella finally cries for mercy, she receives a "penance" of exact payment,
to save as many as before she slew, life for life, eye for eye, tooth for tooth
(vii.34–37). She gets from Cupid, the pagan, natural god of love, a "kindly"
penance which she can never perform and to which she blindly clings. It
would be difficult to imagine a better analogy for the destined damnation
that results from one's own inexcusable blindness than her dignified refusal
of Arthur's offer, a self-canceling refusal of her own dignity, her own human
right to redemption. Her refusal of Arthur's courtesy is superficially polite
but fundamentally discourteous. From one viewpoint it is willful, from

another will-less. Mirabella is pathetic, as Orgoglio is not, but she shares something of his complacent arrogance.[44]

Arthur's significance in this scene is debatable in a way that it is not in Books I and II. It is far more a matter of occasional nuance than of explicit and consistent allusion; our reading of it results more from a total picture of the poem, from the nearer pressures of context, and quite bluntly, then, from an individualized interpretation. As Arthur's significance becomes more simply natural and is assimilated into a more ostensibly secular narrative, it becomes more elusive. The materials for interpretation remain, of course, in the poem, but they no longer have the slight resemblance to signposts that they had before. The conceit has darkened, become in some sense denser. The poem itself has come closer to an image of the complex human world as it is, rather than of a structure, even an essentially human structure, abstracted from it. The meaning implicit in this image or in this world is less visible but more real and therefore, from another perspective, more visible, given eyes to see it.

These changes, evident in Arthur's role, are part of the personalizing of vision in The Faerie Queene. They become explicitly and crucially thematic in Spenser's treatment of Melibee's vision and Calidore's rescue of Pastorella, which Melibee never gets to see. These changes are part of a process not simply to be discovered by readers of Book VI but written self-consciously into this Book by the poet. This fact is sufficiently important to an understanding of the poet's own role in the final Books of The Faerie Queene that it will be considered in greater detail before I turn to the way the concerns and methods of Books V and VI have affected the poet's role, which has proved responsive to the changing roles of his characters throughout the poem.

MELIBEE: "But all the night in siluer sleepe I spend . . ."

Melibee is a sufficiently humane and sympathetic character to make his death at the hands of brigands seem harsh, a fate we do not entirely forget in the survival of his foster-child, Pastorella. The old shepherd has a dignity born of simple wants, kindness, and conscious convictions that are in harmony with the natural world. This harmony is their strength but, unfortunately, also their weakness. We first hear of his generosity to Pastorella, the foundling whom he has reared as his own child, and then see it extended to Calidore, whom he willingly takes into his house. Melibee's stern refusal of the gold Calidore offers him in return may be as unrealistic as Guyon's refusal of Mammon's offers, but it is not allowed to appear so. The poem makes it sincere and convincing. Melibee's Boethian stoicism is worthy of a more heroic figure and, in fact, is to be echoed by more than one of them—

Lear, for example, or Milton's Satan. It is "In vaine," Melibee tells Calidore
that "men / The heauens of their fortunes fault accuse," for each man "hath
his fortune in his brest" (ix.29). He continues, "It is the mynd, that maketh
good or ill, / That maketh wretch or happie, rich or poore":

> For wisedome is most riches; fooles therefore
> They are, which fortunes doe by vowes deuize,
> Sith each vnto himselfe his life may fortunize.
>
> [VI.ix.30]

Each statement is admirable in isolation, but other sides of Melibee's nature,
which provide the context for these lines, let us hear the irony he does not
intend to be in them, an irony which his murder by brigands dramatizes.

Melibee's vulnerability to misfortune does not come without warning.
His own history suggests it when he indicates that he has withdrawn, indeed
retreated, from a larger, more complex world to the peace and privacy of
his birthplace, of the nature he inherits (ix.24–25). The effect of his words on
Calidore gives us reason to examine this nature more closely. Hearing
Melibee and looking on Pastorella, "twixt his pleasing tongue, and her faire
hew," Calidore "lost himselfe, and like one halfe entraunced grew" (26).
Calidore at least thinks that he hears in Melibee's words the promise of an
earthly paradise, for his final assent to them echoes with remarkable closeness
the offer of ease and rest which the King of Eden held out to Redcrosse,
who wisely refused it (I.xii.17, VI.ix.31). It is true that Calidore's response is
primarily his responsibility, not Melibee's, that his response is partly to
Pastorella, and that by staying with the shepherds he will see Mount Acidale;
but it is also true that the words and rhythms of Melibee's speeches have the
strange, lovely power of enchantment.

We first and most memorably heard this power when Despair spoke "his
charmed speeches" to Redcrosse (I.ix.30), a power recalled in the Song of
Acrasia's Bower and echoed more distantly in the pastoral image of Cymoent's grieving. Melibee's name, "honey drinker" or "honey tone," stirs
the memory of Despair's haunting power in Book I, where "His subtill
tongue, like dropping honny, mealt'h / Into the hart" (ix.31).[45] Melibee's
conscious intentions are honorable and benign rather than evil; yet the
"sensefull words" from "his melting mouth" pierce Calidore's "hart so
neare, / That he was rapt with double rauishment" (ix.26). The word
sensefull—sensible, sensuous, or sensual—is triple-edged. The element of
retreat suggested by Melibee's personal history, his retirement from the
"Princes gardin" to his own, becomes explicit in Calidore's words when he
accepts the shepherd's condition (ix.31, verse 7). In this element, too, there

are memories of despair. Melibee's history is a movement from the past to the present; we should note in passing that it is thereby potentially an image for the development of Spenser's poem as a whole and of his own role in particular.

Melibee lacks a sense of proportion and a sense of related dimensions. Langland puts the same problem simply: "The man that moche hony eteth, his mawe it engleymeth" (xv.56). Langland is paraphrasing Proverbs 25:16, 27, and is therefore not necessarily supplying a Spenserian source; yet it is noteworthy that the lines that follow his paraphrase afford the appropriate epitaph for Melibee's Boethian stoicism: "And the more that a man of good mater hereth, / But he do ther-after, it doth hym double scathe" (xv.57–58). Melibee's first and longest speech is full of the ambiguously "sensefull" words which depict his condition. As he explains to Calidore, he contents himself with what he has, "So taught of nature, which doth litle need / Of forreine helpes to lifes due nourishment" (20). Yearly his lambs increase in number, and he adds, "my flockes father daily doth amend it. / What haue I, but to praise th'Almighty, that doth send it?" (ix.21).[46] These are two of the most serenely, comically irresponsible lines in *The Faerie Queene*. The identity of the flock's father in the first line is not immediately clear, and whether in reading we quietly assume that it is either the ram or the Deity, we find in the second line that Melibee cannot quite keep their roles apart. The ready ease of Melibee's question in this line reinforces its cheerful complacency, and the disyllabic rhyme (amend it/send it) enforces its comic cast. Consciously and knowingly, Melibee would never dream of making nature his goddess, but through oversight, a confused perception, she has in fact become so.

The landscape Melibee sees is one-dimensional. His mind has become so completely its own place that it is blind to the reality of anything beyond its own easy control and desires. He forgives the ambitions, follies, and great affairs of the world to those "that list" them but disdains personal involvement. He does what he wishes:

> Me no such cares nor combrous thoughts offend,
> Ne once my minds vnmoued quiet grieue,
> But all the night in siluer sleepe I spend,
> And all the day, to what I list, I doe attend.

> [vi.ix.22]

These are not unnatural or unreal desires, but life given over completely to them is, for they are merely natural and also self-centered. The landscape Melibee creates with them is an image of his condition, his existence, and when that landscape is destroyed, as it is by the brigands, it quite naturally means death. That is the final reality of his mind's unmoved quiet and of its silver sleep.

Melibee's landscape is symbolic in a special, personal way. He elaborates his nature in explaining to Calidore how he spends his days doing what he "lists":

> Sometimes I hunt the Fox, the vowed foe
>   Vnto my Lambes, and him dislodge away;
>   Sometime the fawne I practise from the Doe,
>   Or from the Goat her kidde how to conuay;
>   Another while I baytes and nets display,
>   The birds to catch, or fishes to beguyle:
>   And when I wearie am, I downe doe lay
>   My limbes in euery shade, to rest from toyle,
> And drinke of euery brooke, when thirst my throte doth boyle.
>
> [vi.ix.23]

This landscape embodies desire and corresponds to nothing real we recognize besides that, until we recognize its real danger. The reader of Spenser's whole poem is likely to note specific threats in the illusory image of nature which Melibee has made himself. From the time that Redcrosse had his dreams at Archimago's hermitage, nearly every sleeper in the poem has met with grief; mere relaxation in Book vi repeatedly brings trouble. The "shade" in this poem usually trembles with dark meanings, and an indiscriminate draught from every brook is likely to end in the appearance of Orgoglio or in that other "image of mortalitie," Mordant and Amavia (ii.i.57). The landscape of the poem, which images life, is charged with meanings Melibee has left out; in fact, Melibee seems to have left out the allegory. Allegory does not have to be spiritual, though one is conditioned to expect that it might be in *The Faerie Queene,* but it has to be multidimensional, and the landscape Melibee sees is not. The landscape he sees is symbolic but *consists* of the symbols which merely natural desires create. Nothing would be wrong with it if Melibee did not think it to be truly real. In a paradoxical way we have seen that it is real, as desire and as danger, but its reality is quietly shown to be a desire for death, which is what Despair wanted in Book i and what Redcrosse, from his cry for death in Orgoglio's dungeon until his narrow escape from Despair, progressively wanted, too. "It is the mynd, that maketh good or ill," and Melibee is dead-right after all.

It is with Melibee in mind that the poem gives us the imprisonment and rescue of Pastorella, the child of nature and of art, both the foundling of fortune and the scion of a noble, or courteous, family. Her rescue is denied poor Melibee because he is dead; he can't see it. Her imprisonment, however, is not beyond his ken, for it is an existence now reduced for him and "his people" (x.40) to the single dimension of death, a physical darkness indistinguishable from a spiritual, or inner, one:

> ... darkenesse dred and daily night did houer
> Through all the inner parts, wherein they dwelt.
> Ne lightned was with window, nor with louer,
> But with continuall candlelight, which delt
> A doubtfull sense of things, not so well seene, as felt.
>
> [VI.x.42]

In this darkness visible of the mind's own place, Pastorella "thought her self in hell, / Where with such damned fiends she should in darknesse dwell" (x.43). Pastorella is one of Melibee's people but she is so only by adoption, not by birth. "Shut vp in deadly shade," she participates in the condition of natural decay, wasting "her goodly beauty, which did fade / Like to a flowre, that feeles no hete of sunne" (x.44). Yet she is throughout her imprisonment the only spark of love and light present—"A Diamond of rich regard" shining with "starrie beames" in the "doubtfull shadow" (xi.13, 21). Coridon will escape the cave to return to his former life, now transformed to a condition of fear, human loss, and loneliness—in short, of selfishness. Pastorella alone will be saved from the cave through Calidore's love and lifted into a new condition, which will also be the recovery of her true birthright (xii.16–21).

Pastorella's is another rescue through the power of love, and it is a rebirth. Bringing her forth "to the ioyous light," Calidore devises means to drive away her sad memories: "So her vneath at last he did reuiue, / That long had lyen dead, and made againe aliue" (xi.50). The symbolism of this rescue resembles that of many a Shakespearean romance. Pastorella's rebirth is preeminently a human and natural scene, simply enriched by the emotional weight of mythological and theological contexts. This is one way to read the scene and the scenes of deadly imprisonment which precede it as well. Thus the world is infused with suggestive meaning, with the promise and the hope of *human* redemption. The meaning of such redemption is inclusive and open-ended, not specified as it was in Book I. We recognize what it means—or do we really? Is it not equally true in this scene of rebirth that meaning is being taken over by the natural world, being subsumed into an exclusively human context; and if so, that it is likely to be equated with this world, obscured by it or reduced to it? We know the history of such emo-

tionally charged human symbols; they become naturalized or secularized
—debatably perhaps—in a few of Shakespeare's plays, but clearly in Wordsworth's poetry. The processes of spiritualizing the world and secularizing
the Spirit from this viewpoint look the same.

There has been a basic shift in the nature of symbolism in the course of
The Faerie Queene. As we have seen in the case of Arthur, it no longer indicates
supernatural meaning so pointedly but more darkly acknowledges its
presence. It is more problematical and more personal. This is the reason
that the poem gives so much emphasis to the figure of Melibee before
Calidore's rescue of Pastorella, and the reason that the old man is gone
when her rebirth occurs. In Melibee the theme of will and vision, present in
connection with fortune from the outset of Book VI, crystallizes. Melibee
is denied this vision of rebirth because he himself has already denied it and
in doing so has denied his life, as this poem conceives of life. The details
of Calidore's rescue suggest why. They are allusive but most elusively so;
they glance—and only glance—at more specifically Christian meaning.
When Calidore fights the brigands, they swarm around him like "flyes,"
harassing his flesh with "their litle stings," an image calculated in this context
to recall Redcrosse with Error and Archimago, then Guyon and Arthur
facing the forces of Maleger (I.i.23, 38; II.ix.16).[47] Of course, in fighting
them Calidore is said to fight "theeues," one of the most traditional rep-
resentations of sinners, of the old Adam, and even of the author of sin in
theological writings, and one to which the poet has alluded in earlier Books.[48]
As Melibee's imprisonment might already have been seen to suggest, in
fighting the old man's captors, Calidore also fights the enslavement of
human nature by sin and death, corruption expressed in the more realistic
(naturalistic) form of brigands yet in a form recognizably "sib" to that
fantastic giant, Orgoglio.

It has been suggested that one allusion is still more specific: coming to
the brigands' cave, Calidore "with huge resistlesse might, / The dores
assayled, and the locks vpbrast" (xi.43). These lines allude so darkly, so
fleetingly to the traditional context of Christian redemption that their
meaning was unremarked until Maurice Evans saw in them a reference to
the Harrowing of Hell.[49] I do not mean to be entirely facetious in suggesting
that the expression "Now you see it, now you don't" describes a quality
present in these two lines. The Pauline notion of seeing through a glass
darkly, to which Spenser makes a curiously pointed allusion in the Proem
to Book VI (v), suggests the same quality, though in a more dignified way. A
reader could reasonably be reluctant to believe that Evans's allusion is
demonstrably present in the two lines cited. The meaning of Calidore's

action is substantial and fully developed on the level of human love and romance narrative without it. To my mind, the pressures of context make the reality of this allusion more than likely—that is, the pressures from the immediate context of the rescue, from the total context of the poem, and from the still larger context of "antique" descriptions of Christ's breaking open the gates of hell, certainly including Langland's.[50] The fullest significance of Calidore's entry into the cave makes demands on our recognition, indeed on our vision, greater than those made in earlier Books.

Every Book of *The Faerie Queene* is a perceptual experience and in some way treats human perception, but Book VI is more immediately perceptual and treats perception more directly. There are instances of blindness in Book I similar to Melibee's, for example, but they are also dissimilar in important ways. Redcrosse's behavior between his escape from the House of Pride and his defeat by Orgoglio is particularly close to Melibee's condition. At this point, experience simply lacks a spiritual meaning for Redcrosse. When he leaves the House of Pride, he wipes his brow in relief, not quite daring to rejoice in escape from "his foole-happie ouersight" and in his evidently inexplicable good fortune (I.vi.1–2). He is unaware of what his experience in the House of Pride has meant; he does not, so to speak, know how to read its allegory.

Redcrosse's next foolish act is to take off the armor identified symbolically with his virtue or special power. He does not remove his armor as a conscious rejection of Christianity but merely because he is weary. For him the armor has become mere armor, a dead, flat, physical burden without further significance, and the armor symbolizes what life is becoming for him, too. When Redcrosse disarms, however, he finds or, more accurately, loses himself in a landscape infused with meaning, not, like Melibee's, one infused with its absence. The leaves tremble, as they do on several ominous occasions after Fradubio tells his story, and the birds sing with the same significance heard in the Wandering Wood. The meaning is clearly present in the armor and landscape despite Redcrosse and with minimal recall on the reader's part. His is a failure to see, but it is an unconscious and negative failure.

Melibee's failure is consciously willed and positive. Melibee creates his own landscape out of desire, and *his* voice, not the narrator's, gives it substance. He is actively engaged in a visual venture. Redcrosse's problem is one of faith and therefore of vision. Melibee, a confused but convinced believer in the Almighty, indulges a failure of vision and therefore of faith. Melibee fails to make himself a real landscape and a true life. Redcrosse mistakenly thinks that his landscape and his armor are merely natural or realistic.

Redcrosse forgets or misunderstands eternal truths. Melibee misunderstands life; he fails to live the truths he knows. He loses them really and irreparably, as Redcrosse does not. As for us, we might miss the problem of vision in Book I, but in Book VI we might more easily miss the problem of faith. Between these Books the priorities have indeed shifted, and yet they have shifted only apparently. The priorities are really still the same, but in Book VI their context has become more lifelike, and the recognition of them has become more personal.

PAST, PRESENT, AND POET

The poet's role in Book VI complements his role in Book V, much as other aspects of these Books are mutually complementary. In both Books, he has a more dramatic role—simply more of a role by qualitative standards. In comparison to the first two Books of the poem, his role is not so disembodied, so choric and self-effacing. It is not so exclusively a stand-in for the proper response or a guide to the desirable one, in either case a negative role, or perhaps more charitably viewed, a humble one. In this connection we might recall the ambiguously "lewed" vicar, the puzzled Conscience, or the self-defining figure of Need in the final Passūs of *Piers Plowman*. There the poet's role, along with his characters, becomes embedded in life, and as a result proves less impersonally exemplary, more private but more complexly symbolic. The same can be said of the poet's role in the final Books of *The Faerie Queene*.

In the Proem to Book V, the poet wears an ironic mask. His voice is persuasively dramatized and its dominant tone is pessimistic. Here he laments the "state," the condition "of present time," when he compares it to the "image of the antique world," which he defines as a primal age of virtue. Everywhere he sees degeneration, but finds it especially in the heavens, whose stars have throughout the poem been images of steady faith, conviction, and divine guidance. He sounds defensive, self-justifying—"Let none then blame me," if I do what to me seems right (3)—and like most people who present themselves this way, he soon sounds as though he is talking to himself, borne on a current of thought to which there is no sensible alternative:

> For that which all men then did vertue call,
>   Is now cald vice; and that which vice was hight,
>   Is now hight vertue, and so vs'd of all:
>   Right now is wrong, and wrong that was is right,
>   As all things else in time are chaunged quight.

Ne wonder; for the heauens reuolution
Is wandred farre from where it first was pight,
And so doe make contrarie constitution
Of all this lower world, toward his dissolution.

[v.Pro.iv]

The first stanza begins with the drama of a sonnet—"So oft as I with state of present time, / The image of the antique world compare"—and the next eight stanzas begin with conjunctive expressions which give their thought the pacing of familiar argument: "And if to those Ægyptian wisards old, . . . Faith may be giuen, it is by them told." Only in the last two stanzas of this unusually long Proem does the speaker return, at least superficially, to idealism in order to celebrate the virtue of justice, and even here the uneasiness of the earlier stanzas casts its shadow. His idealism is too sudden and is further qualified by the tension between the extremity of his enthusiam and his lack of decisiveness as to the identity of the "Dread Souerayne Goddesse [Justice? Astrea? Elizabeth? Gloriana?], that doest highest sit" (xi). In the contexts of Spenser's earliest Books, such openness of meaning has been enriching and hopeful; as a conclusion to the anxiety of this Proem, it is strained and puzzling.

The apparently inexplicable movements of the heavens to which the speaker of the Proem devotes most time were understood to be rational by Spenser's educated contemporaries, who saw them as cyclic occurrences. *Epithalamion* indicates that Spenser was astronomically knowledgeable and lends credence to the likelihood of his acquaintance with explanations of the precession of the equinoxes and of the apparently retrograde orbits of planets, phenomena which either the Ptolemaic or the Copernican hypothesis could "save" or account for adequately.[51] Yet he refers to these phenomena at length in the fifth Proem as evidence of random, irrational movement (v–vi, viii, vv. 8–9). With a straight face, he repeats the arguments from appearances used in his day to prove that the world was declining, including those about which we have every reason to believe he knew better. Further, he relates these arguments to a context of hearsay and wizard's tales (viii) and unjustified fear and doubt. The world, according to many of Spenser's contemporaries, especially to the numerous readers of Regiomontanus in the second half of the sixteenth century, was going to hell, and in this Proem, he considers, or rather presents for judgment, the justice of their claims.[52]

The emphasis on sight, on appearance, and quantitative measurement in this Proem is paralleled by the opinions of the leveling Giant whom Artegall destroys early in Book v. This parallel suggests that the poet's observations in the Proem are complexly ironic, serious and not serious at the same time. The speaker of the Proem, referring to the zodiac, says that the Ram has shouldered the Bull, the Bull the Gemini, the Gemini the Crab, and the Crab the Lion—rather systematic disorder at that. The Giant claims in his turn that the waters of the earth have encroached on the land, and the fire on the air, and so he proposes to repair all things "as they were formed aunciently" (ii.32).

The pathetically foolish Giant is annihilated because he tries to tamper with just order for wrong reasons and in wrong ways. He is an active leveler, as the merely observant speaker in the Proem is not; yet the disconcerting similarities between his views and the poet's observations in the Proem make the complexity of the poet's ironic role there more obvious. Artegall's victory over the Giant is qualified by Artegall's answers to him—"All change is perillous, and all chaunce vnsound"[53]—and further qualified by Talus's putting a peremptory end to their argument by shouldering the wretched Giant from cliff to ragged rocks below, thus leveling him. It be-becomes even clearer that the poet's role in the Proem is not merely that of a straw man when Nature begins her answer in the Mutability Cantos: "all things stedfastnes doe hate / And changed be . . ." (vii.58). The Giantess Mutability will offer arguments basically similar to those of the Proem and of the Giant in Book v, and her unwittingly ironic challenge will offer the best comment on their materialism, "But what we see not, who shall vs perswade?" (vii.49).

In Book v the poet plays a complexly ironic persona; by putting on his own pastoral persona in Book vi, he more simply plays himself. In the tenth canto of Book vi, between the introduction of Melibee and Calidore's rescue of Pastorella, Spenser gives us the vision of the Graces on Mount Acidale. There Colin, Calidore, and their creator participate in the union of fortune with desire, of the experience given with the experience sought. When Colin pipes to the Graces, song and dancers embody the harmony of actors and events and of impulse and order. The vision realizes the union of grace with humanity, with human awareness and creative activity, and in short, with human life.

These Graces are the daughters of Jove and Ocean's daughter Eurynome, of sky and water, heaven and earth. They were begot as Jove came from the wedding of Thetis and Peleus, the mortal who won his sea-goddess by holding on to her in all her changing shapes and from whose union Achilles was born (x.22); hence their birth was sequent on that conjunction of mortal and immortal and of mutability and unity which was to result in human heroism.

The Graces of Colin's vision bestow on men "all gracious gifts . . . Which decke the body or adorne the mynde," and so they make men courteous, teaching "vs, how to each degree and kynde / We should our selues demeane, to low, to hie" (x.23). The country lass they choose to grace shows "Diuine resemblaunce, beauty soueraine rare, / Firme Chastity, that spight ne blemish dare" (x.27). As these quotations suggest, the Graces embody the sense of proportion and of related dimensions which Melibee lacked and provide the transitional link between his views and Calidore's rescue of Pastorella.

Like many incidents in Book vi, the vision on Mount Acidale invites us to recall Book i, more particularly the vision of poet and knight on the Mount of Contemplation in canto x. Contemplation holds the promise which Acidale fulfills. We might distinguish the later from the earlier vision in terms of fullness, freedom, and confidence. The vision on Mount Acidale is pure symbol—so rich that it seems limitless in meaning. It is more purely—more directly and fully—the corollary and embodiment of an emotional and spiritual experience, and speaks to us first and most powerfully in affective, intuitive terms. More than any other passage so far in *The Faerie Queene,* this vision originates in imaginative power "all compact" and its excitement is dependent on the tones of immediate, personal involvement: "*Looke* how the Crowne . . . *now* placed in the firmament" and "Pype iolly shepheard, pype thou now apace / Vnto thy loue." On Mount Acidale, Colin's love is "present," seen "there with thee in place, / Thy loue is there aduaunst to be another Grace" (x.13, 16; my italics).

In comparison with Book i, the splendid vision of Book vi is not specifically religious, though it powerfully suggests that the union of grace with human life, indeed courtesy itself, is essentially so. Mount Acidale rather than the Mount of Contemplation—the Book of Courtesy rather than the Book of Holiness—is the greater moment of unity in *The Faerie Queene.* As in most parallels between the first and last Books, however, Book i provides a detailed model for real wholeness. The experiences in both Books have three stages of vision and three "seers": the poet, Contemplation, and Redcrosse; the poet, Colin, and Calidore. The visionary experience in Book vi, like the earlier one, is rightly not allowed to last; if it were, Mount Acidale would really be more of a Paradise than we ever find in Book i, and Spenser would be Melibee. The poet's voice takes an active part in the tenth canto of both Books. In Book i, as we have seen in the second chapter, there is a sudden quickening of imaginative power as the poet speaks of Sinai, Olivet, and Parnassus, but this brief glimpse of power ceases abruptly, and the poem moves on to the soberer, more restrained view (and understanding) of the New Jerusalem which Contemplation shows Redcrosse, until it, too, is ended and the knight returns to his quest.

In Book VI the poet first narrates how Calidore happened to see "An hundred naked maidens lilly white, / All raunged in a ring, and dauncing in delight," a sight so pleasing to the knight that he envies the power granted his own eyes to see it; thus he feels a kind of pain, a slight self-tearing at its loveliness (11). The lines just quoted attribute this sight directly to Calidore. In the lines immediately following them, the poet emphasizes this initial impression by repeating words and phrases—"All they without were raunged in a ring, / And daunced round"—but he no longer speaks specifically of Calidore. His repetition suggests that this sight is becoming his own vision more directly, that he, like Calidore, has in some sense happened upon it. As the poet's attention is increasingly possessed by the vision, Calidore simply disappears. The poet's own voice takes the vision over as its beauty sweeps over him. He speaks in rhythmically recurrent words and sounds and in balanced verbal patterns. They have the effect of suspending forward movement, even while participating in it; they poise and intensify imaginative suggestion, concentrating attention on the vision there on Mount Acidale but also bringing it here, before us.

Soon the poet speaks directly, as if to himself but equally to us, as if he now feels both present and attentive: "Looke how the Crowne, which *Ariadne* wore / Vpon her yuory forehead that same day"—not the less immediate phrasing, "Like as the Crown" but "Looke," or remember, be mindful, and in a moment, look there and imagine, indeed *see,* how that Crown

> Being now placed in the firmament,
> Through the bright heauen doth her beams display,
> And is vnto the starres an ornament,
> Which round about her moue in order excellent.

> [VI.x.13]

It seems more than mere chance that this same crown, according to Spenser's excited conflation of myths, was worn on that day when Theseus took Ariadne as his bride, "When the bold *Centaures* made that bloudy fray / With the fierce *Lapithes,* which did them dismay." (Note the demonstrative adjective *that,* rather than the less specific, less immediately forceful word *the.*) This was the day last called to mind in Ate's dwelling in Book IV, in that place of broken dreams, broken ideals, and broken civilizations:

> . . . there the relicks of the drunken fray,
> The which amongst the *Lapithees* befell,

> And of the bloodie feast, which sent away
> So many *Centaures* drunken soules to hell . . .
>
> [IV.i.23]

Now that same memory is transformed to a bright crown of stars which shines in the firmament and graces a region of "order excellent."[54]

The poet's vision remains so real that he reaches out to it, identifying and addressing Colin: "Pype iolly shepheard, pype thou now apace / Vnto thy loue, that made thee low to lout" (16). First Calidore recedes from the foreground; then the vision becomes the poet's and now more directly Colin's. The continuity among all three of these figures is vital to the meaning of canto x, but for the present we might follow the poet's lead in concentrating on Colin; for it is at this moment that the poet so pointedly asks us to recognize the shepherd. He asks, lest we miss the reunion between himself and his pastoral persona, "who knowes not *Colin Clout?*" And who does not in Spenser's minor poems, or at least in his own dreams and desires? The poet's question alludes to his own past, now realized and reaffirmed as an aspect of his present, and it alludes to ours as well.

After this moment of recognition and of actual repossession, Calidore intrudes on the vision, causing it to disappear. The vision flees in an instant, but its power lingers. Approaching Colin, Calidore asks him what the experience has meant. He needs to be persuaded of its nature, and (once more to borrow Mutability's words) because he has been fortunate enough to see it, he can be persuaded. Colin's explanation is said "to dilate" (21) the vision. It amplifies, yet parallels, the poet's presentation of the vision itself and thus further enforces our sense of a continuity between them.

Colin's explanation is more discursive and at first more definitive and explicitly didactic than the poet's; yet it, too, soon becomes more personal. Colin is the figure who pipes to his own love, and when his explanation of the vision comes to her presence in it, his tone echoes, but only echoes, the verbal music at the height of the earlier vision:

> So farre as doth the daughter of the day,
> All other lesser lights in light excell,
> So farre doth she in beautyfull array,
> Aboue all other lasses beare the bell . . .
>
> [VI.x.26]

The homely image in the last line remains to limit and to specify the subject's nature: the shepherd's love may be a goddess and a fourth Grace, but she is "certes but a countrey lasse" (25). Colin spends three stanzas glorifying his country lass, whereupon he suddenly, intensely addresses Gloriana:

> Sunne of the world, great glory of the sky,
>> That all the earth doest lighten with thy rayes,
>> Great *Gloriana,* greatest Maiesty,
>> Pardon thy shepheard, mongst so many layes,
>> As he hath sung of thee in all his dayes,
>> To make one minime of thy poore handmayd,
>> And vnderneath thy feete to place her prayse,
>> That when thy glory shall be farre displayd
> To future age of her this mention may be made.
>
> [VI.x.28]

For a moment Colin speaks as if he were the author of this poem, and in doing so, he enforces the continuity between pastoral and epic and the essential continuity of all the poet's roles.[55] The poet who announced his epic intentions in the Proem to Book I recovers in Colin something of himself and finds in a pastoral voice one truly his own. The Plotinian notion that "awareness of self is the foundation of memory" is an idea Langland discovers in *Piers Plowman* and one that Spenser explores in earlier Books but now, in the presence of Colin, finds actually and personally true.[56]

Langland's discovery occurs when Imaginative joins the Dreamer's past to his present in the birth of a new understanding, which deepens profoundly as other figures—Conscience, Anima, and Piers—lead him to realize knowledge of Being and of his own figurative being as a plowman, which he had had in some sense before but had not truly possessed. Introducing the pastoral episodes of the sixth Book, Spenser's conception of his own poetic art returns to the past, to the pastoral image of plowing:

> Now turne againe my teme thou iolly swayne,
>> Backe to the furrow which I lately left;
>> I lately left a furrow, one or twayne
>> Vnplough'd, the which my coulter hath not cleft . . .
>
> [VI.ix.1]

The poet of Mount Acidale has no more left this conception behind him than he has ever left behind the image of the Redcrosse Knight in Book I, the image of Colin Clout in *The Shepheardes Calender,* and all that these symbols, Redcrosse and Colin, imply: his personal past as religious, moral, and pastoral poet; his national past as an Englishman writing in the tradition of the great poets who preceded him, conspicuous among them the poet whose image of life's pilgrim was a plowman named Piers; his past as a son of earth and of Adam. It is right—in the very deepest and broadest sense, "kindly"

—that Colin, an allusion not only to pastoral but specifically to Spenser's pastoral poems and particularly to *The Shepheardes Calender,* should be situated at the heart of Spenser's poetic vision.

Calidore's presence is as integral to the meaning of the vision in canto x as is the poet's or Colin's. With the exception of his dispelling the immediate vision, his role is more passive than theirs, but his experiences with Melibee and Pastorella frame the sight on Mount Acidale and adjust the perspective in which we understand it. His presence contributes vitally to the sense we have of moving through various kinds of experience to its heart on the Mount itself. The poet gets to Mount Acidale, as we do, with Calidore and by first passing through Melibee's pastoral landscape.[57] Melibee and Colin are analogous in some respects. The situations of both shepherds are withdrawn—the first in its rural simplicity and shortsightedness, the second in its visionary fullness and freedom—and both exist on the level of conscious choice and creation.

Mount Acidale is said "to ouerlooke the lowly vale" (8), a description which emphasizes at once its immanence and its distance, its nearness and its removal. The name "Acidale" associates the Mount with Venus; if it also means both "freedom from care" and "valley view," as Donald Cheney suggests, then it means carelessness and over-look in senses no further defined, hence senses which embrace the bliss of perfect contentment but still recall the dangers of irresponsibility.[58] There is the possibility, raised by William Nelson, that its name may even have a connection with the Latin *accidia,* sloth or despair.[59] We have already seen that Mount Acidale embodies a sense of proportion and related dimensions; it is a place of potency, a richly and ambiguously poised condition, a paradise hedged with warnings and controls. This is one reason that Calidore is there to see it. Mount Acidale resembles a Shakespearean forest, a place of opportunity wisely guarded and, if embraced wholeheartedly, then embraced by the wise with self-awareness, in disguise, or for a limited time. Melibee's illusions play a necessary part in reaching the Mount. They provide the conditions of withdrawal in which it becomes available, even though these conditions themselves must finally be destroyed or rejected.

When Calidore decides to try Melibee's condition and at least for the time being to abandon his quest for the Blatant Beast (ix.31), his reasons, as the narrator explains them, bear a distinct resemblance to Melibee's own. First we learn why Melibee chose to leave and then to return to the country:

> For further fortune then I would inquire.
> And leauing home, to roiall court I sought;

Where I did sell my selfe for yearely hire,
And in the Princes gardin daily wrought:
There I beheld such vainenesse, as I neuer thought.

With sight whereof soone cloyd, and long deluded
With idle hopes, which them doe entertaine,
After I had ten yeares my selfe excluded
From natiue home, and spent my youth in vaine,
I gan my follies to my selfe to plaine,
And this sweet peace, whose lacke did then appeare.

[VI.ix.24–25]

Then we learn the reasons imputed to Calidore for deciding "no more to sew / His former quest, so full of toile and paine." This knight has "Another quest, another game in vew / . . . the guerdon of his loue to gaine":

And set his rest amongst the rusticke sort,
Rather then hunt still after shadowes vaine
Of courtly fauour, fed with light report
Of euery blaste, and sayling alwaies on the port.

Ne certes mote he greatly blamed be,
From so high step to stoupe vnto so low.
For who had tasted once (as oft did he)
The happy peace, which there doth ouerflow,
And prou'd the perfect pleasures, which doe grow
Amongst poore hyndes, in hils, in woods, in dales,
Would neuer more delight in painted show
Of such false blisse, as there is set for stales,
T'entrap vnwary fooles in their eternall bales.

[VI.x.2–3]

The narrator's sympathy for Calidore's position is remarkable. He states its weakness forthrightly (x.i), but his criticism lacks the emphasis and ironic zest to which other truants, including even Artegall, have been exposed. After one stanza about Calidore's delinquency, the narrator begins to excuse and to justify it; and little wonder that he does, since Calidore's position resembles Colin's in *Colin Clovts Come Home Againe* as well as it resembles Melibee's:

But selfe-regard of priuate good or ill,
Moues me of each, so as I found, to tell
And eke to warne yong shepheards wandring wit,

> Which through report of that liues painted blisse,
> Abandon quiet home, to seeke for it,
> And leaue their lambes to losse misled amisse.[60]

[682–87]

We might also, if distantly, recall the whole tale of Diggon Davie in the September Eclogue of *The Shepheardes Calender,* a story in which one of the earliest references to a type of the Blatant Beast occurs (121). This story lacks the force and biting immediacy of criticisms of the court in Spenser's later poems, yet it tells a history of "vayne desyre, and hope to be enricht" (75) which ultimately leads the chastened Diggon and his interlocutor Hobbinoll to conclusions that anticipate the concerns of Book VI:

> *Diggon.* How, but with heede and watchfulnesse,
>   Forstallen hem of their wilinesse?
>   For thy with shepheard sittes not playe,
>   Or sleepe, as some doen, all the long day:
>   But euer liggen in watch and ward,
>   From soddein force theyr flocks for to gard.
> *Hobbin.* Ah Diggon, thilke same rule were too straight,
>   All the cold season to wach and waite.
>   We ben of fleshe, men as other bee,
>   Why should we be bound to such miseree?
>   What euer thing lacketh chaungeable rest,
>   Mought needes decay, when it is at best.

[230–41][61]

In a Book which explicitly asks, "Who knowes not *Colin Clout?*" we have a right to these memories. They are as legitimate a part of the meaning of this poem as other memories it has invited us to have of Ariosto, Ovid, or the Bible. Given the allusion in Calidore's position to Colin's, we might again call to mind the irony, the doubleness, of the Proem to Book V, which takes a more dramatic form in Artegall's argument with the leveling Giant. In these passages, as well as in the stanzas about Calidore most recently cited, there is a personal element present, as there even more clearly is in the figure of Colin himself. In Colin this element becomes virtually autobiographical— virtually, because Colin Clout remains at a nominal remove from Edmund Spenser.

With Calidore's relation to Melibee and to the poet now in mind, we might look more closely at his effect on the vision of the Graces. His disruption of this vision is perhaps inevitable because it is humanly necessary. Calidore approaches the vision too nearly, too insistently. Mistaking its nature, he tries to encroach on its spontaneity, its freedom and graciousness, and so its mystery eludes him. The dancers flee at once from his intrusive presence, "their vew" of him, and from "his sight," or vision (x.18). Calidore asserts his presence because he questions the nature of what he sees, even doubting that he really sees it at all. He begins to wonder

> Whether it were the traine of beauties Queene,
> Or Nymphes, or Faeries, or enchaunted show,
> With which his eyes mote haue deluded beene.
> Therefore resoluing, what it was, to know,
> Out of the wood he rose, and toward them did go.
>
> [VI.x.17]

There will be no more wishing and guessing for Calidore. He wants definite knowledge and pursues it resolutely. His act is an intention to touch the vision, to grasp and assay its mysterious beauty. He does not as yet realize that this is an intention, in reality, to dispel it. At his sight—insistent, rational, and realistic—vision vanishes.

The impulse to assay, to poke and to prod the vision is hard for anyone to deny. Is it, after all, a vision or a waking dream? The question is bound eventually to come, though not to be answered. It is a sensible question which expresses a natural psychological need, and Calidore, in truth the knight with a quest to fulfill in the active world, is its representative. In being so, he is also, like Colin, one of our representatives and, more immediately, one of the poet's. He has behind him the tradition of fictional projection by the author which derives from the psychological allegory of the dream vision, a tradition we see so well in *Piers Plowman,* where the poet meets (and shows that he wants us to see that he meets) aspects of himself—Will, Thought, Imaginative, Conscience, *Spes*/Moses, and eventually even Piers/Christ.[62] There is some difference between Langland's writing, " 'I haue lyued in londe,' quod I, 'my name is Longe Wille' " (xv.148), and Spenser's writing, "who knowes not *Colin Clout?*" but it is reduced by the fact that Will is a fictional character and an aspect of the human psyche, as well as an authorial signature, and by the fact that the creator of Colin also signed his name to poems he published, in effect putting his special mark on this fictional and allusively personal character.[63] There is a fictional remove between the two poets' signatures within the poems, but it is no more arresting than a fictional nearness.

The reassertion of Calidore's presence is not just a loss in Book VI but also a renewed beginning. It is primarily for Calidore that the vision is explained or dilated. The affective immediacy of the experience is lessened, but its special significance is enlarged. Moreover, it is for Calidore to return to the quest, as Redcrosse returned form the Mount of Contemplation, his further actions in a figurative sense made possible because vision is renewed and heightened in what he has seen. Calidore's presence on Mount Acidale, as well as Colin's and the poet's, makes possible the vision of canto xi: Calidore is the narrative symbol, the carrier, of continuity from Mount Acidale to the rescue of Pastorella.

Calidore's need to leave Mount Acidale frames the vision of the Graces on its farther side. Love brings him from the Mount, and it is love not seen primarily as an ideal but as a component of worldly reality, as "that enuenimd sting, the which of yore, / His poysnous point deepe fixed in his hart" (x.31). Love sounds here as venomous as the Blatant Beast, whom Calidore has chased from court to cities, to towns, to the country, to private farms, a route which parallels in striking detail that taken by Venus in search of an armed and wayward Cupid in Book III (vi.11–15). The quest for love and the defeat of the Beast are, in fact, intimately related. If Calidore remained on Mount Acidale, his quest both for love (Pastorella) and for honor (Beast) would be gone. He would lose her and lose fame, "the name of noble wight" (vi.1), and therefore in effect would become prey for the Blatant Beast. The love which brings him back to the plain may hurt, but unlike the Beast, it has the positive power to restore him. He returns from Acidale, "Like as the wounded Whale to shore flies from the maine" (x.31). This image for love's action on him is hardly elevating, but it suggests a force instinctively natural. The action of his love, in which this force is implicit, is soon to be seen ennobling the spirit and by its virtue redeeming life in Pastorella's rescue. A love which touches Mount Acidale and Cupid's envenomed sting—ideal and instinct, vision and flesh, spirit and nature—invests Calidore with the power to rescue Pastorella, little pastoral, seemingly the mere child of nature; and only then, his love thus reborn to light out of darkness and "nature" restored to her rightful inheritance, is he able to catch and to subdue the Blatant Beast.

The paradoxical relationship of Cupid's envenomed sting to "the poysnous sting" of the Blatant Beast (vi.1) finds a parallel in one of the strangest passages of *Piers Plowman*. There Mercy hopes through her experience that men will be saved, "For venym for-doth venym" (xviii.151–52):

> For of alle venymes foulest is the scorpioun,
> May no medcyne helpe the place there he styngeth
> Tyl he be ded and do ther-to the yuel he destroyeth,
> The fyrst venymouste thorw venym of hym-self.[64]
>
> [xviii.153–56]

If Mercy stopped here, we should merely have an apt illustration of a notion common to medieval and Renaissance times. But the application of her proof, which follows immediately on the lines just cited, makes the possibility that this passage might once have caught Spenser's eye and imagination a little more likely:

> So shal this deth [Christ's] for-do, I dar my lyf legge,
> Al that Deth fordyd furste thorw the deuelles entysynge;
> And ri3t as thorw gyle man was bigyled,[65]
> So shal grace that bigan make a good sleighte;[66]
> *Ars ut artem falleret.*
>
> [XVIII.157–60]

At the end of Book VI, Calidore's nature, part of him even to the envenomed sting of instinct, possesses a redemptive, Christ-like power of love, which alone can overcome the poison of the unkind, unnatural Beast. In Calidore's experience, nature is redeemed and redefined, while remaining perfectly natural. "I were an vnkynde kinge but I my kynde holpe": Langland's idea is fundamentally the same here as Spenser's.

Calidore's return from the mountain is not in any simple sense a return to reality. It is a return both from and to the reality of love's working, a return from a more purely imagined, ideal experience to experiences more care-ful— more tangible, mixed, temporal, and in these senses, real. Like Arthur in the late cantos of Book V, Calidore meets unmitigated success once he puts on his armor again, the symbol of his quest (or of both his quests, which are now continuous). He defeats the brigands, wins Pastorella, restores her by good fortune to her stolen birthright, and muzzles the Blatant Beast.

Yet Book VI splits finally, as did Book V, between mythic success and palpable disappointment. At its end, the Beast that Calidore has tamed breaks loose, "whether wicked fate so framed, / Or fault of men" (xii.38). "Now," we hear, "he raungeth through the world againe, / And rageth sore in each degree and state"; he seems to reserve a special venom for "learned wits" and "gentle Poets rime," rending "without regard of person or of time" (xii.40):

> Ne may this homely verse, of many meanest,
>   Hope to escape his venemous despite,
>   More then my former writs, all were they cleanest
> From blamefull blot, and free from all that wite,
> With which some wicked tongues did it backebite,
> And bring into a mighty Peres displeasure,
> That neuer so deserued to endite.

> Therfore do you my rimes keep better measure,
> And seeke to please, that now is counted wisemens threasure.
>
> [VI.xii.41]

At the end of Book VI, within a canto and therefore within the usual con-
fines of the fiction itself, we hear a voice that specifically locates itself in
Elizabethan history, a voice no less an aspect of the poet than Colin and
Calidore. This voice is disillusioned and in the last two lines bites with a
bitterness approaching cynicism. The Beast here seems loosed in every
sense, even this last self-referential one. Like Langland, Spenser wakes up,
too, at the end of this Book, and because he does not pretend to have been
dreaming, he appears to wake up more rudely.

This last voice is so immediate that it is easy to lose the perspective on it,
easy to forget for a moment the promise of recovery in the rest of Book VI.
The whole poem, especially since the beginning of Book VI, has been about
the recovery of true vision, a recovery at once recurrent and progressive. Its
memory outweighs the voice at the end of Book VI, a sharp and sudden
sound but also a very short-lived one. We have seen the vision on Mount
Acidale, and while we have to hear this final voice because it, too, is real, its
reality is unlikely to persuade us that the other voices are not real as well.
Spenser's poem is no more committed to a cycle of admirable futility, of
recurrence without progress, than Langland's. Book VI may repeat the split
between myth and history which ends Book V, but we no longer understand
it in quite the same way; or rather, since this poem has been, like *Piers
Plowman*, a search for understanding, the choice of understanding it truly at
the end is our own.

8

Conclusion: Change or Dilation

The only cantos of *The Faerie Queene* we have beyond Book VI realize, once more in recurrence *and* progression, the promise of recovery which Courtesy offers. In the Mutability Cantos, this last step forward, though foreseeable in retrospect, takes what was probably once, for most of us, an unforeseen direction. The figure of Mutability might be said to embody disillusionment; in her presence Spenser's fiction is dilated to include more fully the threat to its own vision of Truth that we have noted at the end of Book VI. Like Melibee, Mutability has her real, "sensefull" attractions, as Jove so lecherously appreciates, but she threatens our confidence in life. She becomes an assertion of a lower nature which flatly denies permanence and stability and thus the reality of a higher nature. With all her vigor and vitality, she finally stands for a death-in-life, death of the body and of the spirit. She argues that man is the slave of time, that "man and beasts,"

> The beasts we daily see massacred dy,
> As thralls and vassalls vnto mens beheasts:
> And men themselues doe change continually,
> From youth to eld, from wealth to pouerty,
> From good to bad, from bad to worst of all.
> Ne doe their bodies only flit and fly:
> But eeke their minds (which they immortall call)
> Still change and vary thoughts, as new occasions fall.
>
> [VII.vii.19]

In the figure of Mutability, the voice we heard at the end of Book VI takes a more persuasive and more visible form.

The Mutability Cantos, in manner and matter so quintessentially Renaissance, are in one respect closer to the poetic life of *Piers Plowman* than anything else Spenser wrote, and in being so, they clarify the action and the presence which at first we sense distantly or glimpse briefly in *The Faerie Queene* but of which we become increasingly aware with every Book. In these cantos the action of the poet's own mind is continuous with that of his poem to an extent more deliberate and sustained even than in Book VI.[1] The Mutability Cantos are a continuous process of thought realized immediately before us. This process is not a mere exercise in perception, a sort of flexing of the perceptual muscles as in the Wandering Wood, but the exercise of a fully self-conscious creative vision, a vision which reveals and discovers itself simultaneously as it discovers and unfolds meaning. If the Mutability Cantos diffuse the concentrated radiance of Mount Acidale, they also extend and perpetuate its immediate perceptual life. They are in their entirety essentially a perceptual action, and they are finally Life perceived directly and whole for this poet.

The Mutability Cantos have no representatively human hero like Redcrosse, Britomart, or Calidore, no figure who is our surrogate except the poet himself, and no landscape—not even Arlo Hill—apart from his mind's. As they stand (which is the only way we can deal with them), they have no introduction or proem, no framing story or context. From beginning to end they are themselves. This fact receives dramatic expression within them when we see the personifying of Mutability, the deliberate creating of her as a character, at the beginning of canto vi, and again when we watch Nature vanish at the end of canto vii as only an image, a Nature the mind makes, could vanish. Her vanishing in a breath and without a narrative intruder emphasizes the fact that she is mind-made, a fact that her authority, like Lady Holy Church's or Kind's in *Piers Plowman,* makes easy to forget.[2] Each of the Mutability Cantos is a different invention and a variant form—a fable alluding to classical forms in the first, a pageant alluding to medieval forms in the second, a private meditation and personal prayer in the third. Each is an intricately woven network of memories from all the preceding Books of the poem, as the poet, like Peleus, endeavors to embrace Nature in all her shapes, so to wed immortality.

The first of these cantos achieves no resolution. The argument between Jove and Mutability is referred to a higher court. Meanwhile Diana and Faunus, alternative expressions of the conflicting principles of reality impersonated in Jove and Mutability, are not reconciled. They fly off in opposite directions, and with their flight the land reverts to lawlessness, anarchy, dark disorder. The resolutions in the last two cantos—first Nature's, then the poet's own—resemble the split encountered in the conclusion of Books v and vi: the confident assertion of mythic success offset by temporal failure and personal disappointment. The resemblance is real, but it exists this time to show how apparent opposition can be continuity and apparent duality can be univocal.

Nature's answer to Mutability naturally does not deny the latter's existence, while it rejects her claim that she is exclusively real. Nature recognizes Mutability first as a vitalizing part of the larger pattern of cyclic recurrence:

> I well consider all that ye haue sayd,
>> And find that all things stedfastnes doe hate
>> And changed be: yet being rightly wayd
>> They are not changed from their first estate;
>> But by their change their being doe dilate:
>> And turning to themselues at length againe,
>> Doe worke their owne perfection so by fate:
>> Then ouer them Change doth not rule and raigne;
>> But they raigne ouer change, and doe their states maintaine.
>
>   [VII.vii.58]

This is the center of Nature's answer, the part of it which most assuredly puts Mutability in her place. It is a demonstrable position and also a cyclical one, but as Spenser's Nature herself seems to realize, the cycle is finally not an answer. Nature goes on to speak of time to "come that all shall changed bee, / And from thenceforth, none no more change shall see" (vii.59). Thus, at least in thought, Nature touches eternity, a future in which change will become unnatural, indeed, nonexistent.

The trouble with Nature's cyclical answer is obvious. The fullness of the end may be implicit in the beginning, as it is in *The Faerie Queene* itself, and the essential nature of the beginning may likewise be recognized, after seemingly infinite expansions, in the end; yet Nature's answer depends ultimately for its meaning on what you begin with. What if it is dust and materialism rather than spirit and faith? Her answer finally depends on what we have seen and therefore believe expressions such as "perfectly natural" or "human," and above all the word "life" to mean. The problem here is still vision.

Once Nature has spoken, the poet turns—as Nature says all things at last do—to himself. He speaks easily and quietly about his private thoughts:

> When I bethinke me on that speech whyleare,
>> Of *Mutability*, and well it way:
>> Me seemes, that though she all vnworthy were
>> Of the Heav'ns Rule; yet very sooth to say,
>> In all things else she beares the greatest sway.
>> Which makes me loath this state of life so tickle,
>> And loue of things so vaine to cast away;
>> Whose flowring pride, so fading and so fickle,
>> Short *Time* shall soon cut down with his consuming sickle.
>
>   [VII.viii.1]

In a phrase that recalls the Giant's balances in Book v, which were unable rightly to weigh thoughts and words, and more immediately echoes Nature's answer, the poet weighs well her words. Evidently, for him the cyclical part of her answer has not been sufficient; instead of finding reassurance in her affirmation of temporal stability, he dwells on brevity, loss, and death. What he responds to is the reality of Mutability's *presence,* which Nature has also affirmed; he seems to feel Mutability's individually overwhelming power.

As we saw in chapter 2, the poet's words in this stanza are informed with ambiguity: "Which makes me loath this state of life so tickle (,) / And loue of things so vaine to cast away." The word *loath* could be either an adjective or a verb; the comma after *tickle,* like other marks of punctuation in an early seventeenth-century edition, in this case a posthumous edition to boot, lacks definitive authority; the word *vaine* can be read as an adjective modifying *love* or *things,* or as the adverbial modifier of the infinitive *to cast:* love so vain, things so vain, makes me loath so vainly to cast away.[3] The poet's words, perhaps despite him, still reflect the doubleness of man's condition, the tension we have noticed repeatedly in the poem between "sensefull" loveliness and enervation, between innocence and destruction, attraction and ugliness.

This tension is inherent potentially in all experience and is especially noticeable in its profoundly Christian forms. We saw something like it in Langland's less romantic awareness of the inescapable reality of physical and material needs and desires, and we find moving expressions of it in as stern a moralist as Calvin.[4] The immediate problem, however, is what these ambiguous words are doing in the poet's mouth at the outset of canto viii. It simply does not make emotional or tonal sense at this moment for the speaker—the poet speaking of and for himself—to feel self-torn in an entirely conscious way between the beauty and the mortality he discerns around him. Still less would it be humanly credible for the speaker now to be undermining himself with the ironical perspective of opposite meanings which as a narrator he used so often on figures at a greater remove from himself, and even used on himself in the Proem to Book v. His statement, as it develops in the last two lines of the stanza in question, is too persuasively weighted in a negative direction to sustain the tension of a few verbal ambiguities.

Yet the ambiguities are there; his words are informed paradoxically with their tension. As a result, these ambiguities give the impression of being totally natural, not only unforced but present without the speaker's deliberate help and conscious desire. He no longer feels the attraction of the world's loveliness in the same direct way; it is real but faded for him, literally subliminal. For once, moreover, the impression of subliminal meaning is real and unqualified, even though we shall never know whether the man who wrote these ambiguous words, rather than the one who speaks them, chose them accidentally, intuitively, or with immense care. Their ambiguity is quite simply *fortuitous:* in them we are to see the inherence of such tension in everything we perceive in life and its inseparability from everything we touch, even words and poetic visions.

In the final stanza of the Mutability Cantos, the poet's thoughts turn to Nature's concluding remarks about

> . . . that same time when no more *Change* shall be,
> But stedfast rest of all things firmely stayd,
> Vpon the pillours of Eternity,
> That is contrayr to *Mutabilitie:*
> For, all that moueth, doth in *Change* delight . . .
>
> [vii.viii.2]

"All that moueth," then everything that lives, *delights* in change. "But," the poet continues,

> . . . thence-forth all shall rest eternally
> With Him that is the God of Sabbaoth hight:
> O! that great Sabbaoth God, grant me that Saboaths sight.
>
> [vii.viii.2]

His final prayer is for sight, for vision, and for its "site," its place or condition. It becomes a prayer only in the last line and a direct address to God only in its last five words. This final plea remains poised between the earthly present and the time to come, between having and not-having, between a moving assertion of faith and desire and the utter elusiveness of its fruition.

This ending is not so abrupt as Langland's, "sitthe he [Conscience] gradde after grace til I gan awake," and it is in a technical sense more *simply* personal. In the last two stanzas of Spenser's Cantos, we find a single speaker whose fully developed voice separates itself easily and deliberately from the fiction that precedes it. This speaker therefore asserts the autonomy of his own being more unmistakably than did Langland. He similarly asserts its unity, however slightly that unity is qualified by the ambiguities, the subliminal doubleness of words in the stanza preceding. Indeed, if Upton's attractive suggestion is right—that the last line of stanza viii refers first to the "Sabaoth God," the God of Hosts or Armies active in the natural world, and then to the "Sabbath God," the God of eternal Rest[5]—we can see in these references, as well as in the ambiguity of "sight," an allusion to the split between history and myth, time and eternity, which we have observed at the ends of Books v and vi and in Nature's answer. But this time the opposition, the doubleness, is held in a single voice and in two forms of a single Word; it is implicitly resolved in God, where alone for both Middle Ages and Renaissance contraries meet without contradiction.

At the end of Spenser's poem, as at the end of Langland's, we see a final personalizing of the vision and see it come down to an individual realization of faith in one's God. Spenser's may be a more personal, interiorized realization, and his God likewise may be a more distanced person and impersonal power than is Piers Plowman; notwithstanding, in both poems there will finally be no site and no vision unless they are truly realized in the poet himself. We hear at the end of the Mutability Cantos the simple reality and solitude which give life to the strength and loneliness of one person. Alone and at the end, in a moment of personal realization, a voice we have never heard quite this way before in the poem seems to reach across two centuries, still searching for the immediacy of the promise that Will called Piers Plowman.

Notes

1 "The Printer to the Reader" in *The vision of Pierce Plowman, nowe the seconde time imprinted by Roberte Crowley . . .* (London, 1550).

2 Walter W. Skeat, ed., *The Vision of William concerning Piers Plowman,* by William Langland, EETS 81 (London, 1884), pt. 4, sect. 2, pp. 864–69, lists numerous references to *Piers Plowman* both before and after Crowley. I should add Abraham Fraunce to them and should note the existence of a signed and annotated copy of *Piers Plowman* which belonged to Gabriel Harvey's brother Richard (in the Beinecke Library, Yale University): for Fraunce, see *The Arcadian Rhetoric* (Menston, Eng., Scolar Press Facsimile rpt., 1969), Bk. 1, cap. 25, sig. E4².

3 All references to Spenser's works are to *The Works of Edmund Spenser: A Variorum Edition,* ed. Edwin A. Greenlaw and others, 11 vols. (Baltimore, 1932–57), cited hereinafter as *Var.; The Faerie Queene* is cited as *FQ.* Unless otherwise specified, references to Langland's poem are to *The Vision of William concerning Piers the Plowman in Three Parallel Texts,* ed. Walter W. Skeat, 2 vols, (Oxford, 1886); the B-text is cited hereafter as *PP.* (I have removed Skeat's medial dot from all citations and have altered his punctuation where I judged desirable.)

4 Bk. v.1786: *Works,* ed. F. N. Robinson, 2d ed. (Boston, 1957); subsequent reference is to this edition.

5 "Febrvarie," v. 92, gloss, p. 27; "June," v. 81, gloss, p. 64; "December," v. 4, gloss, p. 118. The Envoy, without gloss, follows E. K.'s notes to the December Eclogue. It is conceivable that *Tityrus* refers to the "Romish Tityrus," Vergil ("October," v. 55), as well as to Chaucer, but in view of Spenser's unmistakable allusion to the *Troilus,* Chaucer cannot be excluded from the reference to Tityrus and must be considered the primary intention of it. Given the additional fact that E. K., who is our authority in this matter, has identified an unmodified Tityrus as Chaucer repeatedly before, Tityrus refers here without confusion (or conflation) to Chaucer, and only with it to Vergil.

6 The final line does not refer to the poet of *The Plowman's Tale* for these reasons: (1) The sixteenth century generally thought that Chaucer, i.e. Tityrus, had written *The Plowman's Tale;* (2) although some of its lines alliterate, *The Tale* is not written essentially or distinctively in alliterative verse; (3) it is implausible that Spenser would *single out* the relatively few and undistinguished verses of *The Tale*—rather than those of Langland, Skelton (whence, after all, Colin Clout), or another substantial poet—to represent one of the two poets whose steps he follows humbly; (4) reference to *The Tale* requires the harder reading of the line (see n. 7, below); thus, even if Spenser—unlike Thynne and Stowe, compilers of the editions of Chaucer which Spenser most likely read—realized that *The Tale* is non-Chaucerian work, we should have to strain to see him using his special knowledge in a cryptic

allusion here. For further discussion, see Edwin A. Greenlaw, "The Shepheards Calender," *PMLA* 26 (1911): 442, 444–45 n.; the introduction to *The Plowman's Tale* in *Chaucerian and Other Pieces,* ed. Walter W. Skeat (Oxford, 1897), pp. xxxi–xxxv; Alice S. Miskimin, *The Renaissance Chaucer* (New Haven, Conn., 1975), p. 249; cf. pp. 93, 290, on *Plowman's Tale,* allusions to which Spenser includes in his tribute to Chaucer; and A. Kent Hieatt, *Chaucer, Spenser, Milton: Mythopoeic Continuities and Transformations* (Montreal, 1975), p. 24.

7 An alternative but harder reading of the line awkwardly reverses the usual syntax of English to have Spenser not daring to vie with the plowman who played the role of a pilgrim for awhile. Greenlaw, *"Shepheards Calender,"* reading the line this way, interprets it as a reference to *Piers Plowman* because Piers says he will "apparaille" himself "in pilgrimes wise" (B.VI.59). Greenlaw does not mention a possible difficulty in the implication, in this case, that Piers was piping. Of course if Spenser shared the liberty of his contemporaries, William Webbe, Francis Meres, and Michael Drayton (whose knowledge of *Piers Plowman* is incontestable), in referring to the author of "The vision of Pierce Plowman" as Piers, no difficulty exists. (Skeat, EETS 81, 867–68, cites relevant passages in Webbe, Meres, Drayton.) In Spenser's time—indeed, until very recently—Langland's identity was a considerable puzzle; it served convenience for Spenser's contemporaries to refer to him in a form briefer than "He that made the booke called *Pierce Plowman*" (Fraunce, n. 2, above).

8 I should subscribe to Edgar Wind's apology in *Pagan Mysteries in the Renaissance,* rev. ed. (Middlesex, Eng.: Penguin, 1967), p. 238: "it seems to be a lesson of history that the commonplace may be understood as a reduction of the exceptional, but that the exceptional cannot be understood [merely] by amplifying the commonplace. Both logically and causally the exception is crucial, because it introduces . . . the more comprehensive category."

9 "Convention as Structure: The *Prologue* to the *Canterbury Tales,*" *Tradition and Poetic Structure* (Denver, 1960); rpt. in *Geoffrey Chaucer,* ed. J. A. Burrow (Baltimore, 1969), p. 221.

10 "The Visions of *Piers Plowman* and *The Faerie Queene,*" *Form and Convention in the Poetry of Edmund Spenser,* ed. William Nelson (New York, 1961), pp. 1–34; quotations below are from pp. 30–31.

11 Paul J. Alpers's important reassessment of rhetorical, as distinct from really visual, elements in Spenser's poetry is centrally responsible for this fact: pp. 11–19 of *The Poetry of "The Faerie Queene"* (Princeton, 1967) are especially pertinent. John B. Bender, *Spenser and Literary Pictorialism* (Princeton, 1972), modifies the definition of visual experience in *The Faerie Queene,* but his position is, as he explains, not sharply opposed to Alpers's (pp. 22–23 n.). He uses the word *visual* in a metaphorical sense that often means more generally and inclusively "perceptual" or even "conceptual."

12 In some instances the Kane-Donaldson edition (*Piers Plowman: The B Version,* London, 1975) uses a reading from manuscripts of the A-, B-, or C-texts which is neither in Crowley not in Skeat but was hypothetically available in manuscript to the sixteenth century; at other times its readings are conjectural.

CHAPTER I

1 "Construe ho-so wolde," the clause immediately preceding line 145, asks recognition of the ambiguity of the Latin here. E. Talbot Donaldson's suggestion that this passage reflects a coronation *ordo* indicates at least the possibility of reading the line affirmatively: *Piers Plowman: The C-Text and Its Poet* (New Haven, Conn., 1949), p. 118. D. W. Robertson, Jr., and Bernard F. Huppé note only an ironic intention in introducing the Rat Parliament: *Piers Plowman and Scriptural Tradition* (Princeton, 1951), p. 30. P. M. Kean, citing general but not precisely verbal similarities between the same line and traditional legal opinion, denies it any ironic intention; she leaves the significant word *vincula* unexplained: "Love, Law, and *Lewte* in *Piers Plowman*," *RES*, n.s. 15 (1964), rpt. in *Style and Symbolism in "Piers Plowman": A Modern Critical Anthology*, ed. Robert J. Blanch (Knoxville, Tenn., 1969), pp. 139–40. Such critical variance would appear to make the line's ambiguity even more obvious. Like several other verbally and politically ambiguous passages in the B-text, this one is omitted in C.

2 John Lawlor, "The Imaginative Unity of *Piers Plowman*," affords a generally accepted view of the poem; he emphasizes "the mind, not behind, but *in* the poem . . . a poem piercingly clear in its central issues . . . [yet] multiple in its implications": *RES*, n.s. 8 (1957), rpt. in *Style and Symbolism*, p. 114.

3 It is instructive to compare the shifting relations of Langland's words to realities (e.g. cardinal, *vincula legis*) with a more radical fragmentation (or more precise delimitation) of meaning in Martin Luther's *De Servo Arbitrio*: thus "Satan et homo . . . non possunt velle bonum, hoc est ea quae Deo placent aut quae Deus vult," even though "liberum arbitrium per conatum suum aliquo posse promoveri, videlicet ad opera bona vel ad iustitiam legis civilis vel moralis": *Werke: Kritische Gesamtausgabe* (Weimar, 1883–1948), 18: 709, 767. Luther refers to the Reformation belief in justification only by grace through faith; the wedge he drives between a good act (Dowel) and real or ultimate goodness is not unknown to Langland but is what the poet strives to find invalid and unreal.

4 Crowley reads *troweth* for *troneth.*

5 Crowley reads *for sinne* for *of heuene* (146), *of all* for *and . . . heuene* (149), *plant* for *plente* (150), *yoten it selue* for *yeten his fylle* (152), *cometh* for *comseth* (161), *wyll* for *welle* (162). In lines 150 and 152, where Crowley readings are essentially the same as Kane-Donaldson (and not unlike the C-text) and also make better sense than Skeat, I have inserted them. In the other instances Skeat is preferable to Crowley both on editorial and artistic grounds.

6 Ben H. Smith, Jr., *Traditional Imagery of Charity in "Piers Plowman"* (The Hague, 1966), pp. 21–40; and P. M. Kean, "Langland on the Incarnation," *RES*, n.s. 16 (1965): 349–63, trace the sources of imagery for this speech. Kean pays particular attention to the tradition behind the "plant of peace." The most suggestive biblical source is Isaiah 53 : 2, 5, as indicated by J. F. Goodridge, trans., *Piers the Ploughman*, by William Langland, rev. ed. (Baltimore, 1966), p. 266, n. 17.

7 On *Yoten* (152), see *OED*, s.v. *Yet v.*, 1, d; 3, a, b; also s.v. *Yoten*: the phrasing *yoten* itself *of the erthe* may loosely imply *infused* itself, as *OED* suggests, but more accurately means *cast, found*, hence *alloyed*, itself.

8 On "kynde knowyng," see Edward Vasta, *The Spiritual Basis of "Piers Plowman"*

(The Hague, 1965), pp. 87, 97: "Lady Church's claim that man naturally knows he ought to love God is important, because it means that love of God is already in the heart but is not aware of itself." See also Sister Mary Clemente Davlin, "*Kynde Knowyng* as a Major Theme in *Piers Plowman B, RES,* n.s. 22 (1971): 1–19; and Elizabeth D. Kirk, *The Dream Thought of "Piers Plowman"* (New Haven, Conn., 1972), pp. 37–38. In attempting to deal with Langland's terms, it is useful to remember that our lexical age tends to rationalize, to fix, the meanings of words rather than to experience, modify, and develop them. Words mean, of course, for Langland—indeed mean more than for us—but they mean gradually, fluidly, and fully only in the fullness of time and of the person.

9 Among medieval dream poems, a series of dreams, laced with inner dreams and with periodic waking intervals, is peculiar only to *Piers Plowman,* a fact to prove of interest in connection with *The Faerie Queene.* On medieval dream forms and theories, see Morton Bloomfield, *Piers Plowman as a Fourteenth-century Apocalypse* (New Brunswick, N.J., 1961), pp. 10–14; and Constance B. Hieatt, *The Realism of Dream Visions: The Poetic Exploitation of the Dream-Experience in Chaucer and his Contemporaries* (The Hague, 1967), passim. William B. Hunter, Jr., "Eve's Demonic Dream," *ELH* 13 (1946): 255–65, offers additional information on medieval, as well as Renaissance, interpretations of dreams.

CHAPTER 2

1 See *Var.,* 1: 173: Upton on the Vergilian echo.
2 Cf. Spenser's personalizing of convention in "Epithalamion" (e.g. fusing of the roles of poet and bridegroom).
3 I have discussed this limitation in "The July Eclogue and the House of Holiness: Perspective in Spenser," *SEL* 10 (1970): 17–32.
4 Spenser's narrative role has become a major subject of investigation in recent years. I have found the following widely varied treatments of particular interest: Alpers, *Poetry of "The Faerie Queene,"* pt. 1, passim, esp. pp. 9, 75–77, 95–98, and pt. 3, pp. 325–33; Harry Berger, Jr., "Spenser's *Faerie Queene,* Book 1: Prelude to Interpretation," *Southern Review: An Australian Journal of Literary Studies* 2 (1966): 18–49; and by the same author, "The Prospect of Imagination: Spenser and the Limits of Poetry," *SEL* 1 (1961): 93–120; Robert M. Durling, *The Figure of the Poet in Renaissance Epic* (Cambridge, Mass., 1965), pp. 1–10, 211–37; Kathleen Williams, "Vision and Rhetoric: The Poet's Voice in *The Faerie Queene,*" *ELH* 36 (1969): 131–44; Jerome S. Dees, "The Narrator of *The Faerie Queene,* Patterns of Response," *TSLL* 12 (1971): 537–68; Thomas H. Cain, "Spenser and the Renaissance Orpheus," *UTQ* 41 (1971): 24–47. Both my debts to these works—specifically to Berger and Alpers—and differences from them will be evident in succeeding pages.
5 *OED,* s.v. *Pride sb¹,* II. 7, 9. Cf. "proud humility" in "Epithalamion," v. 306; and "modest pride" in *Paradise Lost,* Bk. IV.310: John Milton, *Complete Poems and Major Prose,* ed. Merritt Y. Hughes (New York, 1957); future references to Milton are to this edition.
6 Cf. Alpers, *Poetry of "The Faerie Queene,"* pp. 5, 8, 14; or for a concise summary of Alpers's position, his article "Narrative and Rhetoric in *The Faerie Queene,*" *SEL* 2 (1962): 27–46. I have used the term "narrative presence" rather than such a phrase as "action of his poetry," which would work here, because I do not want all its

probable implications: I should not agree with Alpers that because stanza 7 contains the action of our minds narrative action has no actuality there and, more generally, that the unity of the poem is (unqualifiedly) in the reader's responses.

7   Cf. Donald Cheney, *Spenser's Image of Nature: Wild Man and Shepherd in "The Faerie Queene"* (New Haven, Conn., 1966), pp. 22–25. I do not agree, however, with Cheney's literal ascription of action (choice rather than experience, active projection rather than passive reception) to Redcrosse and Una: "they praise the trees," etc. (pp. 24–25).

8   The rainstorm is sent by an "angry *Ioue*," but pagan imagery in Book I is associated with the merely natural (both good and bad), i.e. pagan, until cantos x–xi. The reference to Jove does add another, more dangerous dimension to the rain; yet the poem has not as yet revealed just what this dimension signifies. Jove's violent, passionate relation to the Earth, his "Leman," or mistress (I.i.6), makes association of him with the Christian Deity most unlikely.

9   Matt. 7 : 13–14; *FQ* I.iv.2.

10 See *FQ* I.i.32, 55, 49; ii.4; also discussion of I.i–ii below, pp. 29 ff.

11 The presence of tensions in the tone of these stanzas finds support on other grounds in the investigations of Blossom Feinstein, *"The Faerie Queene* and Cosmogonies of the Near East," *JHI* 29 (1968): 531–50; and J. E. Hankins, *Source and Meaning in Spenser's Allegory: A Study of "The Faerie Queene"* (Oxford, 1971), pp. 137, 278, 285.

12 *FQ* I.i.34, vv. 8–9; 36, v. 6; 39, v. 2; 40, vv. 8–9; 36, v. 4; ii.I, v. 5; and see Cheney, *Spenser's Image of Nature,* pp. 29–31.

13 Cf. *FQ* I.i.22, vv. 3, 8–9; and I.i.23, vv. 5, 9.

14 Even if unprincipled, Morpheus is comically natural; in contrast, Archimago's activities associate sleep with inherent corruption and diabolic temptation; one of Archimago's sprites gets the dream from Morpheus, and another becomes the false Una. Two views of nature are present here—nature as weakened and vulnerable in Morpheus; nature as corrupt and perverse in Archimago.

15 Spenser refers especially, but not exclusively, to the vision of Una with Flora and the Graces as a "dream." But this single experience, or "dream," blends into the larger experience, or "dream," of which it is a part; it becomes personified and virtually synonymous with one of Archimago's sprites (I.i.46, vv.1–2; 55, vv. 6–9). We hear again of a "dream" at both the end of the third and the beginning of the fourth stages of illusion (I.i.55, ii.2). My usage will follow Spenser's—"dream" meaning at first the single stage, but after exposition of further stages, coming to mean the total experience at Archimago's.

16 *FQ* I.v.18, 17, 21, 11–12, 13–15; I.ii.24, i.19, 14, 36, 21.

17 *OED,* s.v. *Dream sb²,* 1–2. I have discussed the relation of cantos iv and v to canto i more fully in "Redcrosse and the Descent into Hell," *ELH* 36 (1969): 470–92.

18 While Redcrosse is washed in wine and oil and embalmed on every side, "sweet musicke" is dividing "most heauenly melody" (v.17). When Redcrosse fancies that he sees Una crowned by Flora in the dream of canto i, "the *Graces* seemed all to sing," and they dance "all around" (i.48). Given Spenser's interest in archaic words, the fact that the word *dream* also meant "gladness, mirth, rejoicing"; "music, minstrelsy, melody" in Middle English bears suggestively on both these dream sequences (*OED,* s.v. *Dream sb¹,* 1–2).

19 Archimago embodies a force within Redcrosse, but he is also an obvious allusion to

particular facts and forces in contemporary political and ecclesiastical history, as well as in biblical history. The same is even more obviously true of Error. Though Sans Joy is a pagan and the wounds he gives Redcrosse are merely the conditions of illusion, his significance is far more exclusively psychological than Error's or Archimago's.

20 Cf. *FQ* I.v.17.

21 William Nelson's comments on Renaissance interpretations of the forest in *Aeneid* VI are pertinent: "The Vergilian forest . . . becomes a figure variously signifying . . . the activities of this world, the passions of the body, the earthly or fleshly aspect of human life": *Poetry of Edmund Spenser: A Study* (New York, 1963); p. 159.

22 It is useful to recall George Herbert's need to qualify and very nearly to renounce art in *Jordan* II and *The Forerunners* (*Works,* ed. F. E. Hutchinson [Oxford, 1941]), and the profound ambivalence of Milton's attitude to pagan art and classical civilization generally, e.g. *Paradise Lost,* Bk. IV.205–311; *Paradise Regained,* Bk. IV.25 ff. Spenser's "special involvement" in canto v is subtler, perhaps more optimistic, by comparison; it is not so explicit, self-conscious, or nervous.

23 See Kathleen Williams, *Spenser's Faerie Queene: The World of Glass* (London, 1966), p. 14; Alpers, *Poetry of "The Faerie Queene,"* p. 347.

24 Cf. *FQ* I.ix.41. The rhetoric and sentiments of Despair's speeches are also markedly classical: see Kathrine Koller, "Art, Rhetoric, and Holy Dying in the *Faerie Queene,* with special reference to the Despair Canto," *SP* 61 (1964): 130–31, 134–39.

25 Lines 58–63 of Milton's "Lycidas," which likewise employ classical myth (Orpheus), provide a familiar instance of such figurative transcription. The instance in canto v is *like* such a transcription; that is, Spenser has written a narrative, not simply a lyric, or more precisely, he has written a poem which at times (and progressively) combines narrative and lyrical elements in ways which recall and anticipate other poets' achievements but which remain his own, perhaps uniquely.

26 Douglas Bush, *Mythology and the Renaissance Tradition in English Poetry* (Minneapolis, 1932), p. 112 n., suggests that Seneca is the primary source for Spenser's treatment. Henry Gibbons Lotspeich, *Classical Mythology in the Poetry of Edmund Spenser* (1932; rpt. New York, 1965), pp. 69–70, sees Boccaccio as Spenser's main source. Both views are probably right, for Boccaccio himself calls our attention specifically to Seneca: "Esto poetae omnes: & signanter tragoedus Seneca in tragoedia euisdem Hippoliti laceratum atque discerptum omnem asserant & occisum": *Genealogiae Deorum Gentilium Joannis Boccatii . . .* Libri *XV* (Vincenza, Italy, 1487), Bk. x.50.

27 *Seneca's Tragedies,* trans. Frank Justus Miller, 2 vols. (New York: Loeb, 1917), I: 1209–11, 100–03, 112–14; 162–63, 181–84. See also the Nurse's criticism of Hippolytus's failure to love (478 ff.) and Hippolytus's naïve tendency to think that he can live in this world as in a paradise (525 ff.). Miller's translation of *Hippolytus* is reasonably close to Seneca's text and closer to canto v than is the awkward translation by John Studley in the 1581 edition of *Seneca, His Tenne Tragedies* in *The Tenne Tragedies of Seneca,* Spenser Society rpt. (Manchester, Eng., 1887).

28 Cf. the use of pagan imagery in *FQ* I.viii.9 and in xi.33, 51. In the last instance, which canto x adumbrates, such imagery fully reflects the positive effects of redemption (Alpers, *Poetry of "The Faerie Queene,"* pp. 361–69). The significance of Spenser's combining classical and biblical imagery in canto x is further illuminated

by Wind, *Pagan Mysteries in the Renaissance,* pp. 81–83; and James E. Phillips, "Spenser's Syncretistic Religious Imagery," *ELH* 36 (1969): 110–30.

29 Note again the Proem to Book I and the poet's role in hell, canto v. The assertions of the Proem are hopeful and very ambitious yet are tempered by a diffidence which now, in retrospect, becomes much more than *merely* decorous—that is, now becomes decorous in the fully realized moral sense.

30 Referring to II.viii.12, 13, 27, 28, A. C. Hamilton finds a Spenserian pun in the word *carcas,* that is, "fallen flesh" (presumably from *caro* and *cado*): "Our New Poet: Spenser, 'Well of English Undefyld,' " *Essential Articles for the Study of Edmund Spenser,* ed. A. C. Hamilton (Hamden, Conn.: Archon, 1972), p. 501. If Hamilton's suggestion applies to Contemplation's "carcas," it does not cancel the more obvious and familiar meanings active in this passage: *OED,* s.v. *Carcass:* (1) "The dead body," (2) "The living body considered in its material nature," (3) "in application to the human body, dead or alive, [since 1528] it has gradually come to be a term of contempt, ridicule, or indignity"; (4) *fig.* "the lifeless shell or husk."

31 Also *FQ* I.ii.28; ix.51, 53; and n. 21 in this chapter.

32 Una stands at the conclusion of the particular process, the particular stage of the journey which is Book I. In this role she further suggests (symbolizes) absolute unity, even though she more fully actualizes continuity in the poem. Cf. Harry Berger, Jr., "The Spenserian Dynamics," *SEL* 8 (1968): 4, 10.

33 These ambiguities are discussed in detail in chap. 8, pp. 201 ff.

34 The word *shortly* has as imprecise a meaning as the other temporal references in canto x; *in good time* or *in best time* would be suitable equivalents.

35 For the pun *site / sight,* see A. Bartlett Giamatti, *The Earthly Paradise and the Renaissance Epic* (Princeton, 1966), p. 240.

36 *FQ* VI.v.37; vi.3–4; ix.24–31 (Hermit and Melibee) also echo these same lines from Books I and VII, a fact suggesting that the echoes cited here arise from more than mere chance. (In view of the emotion and importance, the memorable qualities, of these passages, mere chance hardly seems a credible explanation in any case.) The role of memory in reading *The Faerie Queene* has cogently been questioned: Alpers, *Poetry of "The Faerie Queene,"* pp. 124–33. But Alpers's questions raise others. On which reading does "the reader" come into being, or which reading do we describe, if that is what we do in criticism? I now remember names, details of plot, stylistic flourishes, words of the poem fairly well. Admittedly these memories expand, even alter, the meaning of the poem for me. Frances A. Yates's study of the Renaissance interest in memory and training in its techniques—*The Art of Memory* (Chicago, 1966)—bears on theoretical questions about the nature of Spenser's poem and practical questions about our reading of it.

37 A number of studies have drawn analogies between the techniques of allegory in *The Faerie Queene* and the phenomena of dreams: notably, Edwin Honig, *Dark Conceit: The Making of Allegory* (Evanston, Ill., 1959), pp. 68–81, et passim; Angus Fletcher, *Allegory: The Theory of a Symbolic Mode* (Ithaca, N.Y., 1964), pp. 348–49, et passim. I do not share the concern of these stimulating works with psychoanalytic realism, whether as origin, effect, or symptom. I refer to the dream as metaphor, deliberate subject, or convention, and ultimately to the relation of metaphor, subject, and convention to the poet's role as consciously expressed in

the poem. Cf. also Graham Hough, *A Preface to "The Faerie Queene"* (New York, 1963), pp. 98, 135–36; and Robert Rawdon Wilson's strictures on Hough's views: "The Deformation of Narrative Time in *The Faerie Queene*," *UTQ* 41 (1971): 55–56.

CHAPTER 3

1 The ·B-text of *Piers Plowman* has the following sections: Prologue, Visio (Passūs I–VII); Vita de Dowel (Passūs VIII–XIV), Vita de Dobet (Passūs XV–XVIII), Vita de Dobest (Passūs XIX–XX).

2 *PP* v.62, 186–87; VII.109, III.64–90; see also VI.321–32.

3 I have discussed this progression in "The Knight and the Palmer in *The Faerie Queene*, Book II," *MLQ* 31 (1970): 160–78.

4 Critical discussion of the Cave has recently been so extended as to make the assumption of a large body of common knowledge both possible and necessary. An equally large debt to recent discussions is present in this assumption, particularly to Harry Berger, Jr., *The Allegorical Temper: Vision and Reality in Book II of Spenser's "Faerie Queene"* (New Haven, Conn., 1957), esp. pp. 3–38; Frank Kermode, "The Cave of Mammon," *Elizabethan Poetry*, ed. John Russell Brown and Bernard Harris, Stratford-Upon-Avon Studies, vol. 2 (London, 1960), rpt. in *The Prince of Poets: Essays on Edmund Spenser*, ed. John R. Elliott, Jr. (New York, 1968), pp. 256–80; Alpers, *Poetry of "The Faerie Queene*," pp. 235–75. K. Williams, *Spenser's Faerie Queene*, pp. 56–62; and M. Pauline Parker, *The Allegory of the "Faerie Queene"* (Oxford, 1960), pp. 129–35, have also proved helpful. In addition to important refinements of the three major interpretations of the Cave (first cited), penetrating summaries and assessments of earlier work can be found in Patrick Cullen, "Guyon Microchristus: The Cave of Mammon Re-examined," *ELH* 37 (1970): 153–74, now recast for his book, *Infernal Triad: The Flesh, the World, and the Devil in Spenser and Milton* (Princeton, 1974), which appeared after this discussion was completed; A. Kent Hieatt, "Three Fearful Symmetries and the Meaning of Faerie Queene II," *A Theatre for Spenserians*, ed. Judith M. Kennedy and James A. Reither (Toronto, 1973), pp. 19–52; Humphrey Tonkin, "Discussing Spenser's Cave of Mammon," *SEL* 13 (1973): 1–13. Since my purpose in treating the Cave is to describe areas and elements analogous to *Piers Plowman*, I shall minimize references to controversies about its more arcane details.

5 Cf. the attraction of false Una as Flora in *FQ* I.i.48 and the "pleasure," "sweete harmony," and "delight" of the Wandering Wood, the experiences which lie behind the dream in I.v (see chap. 2). Our response to the poetic authority of canto vii is more guarded, more swiftly, easily negative than in these passages from Book I. The exchange between Duessa and Night is also more deceptive; the Redcrosse Knight fundamentally and sinfully has lost control of himself in I.v. He is dislocated to an extent that neither Guyon nor the reader is in the Cave of Mammon.

6 The fact that *thee* is a second-person singular form indicates that the narrator speaks here as if addressing Guyon (who was never meant to hear him) and clearly not that he abruptly and familiarly addresses the reader. His cry is part of his own situation and of the reader's experience, however. It is a foretaste, worthy of Langland, of what is to come, and we fully appreciate it only in retrospect or on repeated reading.

7   The link between Tantalus and Pilate has proved difficult. The two appear virtually
     interchangeable in terms of blood-guilt (Pelops and Christ) and in terms of theft,
     perhaps directly from the gods on Tantalus's part, but more generally insofar as
     both figures are notable descendants of the archetypal thief Adam (after Lucifer).
     The thief sins against God by usurpation or denial, by Tantalus's self-seeking or
     Pilate's self-protection—that is, by theft or hoarding—and thus he follows Mammon.
     (The figure of Robert the Robber in *PP* v.469 ff. is instructive; he directly succeeds
     the confessions of the Deadly Sins, for his trade is the biblically historic and symbolic
     summation of them all. See also the Patristic citations on theft in Cullen, "Guyon
     Microchristus," p. 157; and Barbara Raw, "Piers and the Image of God in Man,"
     Piers Plowman: Critical Approaches, ed. S. S. Hussey [London, 1969], pp. 151–52.)
     Whether seen as greed, injustice, pride, or all three, Tantalus's and Pilate's thefts
     are blasphemous forms of selfishness, expressions of the essence of Mammon and
     his Cave, parodies of what is godlike by exhibiting a human materialism which
     denies the spirit. Both figures lie, appropriately, beyond the apple tree (*malus*),
     whose fruit, whatever its material basis, is *malum* simply.

8   *Institutes of the Christian Religion,* trans. Ford Lewis Battles, ed. John T. McNeill,
     2 vols. (London, 1961), vol. 1, Bk. II.i.1–3; for Calvin's original Latin, see *Corpus
     Reformatorum, Opera Calvini,* 59 vols. (Brunswick, 1863–1900), vols. 29–30. See
     also "A Pathway Into the Holy Scripture," written by Tyndale under Lutheran
     influence and relevant both in part to Guyon and in part to Tantalus and to the
     plants, poisonous or symbolizing death, in the Garden of Proserpina: the law
     "only setteth man at variance with God . . . and stirreth him to rail on God, and to
     blaspheme him as a cruel tyrant. For it is not possible for a man, till he be born
     again, to think that God is righteous to make him of so poison a nature, either for
     his own pleasure or for the sin of another man, and to give him a law that is impos-
     sible for him to do, or to consent to; his wit, reason, and will being . . . chained
     unto the will of the devil": *The Work of William Tyndale,* ed. G. E. Duffield (Phil-
     adelphia, 1965), p. 14, cf. pp. 10–15, 17–18. (Subsequent references to Tyndale and
     Calvin are to the editions given here.)

9   J. B. Broadbent's discussion of the nature of Adam's and Eve's innocence in *Paradise
     Lost* is suggestive with respect to Guyon's growing awareness in II.vii: *Some Graver
     Subject: An Essay on Paradise Lost* (New York, 1960), pp. 170, 184–87, 192. Guyon's
     faerie—mythic, nonhistorical—status makes it credible for the poet to keep human
     depths and complexities at a controlled, though progressively decreasing, remove
     from his cognizance.

10   *OED,* s.v. *Regard sb,* II.6–8. Cf. *FQ* I.i.21 and III.vi.8.

11   Spenser's knowledge of Machiavelli and apparent regard for certain of his views
     bear on the seriousness of issues raised both in this exchange and in the debate as a
     whole. See "A vewe of the present state of Irelande," *Var.,* 10: 229, 410, 429, and
     s.v. "Machiavelli," 560; also Edwin A. Greenlaw, "The Influence of Machiavelli
     on Spenser," *MP* 7 (1909): 187–202; and Felix Raab, *The English Face of Machiavelli*
     (London, 1964), pp. 61–76.

12   E.g., "Nichomachean Ethics," trans. W. D. Ross, in *Introduction to Aristotle,* ed.
     Richard McKeon (New York, 1947), IV.i.1120a 32–34, 1121a 30–33—1121b 1–4;
     all references are to this edition (hereinafter referred to as *Nic. Eth.*).

13   See the distinctions between Books I and II posited by A. D. S. Fowler, "The

Image of Mortality: *The Faerie Queene,* II.i–ii," *HLQ* 24 (1961): 109; Maurice Evans, "The Fall of Guyon," *ELH* 28 (1961): 223; Cullen, "Guyon *Microchristus,*" pp. 172–74.

14 See *FQ* II.viii.7, where Guyon is described as the Palmer's "pupill," and Aristotle's discussion of Temperance in terms of a child/tutor relationship: *Nic. Eth.* III.12.1119b 14–16. Book II is an education for Guyon—a very basic one.

15 Crowley reads *world* for *grounde* and *lykned* for *like.*

16 Crowley omits *fende . . . the.*

17 See Jacques Maritain, *Moral Philosophy: An Historical and Critical Survey of the Great Systems,* English language ed. (New York, 1964), p. 49: "In spite of everything," Aristotle's "moral teaching leaves us enclosed in love of ourselves." The pertinence of Tyndale, "Pathway," p. 18, is likewise striking: The law, by which a man's moral impotence by mere nature is shown to him, "pulleth from a man the trust and confidence that he hath in himself, and in his own works, merits, deservings . . . and robbeth him of all his righteousness, and maketh him poor. It killeth him, sendeth him down to hell, and bringeth him to utter desperation, and prepareth the way of the Lord. . . . For it is not possible that Christ should come to a man, as long as he trusteth in himself."

18 E.g. *PP* XVIII.159, 284, 289–90, 332, 337, 345, 351–59. Shifts in context, and concomitantly in the meaning of symbols as time unfolds, are characteristic of many theological allegories, though nowhere as profoundly and dramatically characteristic of an earlier poem as of Langland's.

19 Esp. *PP* v.614–16, 620–23, 625 (my italics):

> And if Grace graunte the to go in in this wise,
> Thow shalt see *in thi-selue Treuthe sitte in thine herte*
> In a cheyne of charyte, as thow a childe were . . .

But if you become proud "to prayse thi-seluen,"

> *The boldnesse of thi bienfetes maketh the blynde thanne,*
> And thanne worstow dryuen oute as dew, and the dore closed,
> Kayed and cliketed to kepe the with-outen [that is, out of
>   "thi-selue"] . . .

Having already made the connection between such self-loss and Adam's sin, the passage continues, "Thus myght thow lesen his loue to late wel by thi-selue." *Var.,* 2: 286, 456, suggests a connection between Langland's Castle of Conscience, to which these lines refer, and Spenser's House of Alma (II.ix).

20 "De Libero Arbitrio Diatribe sive Collatio Desiderii Erasmi Roterodami," *Omnia Opera* (Basel, Froben printing, 1540), IX, 1016: "sed quoniam minimum hoc est, quod per nos agitur, totum deo transcribitur, quemadmodum nauita qui nauim in portum deduxit e graui tempestate incolumem, non dicit, ego seruaui nauim, sed deus seruauit. . . ." Skeat, *PP,* 2: 133, n. 32, refers the friar's parable to the Bible, to St. Augustine (among others), and to *The Kalender of Shepherdes* (1656 edition). Skeat describes the illustration in *The Kalender* and gives one sentence of accompanying text. An earlier edition of *The Kalender* I have consulted carries a variant text under the identical illustration, which shows a fiend behind the steersman (cf. Mammon's fiend behind Guyon) who wants to upset or to wreck the boat.

The text reads: "Man mortel lyuant in thys world qwych is lyknyt to oon shyp aboue the see . . . berand rych marchandys the qwych may cum to the port that the marchant desyrys he shal be happy and rych. The shyp of the qwych entrys in the see wnto the eynd of ys woyage day and nyght ys contynwelly in peryl to be drownyt robyt or takyn of ys ennemys. . . . Sych in the body of man lyuant in the world the marchandys that yt berys ys the saowlys wertus and good werkys. The port ys the deeth and paradys for the good pewpyl to the qwych he that cumys thayr to ys sowerantly rych. The se is the world ful of synnys that he qwych sayl3ys to pas he is in peryl to leys the body and the saowl and al ys goodys and to be drownyt in the see of hel of the qwych god keyp ws": *The Kalender of Shepherdes,* ed. H. Oskar Sommer, 3 vols. (London, 1892), 2: f iiii$^{2-3}$, cf. 3: 80-81. (Vol. 2 is a facsimile of the Paris edition of 1503; vol. 3 is a reprint of R. Pynson's London edition of 1506, based on the Paris edition, and although in better English, much less pertinent to *FQ* II.vii.)

21 E.g. see Robert Kellogg and Oliver Steele, eds. *Books I and II of The Faerie Queene* . . . , by Edmund Spenser (New York, 1965), pp. 302 n., 310–11 n.

22 Cf. Kirk's discussion of the Sins, *Dream Thought,* pp. 51–61: I should agree that the Sins' reformation becomes less credible with each confession, but should add that their efforts to repent and to reform, taken singly or together, are, in contrast to Meed's effortless corruption, an optimistic step forward in the poem.

23 The diagram is reproduced as the frontispiece of *The Macro Plays,* ed. Mark Eccles, EETS 262 (London, 1969); references to *The Castle* are to this edition.

24 This is not to deny that *The Castle* entertained and engrossed its original audience, but to suggest the special and limited nature of its moral and artistic appeal. A justly celebrated legend on the staging diagram of *The Castle* directs that the actor playing Belial "loke þat he haue gunnepowdyr brennynge In pypys in hys handys and in hys erys and in hys ars whanne he gothe to batayl" (p. 1): this devil must have been as much fun as fireworks at a family picnic on the Fourth of July, but this is the fun of complicity.

25 Whatever else the silver stool signifies—scholars are in considerable disagreement— it includes sloth, traditionally identified with despair (as in *PP* v.392–468 [*Accidia*], xx.156–59). Mammon explicitly offers "rest" for Guyon's "wearie person" when he offers the stool. Cf. i.v.35, v. 8: as Book 1 demonstrates, a person gets to sloth and despair by way of the House of Pride. See Harry Rusche, "Pride, Humility, and Grace in Book 1 of *The Faerie Queene,*" *SEL* 7 (1967): 29–39: "Despair, like all the sins that threaten the Christian's quest for salvation, is a result of the egocentrism created by pride" (38–39). Although aimed at Book 1, this article affords a gloss on the closeness of Tantalus and Pilate to the silver seat, Mammon's final offer to Guyon.

26 See A. G. Mitchell, "Lady Meed and the Art of *Piers Plowman,*" University College, London; Chambers Memorial Lecture, 1956; rpt. in *Style and Symbolism,* pp. 174–93: "the apparent mixed nature of Meed . . . is not merely Skeat's or Chambers's imagination, not something that confuses the portrayal, but something insisted upon by Langland himself" (175).

27 Crowley reads *vpward* for *homeward.*

28 Crowley may have found Conscience's distinction fuzzy: his second and third printings read *pore* for *lowe,* even though his first printing reads *lowe.*

29 Mitchell, "Lady Meed," pp. 183–84, understands Conscience's rejection of Meed here by placing emphasis not on the moral condition of laborers and low folk but on the principle of measurable hire. The rejection is thus entirely rational for him. Mitchell argues that Conscience does not distinguish between two kinds of reward, the one heavenly and the other earthly; he apparently takes "an-other mede mesurelees" (245) to mean another besides God's measureless meed, a reading which he grants is different from what Conscience first seems to say. In both cases, he takes meed not as something given but as a principle of giving, one without measure. In this way, meed is banished from merely human affairs. Mitchell's explanation works backward expansively from a principle which Langland's Conscience seems to stumble on, if not to trip over, only at the end. It is a brilliant rationalization of what Conscience actually says, yet I doubt that "measure" is the fundamental answer that Langland's Conscience gives—or can give—us.

   If a rational distinction based on measure resolved the real problem of man's nature —which the verbal and conceptual difficulties of Conscience's speech reflect—we might expect different responses from those paid measurably in plowing Piers's half-acre, and would not expect the problem of alms to be so difficult of resolution there. It is possible that Langland found the reason to alter Conscience's distinctions radically only in the C-text. In revising, he omits the troublesome first distinction (Mitchell's connection) between a heavenly and an earthly meed and greatly expands and modifies the conclusion, the mere opposition of measurable hire to meed; here a grammatical analogy, which is lacking in B, supplies a significant *positive* relation between God's ways *and* means and man's, and the verbal-conceptual difficulties in B are avoided by the introduction of dual terms, *mede* and *mercede,* at the outset.

30 Guyon's "myth," of course, is not specifically biblical; Conscience's use of the distant past, on the other hand, is less inclusively mythic, more exclusively historical, than Guyon's.

31 "The Problem of Free Will in the Renaissance and the Reformation," *JHI*, vol. 10 (1949), rpt. in *Renaissance Essays from the "Journal of the History of Ideas,"* ed. Paul Oskar Kristeller and Philip P. Wiener (New York, 1968), p. 194.

FOREWORD TO PART II

1 G. J. Whitrow, *The Natural Philosophy of Time* (1961; rpt. New York, 1963), p. 96.
2 This development is probably not wholly chronological with respect to the composition of *The Faerie Queene*. See p. 98 and n. 4, chap. 5.
3 R. W. Chambers, *Man's Unconquerable Mind* (London, 1939), p. 136, and Donaldson, *Piers Plowman: The C-Text and Its Poet*, p. 173, attribute the whole passage to the Dreamer. Robert Worth Frank, Jr., *"Piers Plowman" and the Scheme of Salvation* (New Haven, 1957), p. 60 n., argues Trajan is the speaker. Skeat, *PP,* 2: 176, and John Lawlor, *"Piers Plowman": An Essay in Criticism* (London, 1962), p. 138 n., assign it to Lewte. In an essay intended to establish the firm control of a poet "quite separable from his *persona*" in Passūs IX–XII, Joseph S. Wittig assigns the passage in question to Lewte but suggests that it might belong to a deliberate fusion of Trajan with Lewte: *"Piers Plowman* B, Passus IX–XII; Elements in the Design of the Inward Journey," *Traditio,* 28 (1972): 255 n., 279. Kirk, *Dream Thought,* p. 136, argues that the passage is probably Scripture's. Mary Carruthers, *The Search for St. Truth: A*

Study of Meaning in "Piers Plowman" (Evanston, Ill., 1973), p. 99, sees Trajan as an "obvious choice" but regards the problem of attribution as "insoluble."

4   Chambers's theory (pp. 129–48) is immensely appealing; it rationalizes the poet's confusion without attempting to make these passages entirely satisfactory as art. Perhaps Hamlet's "antic" speeches or Lear's madness are contrasting cases in point; there is artistic control, however complex, in either. Cf. Kirk, p. 120, and on the more general question of relationship between poet and poem or poet and Dreamer, see the crucial chapter on "Signatures" in George Kane, *Piers Plowman: The Evidence for Authorship* (London, 1965), esp. pp. 61–65.

5   Cf. Elizabeth Salter and Derek Pearsall, eds., *Piers Plowman*, by William Langland (Evanston, Ill., 1967), pp. 31–32; and Charles Muscatine, *"Piers Plowman:* The Poetry of Crisis," *Poetry and Crisis in the Age of Chaucer* (Notre Dame, Ind., 1972), pp. 91–92. (The latter provides a judicious review of major critical approaches to the poem.)

CHAPTER 4

1   Reason is the faculty but also the reason and the attitude which Reason produces. The Reason of xi.367 ff. *is* in accord with Kind and actually—also ironically, in view of Will's rebuke—shows enigmatic signs of His Wisdom:

> Whi I suffre or nou3t suffre thi-self hast nou3t to done;
> Amende thow it, if thow my3te, for my tyme is to abyde.
> Suffraunce is a souereygne vertue and a swyfte veniaunce.
>
> [xi.368–70]

See Acts 1 : 7 "Dixit [Christus] autem eis: Non est vestrum nosse tempora vel momenta, quae Pater posuit in sua potestate"; also Matt. 24 : 6, John 2 : 4, and esp. 7 : 3–8: "... Nemo quippe in occulto quid facit, et quaerit ipse in palam esse: Si haec facis, manifesta teipsum mundo.... Dicit ergo eis Iesus: Tempus meum nondum advenit: tempus autem vestrum semper est paratum...." Goodridge, trans., *Piers the Ploughman*, p. 290, n. 49, refers v. 369 to 1 Cor. 4 : 5; Skeat, *PP*, 2 : 177, refers v. 370 to Luke 18 : 7. We might infer from Reason's words that a truly reasonable attitude is informed by revelation and likewise that Reason enables one to see revelation more clearly: cf. Étienne Gilson, *Reason and Revelation in the Middle Ages* (New York, 1938), esp. chapter 1. More significantly, Langland's dramatization of the enlightened, or higher, Reason, whose words end the Dreamer's inner sleep, suggests that Reason is the medium of revelation. Cf. *PP*, C xiv.193–94, where Reason distinctly resembles the image, or reflection, of God. (When cited in connection with Langland, biblical references are to the Vulgate.)

2   This is presumably why the adjective *Imaginatyf*, rather than the noun *Imaginacioun*, is used in the poem, and why Imaginative emerges, as it were, out of Reason's presence, conspicuously sharing the conclusion of Passus xi with him. On the relation of imagination to memory, see Bloomfield, *Fourteenth-century Apocalypse*, pp. 59, 171–72; Joseph A. Longo, *"Piers Plowman* and the Tropological Matrix: Passūs xi and xii," *Anglia* 82 (1964): 302; H. S. V. Jones, "Imaginatif in *Piers Plowman, JEGP* 13 (1914): 586–88.

3   Cf. Lawlor, *"Piers Plowman": An Essay*, pp. 113–15. I have also benefited from Wittig's learned discussion of the term *imaginative, "Piers Plowman* B," pp. 264–73; he sees imaginative as an activity involving "the whole psyche," rather than as a single

faculty, and defines this term as "actively or vividly representing to oneself." The more specifically constructive and memorial emphasis of Randolph Quirk's definition—"creative reflection"—nevertheless remains essential to an understanding of the nature of Imaginative's Function in Passus XI: "Vis Imaginativa," *JEGP* 53 (1954): 81–83.

4 "Know-how" is perhaps a useful modern gloss for the term *Clergye*, although what is known in this case must be learned or acquired rather than instinctive or, strictly speaking, inherent. *Clergy* includes clerics and their power to baptize, consecrate, etc. See *OED*, s.v. *Clergy*, I.2, 2a: "The clerical order" as a "body of men" or "construed as *collective plural*"; I.5: " 'Clerkly skill'; learning, scholarship, science."

5 Crowley's second and third printings read *vir* for *vix;* his first printing reads *vix*.

6 James 5 : 7–11. See also Étienne Gilson, *The Christian Philosophy of St. Thomas Aquinas*, trans. L. K. Shook (New York, 1956), pp. 344–45 and 490, n. 30: *Summa Theologica*, pt. II–II, q. 136, a.3, where Aquinas draws directly on Augustine's *De Patientia*.

7 The reading *bouste* (box) for Skeat's and Crowley's *aboute* (XIII.152) is taken from the Kane-Donaldson edition. On the contents of Patience's box, see Smith, *Traditional Imagery of Charity*, pp. 41–55.

8 Cf. Ruth M. Ames, *The Fulfillment of the Scriptures: Abraham, Moses, and Piers* (Evanston, Ill., 1970), p. 175: Clergy's offer to Conscience identifies Clergy's learning with the Old Law at this point.

9 *PP* XX.227, 373.

10 "Langland's Use of *Kynde Wit* and *Inwit*," *JEGP* 52 (1953): 187–88. Like Willi Erzgräber (*William Langlands "Piers Plowman": Eine Interpretation des C-Textes* [Heidelberg, 1957], pp. 118–19), Britton J. Harwood and Ruth F. Smith ("Inwit and the Castle of *Caro* in *Piers Plowman*," *NM* 71 [1970]: 648–54) indentify inwit with synderesis, but as a separate faculty rather than as a perfection of reason. Their refinement is persuasive but does not affect essentially the accuracy of Quirk's discussion: conscience remains inwit in action; and at least for practical purposes, inwit itself remains an aspect of intellect. See also Bloomfield, *Fourteenth-century Apocalypse*, pp. 64, 111–12, 168; and for a recent and comprehensive treatment of Conscience, see Mary C[arruthers] Schroeder, "The Character of Conscience in *Piers Plowman*," *SP* 67 (1970): 13–30.

11 *OED*, s.v. *Conscience*, I.1. See also Schroeder, "Character of Conscience," p. 16: "if *inwit* could be confused with conscience [Quirk, "Kynde Wit and Inwit," p. 187] conscience could also be confused with *inwit* and mean 'consciousness,' 'inward knowledge,' or 'mind' " (three definitions of conscience in *OED*).

12 This is essentially the point made by Stella Maguire, "The Significance of Haukyn, *Activa Vita*, in *Piers Plowman*," *RES* vol. 25 (1949), rpt. in *Style and Symbolism*, pp. 194–208.

13 As was not the case with Piers's sudden emergence in Passus V.

14 Hawkin is mentioned, remembered, in XVI.2 but does not appear as a character.

15 Crowley reads *hym* for *me* and *his* for *my*. Interestingly, however, he makes no effort to rationalize the shifts in person in Hawkin's confession. We might conjecture that an isolated discrepancy seemed merely accidental to him but that patterned, or even recurrent, discrepancies suggested poetic purpose or textual authority.

16 Cf. the pronominal "slippage" in *FQ* I.i, discussed in chap. 2, p. 30. I have else-

where suggested that Martha Craig's demonstration of ties between Spenser's "philosophic realism" and his use of language ("The Secret Wit of Spenser's Language," *Elizabethan Poetry: Modern Essays in Criticism,* ed. Paul J. Alpers [Oxford, 1967], pp. 449–53) might be expanded by reference to the late-classic/medieval grammarians: see "Whatever Happened to Amoret? The Poet's Role in Book IV of *The Faerie Queene,*" *Criticism* 13 (1971): 191–92. The same suggestion pertains forcefully to Langland, whose poem tells us grammar is "the grounde of al" (xv.365); like Spenser's, his apparently careless handling of pronouns in certain contexts may well be rational: e.g. "Donatus says that the pronoun is a part of speech which, set in the place of a noun . . . sometimes assumes person as matter assumes form. And because a pronoun cannot have a definition except by analogy with form as in the case of first matter, Priscian says . . . that the pronoun is a part of speech which is taken in place of a proper name of any substance . . .": taken from *The Summa Modorum Significandi of Siger de Courtrai,* trans. Sister John Marie (St. Louis, Mo., 1943), p. 115. Carruthers, *Search for St. Truth,* p. 119, interprets the pronominal "slippage" in Hawkin's speech to mean that the spots on his coat are speaking.

17 E.g. *PP* vii.181, iii.69; cf. v.17, i.173.

18 The views in this paragraph are particularly congenial to a figural reading of the Pardon Scene; e.g. Ames, *Fulfillment of the Scriptures,* p. 50; Mary C[arruthers] Schroeder, "*Piers Plowman:* The Tearing of the Pardon," *PQ* 49 (1970): 8–18. Cf. also J. A. Burrow on "Langland's attitude to his image" in "Words, Works and Will: Theme and Structure in *Piers Plowman,*" *Critical Approaches,* esp. pp. 120–22. For a significantly different approach to the enigmas of the Pardon Scene, see Kirk, *Dream Thought,* chap. 3; but I should question the emphasis of this provocative reading on the inner responses, or psychology, of Piers himself, and its developing Will's relation to Piers so fully in the Visio, i.e. so early in the poem.

CHAPTER 5

1 E.g. see Alpers, *Poetry of "The Faerie Queene,"* p. 299; and Roger Sale, *Reading Spenser: An Introduction to "The Faerie Queene"* (New York, 1968), pp. 161 ff. Both derogate the quality of Books IV–VI.

2 The final phrase of the alexandrine is not in Tasso, Spenser's direct source for the Song of the Rose (*Var.,* 2: 388–89). Without the characterization informing a Satan or Volpone, the alexandrine, though attributed to the singer (the anonymous "some one"), must remain intrusive—a problem of artistic judgment, if not of moral intention.

3 Harry Berger, Jr., "Book I: Prelude," pp. 24–25. Alpers (*Poetry of "The Faerie Queene,"* pp. 26–29) finds Spenser's "extravagance" in this passage entirely successful and not in the least ironic. (The fact that the passage shows Ariosto's influence further complicates it, although I think not significantly in this case.) K. Williams, "Vision and Rhetoric," pp. 138–39, and Dees, "Narrator of *The Faerie Queene,*" pp. 541, 563–64, afford still other explanations, although they do not discuss this passage directly. Taken together, their views—roughly that Spenser's narrator is a chameleon with respect to story, audience, inspiring vision—persuasively explain a large part of his role in the early Books but do not address the possibility that such a role might (indeed does) at times create artistic difficulties.

More importantly, they do not take into account the great extent to which Spenser's role evolves.

4   See Josephine Waters Bennett, *The Evolution of "The Faerie Queene"* (Chicago, 1942), pp. 1–46, 152–53.

5   See *FQ* II.xii.82, v. 8; the allusion to Verdant in III.i comes only fifteen stanzas later. Surely this is not an accidental echo of a proper name.

6   Guyon's horse is associated with his heroic passions and aspirations in Book II.

7   *FQ* III.ii.4 reads "Guyon," presumably an error for "Redcrosse": see III.ii.16, and the quatrain introducing this canto.

8   Cf. Kathleen Williams, Spenser's *Faerie Queene*, pp. 80–95; and her "Venus and Diana: Some Uses of Myth in *The Faerie Queene*," *ELH*, vol. 28 (1961), rpt. in *Essential Articles*, pp. 202–19.

9   Durling speaks of Ariosto's "absolute dominion" of his poem and distinguishes it from Spenser's general position: *Figure of the Poet*, p. 216.

10 In discussing Book III, my debt to Alpers is considerable (*Poetry of "The Faerie Queene*," pp. 377–97). Although my purposes and many of my readings differ from his, in order to pursue them I cannot avoid some repetition of material he has covered.

11 Preceding quotation is from *The Discovery of the Mind: The Greek Origins of European Thought*, trans. T. G. Rosenmeyer (1953; rpt. New York, 1960), pp. 200–01. The traditional Petrarchan imagery of Britomart's complaint is refreshed and illuminated in the context of her history. (Maurice Evans, *Spenser's Anatomy of Heroism: A Commentary on "The Faerie Queene"* [Cambridge, 1970], p. 159, is not alone in holding a less sympathetic view.) Britomart will outgrow this particular stage and expression, but only after growing into it, the latter an engaging process and a considerable achievement. Harry Berger, Jr., "*The Faerie Queene*, Book III: A General Description," *Criticism*, vol. 11 (1969), rpt. in *Essential Articles*, p. 418, is most pertinent: "Spenser presupposes not only a matrix of 'nature' but also a matrix of convention." In this light consider Richard Hooker's preoccupation with "custom," or convention, both as the voice of nature and potentially as the stifler of that voice: e.g. "Of the Laws of Ecclesiastical Polity," *Works*, ed. John Keble; rev. ed. R. W. Church, 3 vols. (Oxford, 1888), vol. 1, Bk. I.vii.6, viii.3, 11; subsequent reference is to this edition.

12 Marinell's mother is Cymoent, whose name derives from the Greek word for "wave"; his father is an "earthly peare" named Dumarin, or in Old French *du marin*, "of the sailor" or "of the sea": A. Tobler—E. Lommatzsch, *Altfranzösisches Wörterbuch* (Weisbaden, 1925 ff.), s.v. *Marin*, s.m. *Seemann*, and in a separate entry, s.m. *Meer*.

13 There is a further parallel between Britomart/Florimell and Artegall/Marinell, neither of whom apparently knows of the lady's love. Britomart's assault on Marinell thus has additional emotional significance, although, ironically, it is unknown to her.

14 See Lotspeich, *Classical Mythology*, p. 95, s.v. *Paeon*: "This rather vague figure, scantily represented in classical literature . . . was identified, sometimes with Apollo, sometimes with Aesculapius. Making him the son of Apollo, Sp[enser] may be identifying him with Aesculapius." If Lotspeich's speculation is right, then we have

here another tie to Book I. (See chap. 2, pp. 37–40, and my discussion of Aesculapius in "Redcrosse," pp. 489–91.)

15 *Poetry of "The Faerie Queene,"* p. 382: "Spenser brilliantly adapts the rationale of the idyllic pastoral—that nature responds to and is in a sense created by man's desires."

16 Cf. *FQ* i.v.36–40: Cymoent is a much more extensive instance of this presence than we find in the story of Hippolytus. The specific occasion in the poem is still hers, as it was Redcrosse's, however; and it is hers to a greater degree than the Gardens of Adonis will be any fictional character's apart from the poet.

17 Cf. Michael Drayton, 'Amour 45' of "Ideas Mirrovr," 1594, in *Works,* ed. J. William Hebel, with introductions, notes, variant readings by Kathleen Tillotson and Bernard H. Newdigate (Oxford, 1961), vol. I.

18 I.e. Triamond: see Thomas P. Roche, Jr., *The Kindly Flame: A Study of the Third and Fourth Books of Spenser's "Faerie Queene"* (Princeton, 1964), pp. 16–17.

19 See the verbal pointing of this theme in *FQ* iv.i.3, 7, 14, 17; iv.2, 13; xii.35.

20 E.g. the ends of cantos ii, iv, v–xii, plus iv.i and ii.32–34 ("Dan *Chaucer*"), discussed below.

21 The exception is Marinell; it is slight, indeed virtually nominal.

22 In *FQ* iv.Pro., the poet explicitly refers to the Queen only in the third person. Cf. i.Pro.4, ii.Pro.4, iii.Pro.3–4.

23 As the poet's relation to his poem changes, as he becomes a more autonomous voice and figure in Books iii and iv, I have used the word *poet* more extensively than *narrator* and now use the word *narrative* in a sense relatively more external to his own role. I think this usage properly reflects what is happening in the poem, while it maintains the continuity actually present in his developing role and in his developing characters. The poet is still a narrator, we might say, but more nearly a dramatic and personal one.

24 *FQ* i.vii.8–14. Comments by Honig, *Dark Conceit,* p. 81, and by Fletcher, *Allegory,* p. 50, apply helpfully to characters like Orgoglio or Furor/Occasion (ii.iv); yet these same generalizations are at some odds with the poetic facts of Book iv described here.

25 On relations among the three brothers, see Roche, *Kindly Flame,* pp. 15–30; Wind, *Pagan Mysteries in the Renaissance,* p. 210; and *Var.,* iv, 293–95, 327, 330. Clearly there are parallels between such infusings of spirits and the levels, or modes, of being imaged in the characters and places of Book iv, and further ties between such levels and the Renaissance doctrines of friendship reflected in this Book. On the word *dilation* in *The Faerie Queene,* see Rosalie L. Colie's pertinent remarks relating it to Plotinus: *Paradoxia Epidemica* (Princeton, 1966), pp. 345–46.

26 Walter Oakeshott's recent investigation of the Ralegh family's copy of Spenser's works makes the association of Timias with Ralegh even stronger. Oakeshott argues that annotations on *The Faerie Queene* are Sir Walter's; this annotation shows a remarkable interest in Timias and Belphoebe. On the basis of a comment by Ben Jonson (recorded by Drummond), Oakeshott also suggests that Spenser might once have given Ralegh a "key" to certain historical allusions in the poem other than the letter published in 1590: "Carew Ralegh's Copy of Spenser," *Library,* 5th ser., 26 (1971): 1–21. Cf. Roche, pp. 142–43, 207; *Var.,* 4: 205–07.

There is some controversy as to whether cantos vii–viii allude to the Queen's offense at Ralegh's marriage to Elizabeth Throgmorton or at some other slight to her ideal of virginity: see Allan H. Gilbert, "Belphoebe's Misdeeming of Timias," *PMLA* 62 (1947): 627–34; Walter Oakeshott, *The Queen and the Poet* (London, 1960), pp. 89–95; H. M. English, Jr., "Spenser's Accommodation of Allegory to History in the Story of Timias and Belphoebe," *JEGP* 59 (1960): 417–29.

27 E.g. see *FQ* III.v.26.

28 Allusions to such pressures and appeals exist in the Proem (his own disappointments) and in the incident involving Belphoebe, Timias, Amoret (the problems of Spenser's notable friend Ralegh with the Queen). Since both passages glance at difficulties with the Court, it is not hard to imagine why Spenser's indications of their significance are indirect or elusive. In connection with Amoret, see Oakeshott's speculations about Spenser's high regard for Ralegh's wife; Lady Ralegh writes, "E. Throkemorton his [Ralegh's] mistris" beside the adoring lines to an unidentified lady in *Colin Clovts Come Home Againe* (vv. 464–79), a poem Spenser dedicated to Ralegh himself: "Carew Ralegh's . . . Spenser," pp. 4–6.

FOREWORD TO PART III

1 John Duns Scotus, "Opus Oxoniense," *Opera Omnia*, ed. L. Vivès, 26 vols. (Paris, 1891–95), vols. 8–21: Bk. II, d. iii, q. 2, n. 15; Bk. IV, d. xi, q. 3, n. 46; Bk. III, d. i, q. 1, n. 17; cf. Bk. III, d. i, q. 1, n. 5. References are to vols. 12, 14 (Bk. III, d. i–xxii), 17, 20, 21 (Bk. IV, d. xlix–l) of this edition, cited hereafter as *Op. Ox.* Discussions of personality are available in A. Michel, "L'Évolution du concept de 'personne' dans la philosophie chrétienne," *Revue de Philosophie* 26 (1919): 351–83, 487–515; and Heribert Mühlen, *Sein und Person nach Johannes Duns Scotus: Beitrag zur Grundlegung einer Metaphysik der Person* (Werl: Dietrich-Coelde, 1954), esp. pp. 78–128.

2 Cf. Christopher Devlin, *The Psychology of Duns Scotus:* Aquinas Paper 15 of The Aquinas Society of London (Oxford: Blackfriars, 1950): highly pertinent throughout; also Efrem Bettoni, *Duns Scotus: The Basic Principles of His Philosophy,* trans. Bernardine Bonansea (Washington, D.C., 1961), pp. 123, 128; Beraud de Saint Maurice, "Existential Import in the Philosophy of Duns Scotus," *FranS* 9 (1949): 296–97.

CHAPTER 6

1 Crowley reads *womman* for *no man.*

2 Étienne Borne, "D'une Philosophie chrétienne qui serait philosophique," *Esprit* 1, no. 2 (1932): 337: quoted from Walter Roberts, trans., *God and the Ways of Knowing,* by Jean Daniélou (New York, 1957), p. 70; Roberts refers to Borne's article as "Le Problème de la philosophie chrétienne."

3 On the name "Longe Wille," see Kane, *Evidence for Authorship,* pp. 61–62, 67.

4 Robertson and Huppé, *Piers Plowman and Scriptural Tradition,* p. 130, and Wittig, "*Piers Plowman* B," p. 236, cite this passage in connection with Passus XI.8; noting the *Glossa Ordinaria,* they find a negative reference to depravity (sinful nature) in the phrase "*vultum nativitatis suae.*" There is no reason in James's statement itself, however, to insist on a negative interpretation, and the context in which his statement occurs invites a positive one. Further, there is ample reason in *Piers Plowman*

to suppose that its author would use James's reference to man's "kind" in a richly ambiguous sense, potentially positive or negative, and more likely the former.

5 In Luke 11 : 17, Jesus "*vidit cogitationes eorum*," the faithless hostility of the crowd who see Him cast out a devil, an incident which leads to His saying, "*Quinimmo beati, qui audiunt verbum Dei et costodiunt illud*" (11 : 28).

6 Howard William Troyer cites Aquinas in the same connection: "Who Is Piers Plowman," *PMLA*, vol. 47 (1932); rpt. in *Style and Symbolism*, p. 159. As T. P. Dunning points out, *Petrus* means the same as "John Smith" in Troyer's (somewhat different, though related) citation: "*Piers Plowman:*" *An Interpretation of the A-text* (London, 1937), p. 120. But Aquinas's intended meaning fails to eliminate Langland's statement, *Petrus id est Christus*, or adequately to gloss its import in the poem. Langland is talking about Piers (Peter) Plowman, after all, and not about J. Smith; and he is talking about a symbol in a poem, defined by that poem, and not about an actually existent individual. There is, of course, the possibility that Langland misunderstood or misremembered such statements as Aquinas's or that he exploited their associative and imaginative potential, or that he did both.

7 "We say that the Son of God, according to the preceding position, is several men. Still, we concede the validity of this statement: 'Jesus is Peter,' because He is the same by virtue of personal identity; yet He is another through a natural 'otherness.' This argument is therefore invalid: 'He is the same as Peter; therefore He is not another than Peter' " (unless otherwise specified, all translations are mine): "Summa Aurea," III, tr. i, q. 1, 10, *William of Auxerre's Theology of the Hypostatic Union*, ed. Walter Henry Principe (Toronto, 1963), pt. 2, p. 263: q. 1, cap. 5.7. Introduction and part I of this volume (pp. 9–141) offer a lucid, instructive discussion of William's views and of the philosophical elements they employ. This discussion emphasizes the centrality of questions touching "the mode of union in Christ" to the most important issues of medieval theology (e.g. p. 11).

8 "For the supposit subsisting in any nature, as the supposit of the nature, expresses [something that is] formally such according to that nature; now that union is believed to be of such a kind, that through it the Word subsists in human nature, as a supposit does in a nature; therefore through it the Word is formally man. The major premise of this argument is proved by Damascene. . . . But 'God' signifies a name that is both common [to several Persons] and that in any one hypostasis, that is, person, is ordered *denominatively*, just as is the case with [the name] 'man'. For it is God who has divine nature, and man who has human nature. The minor premise is proved by Augustine . . . *That assumption was of such a kind that it would make God man, and man, God*": *Op. Ox.*, Bk. III, d. vii, q. 1, n. 3 (*denominative* not italicized in *Op. Ox.*).

9 Freund's *Latin Dictionary*, rev. Charlton T. Lewis and Charles Short (Oxford, 1879), s.v. *Denominatio*. Principe discusses this term in *William of Auxerre*, p. 212, n. 14.

10 "With respect to the act of the created will, He is nevertheless denominated the Word": *Op. Ox.*, Bk. III, d. xvii, q. 1, n. 5. Scotus refers here to usage deriving from the doctrine of idioms (*communicatio idiomatum*).

11 Crowley reads *for* instead of *tyl*; Kane-Donaldson reads *stille*.

12 Crowley omits this line entirely, as does Kane-Donaldson.

13 Other pertinent examples: *PP* xv.263 ff., 435 ff.

14 In this connection, consider *Op. Ox.*, Bk. IV, d. xliii, q. 2, n. II: "Intellectus potest

percipere actum meum intuitive . . . quodam sensu, id est perceptione interiori experimur," and Sebastian J. Day's discussion of this passage, *Intuitive Cognition: A Key to the Significance of the Later Scholastics* (St. Bonaventure, N.Y.: Franciscan Institute Publication, 1947), p. 127, also pp. 125–39.

15   See A. V. C. Schmidt, "Note on Langland's Conception of 'Anima' and 'Inwit,'" *N&Q* 213 (1968): 363–64; the soul is in the whole body but "more intensely" in the heart and brain, as "life principle" and "rational principle," respectively; see *PP*, A, x.43–45, where Anima is identified with "Lyf" (as Christ is elsewhere) and is said to wander all over the body but to dwell especially in the heart. (*PP*, A, x.46 makes Anima sound very like the "Love" of *PP*, B, 1.140–62.) Cf. Léon Seiller, *L'Activité humaine du Christ selon Duns Scot*, Études de Science Religieuse, 3 (Paris: Les Éditions franciscaines, 1943), p. 69: "'Le coeur . . . est le naturel symbole des purs amours de l'âme'"; Seiller refers to Christ's heart and soul, the model for man's, and quotes J. L. V. Marie Déodat de Basly, "La Mission théologique des Franciscains," *La Bonne Parole*, 1, no. 1 (1906): 56. Smith, *Traditional Imagery of Charity*, has a very useful chapter on "The Tree of Charity"; pp. 59–60 offer support of a different kind for the interpretation of later portions of Passus XVI, which I shall develop.

16   Étienne Gilson, *The Philosophy of St. Bonaventure*, trans. Illtyd Trethowan and F. J. Sheed (New York, 1938), p. 224.

17   This technique of dramatizing recognition or developing perception is analogous to the evolution of the figure Contemplation (*FQ* I.x), to Guyon's growing awareness of Mammon outside the Cave, to the unfolding of time within the Cave, and to the poet's treatment of time and matter in the Gardens (i.e. various stages or views of the Garden) of Adonis.

18   On the three major types of theories about the Hypostatic Union, see Principe, *William of Auxerre*, pp. 64–70; and for specific reference to Aquinas and Scotus, see the penetrating study by Heiko Augustinus Oberman, *The Harvest of Medieval Theology: Gabriel Biel and Late Medieval Nominalism* (Cambridge, Mass., 1963), pp. 251–55.

19   Greta Hort, *Piers Plowman and Contemporary Religious Thought* (London, n.d.), p. 115; Donaldson, *Piers Plowman*, pp. 188–93; and Erzgräber, *William Langlands "Piers Plowman,"* pp. 169–70, 174, 204 ff., illuminate the nature of this cooperation or "union." A broader treatment of *Franciscan Elements in the Thought of "Piers Plowman,"* from which I have profited, is the excellent study by Mother Catherine Elizabeth Maguire (Ph.D. dissertation, Fordham University, 1950).

20   E.g. *Op. Ox.*, Bk. III, d. xiii, q. 4, n. 14: "charitas est quaedam participatio Dei . . ."; and on the distinction between Thomist and Scotist attitudes toward sanctifying grace, see Karl Adam, *The Christ of Faith: The Christology of the Church*, trans. Joyce Crick (1957; rpt. New York, 1962), p. 229: in a Scotist system, such grace "and love are one and the same thing."

21   E.g. *Op. Ox.*, Bk. III, d. vii, q. 3, n. 3–4: "imo ulterius sequeretur absurdius, scilicet quod Deus praedestinando Adam ad gloriam, prius praevidisset ipsum casurum in peccatum quam praedestinasset Christum ad gloriam . . ."; for further discussion, see P. Ephrem Longpré, "Le B. Duns Scot, docteur du Verbe Incarne," *Studi Francescani* 30 (1933): 175–76.

22   Cf. *Op. Ox.*, Bk. III, d. i, q. 1, n. 9–10: "nec tamen haec independentia aptitudinalis

ponit repugnantiam ad dependentiam actualem, quia licet non sit aptitudo talis naturae ad dependendum, est tamen aptitudo obedientiae, quia natura illa est in perfecta obedientia ad dependendum per actionem agentis supernaturalis; et quando datur sibi talis dependentia, personatur personalitate illa ad quam dependet; quando autem non datur, personatur in se ista negatione formaliter, et non aliquo positivo addito ultra illam entitatem positivam, quae est haec natura" (n. 9). Given this theory of personality (i.e. nothing positive need be added to "this nature" in ordinary cases to make it a human person), the "special dependence" (*specialis dependentia:* n. 10) on the uncreated Word which Scotus attributes to the human nature of Christ partakes of the same ambiguity that Langland's term *kind,* or *Kind,* does. This special aptitude or potency can be realized without subtracting anything positive which an ordinary human person possesses.

23 See Daniélou's suggestive discussion of Wisdom's role in the Bible: *God and . . . Knowing,* pp. 153–59; cf. Ames, *Fulfillment of the Scriptures,* pp. 54–55.

24 "The nature which He assumed was in itself capable of sinning because it was not beatified by reason of the power of that union, and it had free will and thus could turn to whichever of the two [i.e. sanctity or sin] it pleases": *Op. Ox.,* Bk. iii, d. xii, q. i, n. 3.

25 He says that "beatitude removed from Him all peccability or possibility of sinning which can be removed through beatitude, granted that the ability to merit by [God's] dispensation remains together with this [removal]; for the plenitude of glory by which He himself was joined to His end, no less than is another blessed one [in heaven]—granted that he could merit—equally excluded every power on His part of turning away from that end, just as in the others [blessed ones]": *Op. Ox.,* Bk. iii, d. xii, q. i, n. 2.

26 "From the very conception, by virtue of which He was made man, through charity and justice and other virtues": *Op. Ox.,* Bk. iii, d. xviii, q. i, *Textus Magistri Sententiarum,* n. B; Lombard's statement is affirmed by Scotus at length (see esp. n. 5–6).

27 "The capacity, perfect grace, the object present through the intellect, namely the whole Trinity, to whom for its own sake He could will good, and He was not impeded from so doing": *Op. Ox.,* Bk. iii, d. xviii, q. i, n. 11.

28 *Op. Ox.,* Bk. iii, d. i, q. i, n. 7: from Damascene ii.25.

29 *Op. Ox.,* Bk. iii, d. xviii, q. i, *Textus Magistri Sententiarum,* n. B: Lombard quotes Gregory.

30 "Now the human will assumed by the Word is a humanly natural will univocally like ours; therefore that will itself cannot achieve fruition without charity": *Op. Ox.,* Bk. iii, d. ii, q. i, n. 4.

31 *Op. Ox.,* Bk. iv, d. xlix, q. 6, n. 9. Aquinas differs from Scotus on this point. His explanations of other points pertaining to the freedom of Christ's human will (meriting, sinning or not sinning, use of charity, likeness to ours) also differ in significant details from Scotus's; e.g. consider Jan Rohof, *La Sainteté substantielle du Christ dans la théologie scolastique: Histoire du problème,* Studia Friburgensia, n.s. 5 (Fribourg, Switzerland: Éditions St. Paul, 1952), pp. 38–40, 46–47: for Aquinas, "L'union hypostatique au point de vue de la grâce ou le don de la grâce d'union consiste en premier lieu *dans l'état où se trouve la nature humaine par l'union au Verbe.*" Thus the grace of union "n'est pas une grâce habituelle"; it effects a "filiation naturelle" with

the Word and is thereby "la *raison d'une sanctification spéciale* que le Christ a possédée dans sa nature humaine. La grâce d'union sanctifie donc le Christ, non pas comme les autres hommes . . . mais d'une manière spéciale qui lui est propre" (p. 38). See *Summa Theologica,* trans. Fathers of the English Dominican Province, 3 vols. (New York, 1947), vol. 2: pt. III, q. vi, a. 6; all references are to this edition.

32 *Op. Ox.,* Bk. III, d. ii, q. 1, n. 12. For additional information about Scotus's view, consult Seiller, *L'Activité humaine du Christ,* pp. 51–52.

33 "Is not a necessity or necessarily a perpetual condition by reason of habits determining potencies toward [their] acts, but only by reason of the habit of glory is it a necessity *secundum quid* [relatively or conditionally, not absolutely], because a habit by nature [only] inclines [to its act]; nor by reason of charity is such a necessity in the will, because such a will can freely use charity, or not use it": *Op. Ox.,* Bk. IV, d. xlix, q. 6, n. 9.

34 Adam, *The Christ of Faith,* pp. 302–04, writes both of Jesus' "*direct vision of the divine essence*" and of the "*intuitive vision* [of His human soul] *into the essence of the Logos* in which it subsists." The significance of Piers's action, as I have described it, could strike modern sensibilities as being audacious, indecorous, or even shocking. It might be suggested, however, that the age which seriously considered such questions as whether or not Christ would have been able to assume a fire, a stone, or an ass (not to mention a woman) was less artificially pious than ours and more easily at home with the profundities of revealed religion. Cf. Oberman, *Harvest of Medieval Theology,* pp. 255–56 ff.

35 Cf. Seiller, p. 33: "l'âme du Christ demeure cause efficiente unique de son agir volitif; elle possède sur son propre vouloir une complète domination." It should be noted that Seiller stresses the necessity of distinguishing between an order that is psychological and one that is metaphysical in treating personality: "Duns Scot entend affirmer de l'individu humain subjoint au Verbe tout ce que nous entrevoyons de perfection et d'activité sous ces mots: personnalité psychologique" (p. 35; cf. p. 25).

36 The word *mod* (*OED,* s.v. *Mood* sb[1]: [1] "Mind, heart, thought, feeling"; [2a] "Fierce courage; spirit," [b] "Anger," [c] "Passionate grief": [3] "A frame of mind or state of feelings") provides a subtler indication of motive for the action described. Although this remains a motive closely related to Piers's "pure tene" in the B-text (XVI.86), it might be argued that this motive is more appropriate to the meaning of that action as I have interpreted it. Yet the word *tene* (*OED,* s.v. *Teen* sb[1]: [1] "Harm inflicted or suffered"; [2] "Irritation, vexation, annoyance; anger, wrath," [b] "Something vexatious") does not present an insuperable problem. Piers seizes the pile "for," or on account of, "tene," phrasing which ensures that "tene" is not the *response* to that seizing, even while it is a motive power with respect to it. Piers's "tene" indicates his vexation, his anger and grief, at the devil's thievery, and perhaps suggests at once the frustration of and the transcendence over his helplessness alone. (See Kirk, *Dream Thought,* p. 170, for a somewhat different reading, yet one that nicely grasps the strange doubleness—human and godlike quality—of Piers's action.) Readers have noticed that Piers also tears the Pardon "for pure tene" (VII.116), an action recalling Moses' breaking of the Tablets in Exodus. In Passus XVI, however, Piers's spirit (or wrath) flares up specifically at the devil, not at a priest or at his misguided people, and in doing so anticipates Christ's debate with the

devil, the author of sin, in Passus XVIII. Clearly, Piers's "tene" correlates in some way with Christ's here. It is a complex, compressed, paradoxical assertion of Justice and Mercy, perhaps suggestively—if necessarily also elusively—correlative as well with the notion that Christ merited "ab ipsa conceptione, ex quo factus est, per charitatem et justitiam et alias virtutes" (n. 26, above). (Cf. Theology's "tene" [II.114] and Study's: "Ac Theologie hath tened me ten score tymes," and "A ful lethy thinge it were, 3if that loue nere" [X.180, 184]. Passus XVI lends Study's remarks a sharper edge: there Love *is,* and love is first truly realized—against a thoroughly theological background.)

37 *Op. Ox.,* Bk. III, d. xviii, q. I, n. 11.

38 Crowley omits *thowgh . . . were* and reads *he might* for *to.*

39 "There were in Christ at least three wills or appetites, namely the uncreated intellectual one, the created rational one, and the irrational or sensitive one; but because the will adds something above appetite [as such], since it [the will] is free appetite together with reason, strictly speaking, there were in Christ only two wills": *Op. Ox.,* Bk. III, d. xvii, q. I, n. 2.

40 "But in some sense Christ was a viator [wayfarer] and was capable of feeling or suffering with respect to the sensitive part of His being and the inferior portion of His will; therefore He had many objects present to His senses and to that inferior portion, about which He could freely will in opposition to merely natural appetition [His affection for what is satisfying, pleasing, or convenient] which is always inclined toward what is agreeable [comfortable] to that being whose it is; therefore by fasting, by being watchful, by praying, and by many other such acts, He could merit": *Op. Ox.,* Bk. III, d. xviii, q. I, n. 5, cf. n. 6. Cf. Seiller, p. 70: "Jésus-Christ, Homme parfait, notre Rédempteur, priait . . . pour nous Dieu le Verbe auquel il est subjoint; Dieu le Verbe et donc aussi Dieu Père et Esprit-Saint" (based on Innocent III). See n. 41, below. On Christ as physician, see also Rudolph Arbesmann, "The Concept of 'Christus Medicus' in St. Augustine," *Traditio* 10 (1954): 1–28.

41 "Semi-reflexive construction" would be the most accurate description. The unique condition which unites Piers and Christ makes the grammatical, indeed real, relation between them uniquely reflexive. Notice that the rest of line 104—"his lyf for to saue"—and lines 105–06 exhibit the same pronominal doubleness, a technique we have seen Langland use before (e.g. in XIII) and one that now achieves special meaning in the context of Passus XVI.

42 *OED,* s.v. *Licham:* "The body; the living body; also the body as the seat of desire and appetite."

43 The preceding discussion of Piers has benefited in numerous ways from earlier efforts to associate Piers with a "divine" element in human nature. Although space does not allow a complete listing, I should especially refer to Donaldson, pp. 184–87; Frank, *"Piers Plowman" and the Scheme of Salvation,* p. 15, et passim; Vasta, *Spiritual Basis of "Piers Plowman,"* pp. 59–60; and for more recent studies, Sister Mary Clemente Davlin, *"Petrus, Id Est, Christus:* Piers the Plowman as 'the Whole Christ,' " *ChauR,* 6 (1972): 280–92 (includes a useful review of scholarship); and Raw's admirable essay, "Piers and the Image of God in Man," esp. pp. 150–68.

44 *Liberum-Arbitrium* again takes Piers's place in C, XIX.181.

45 As suggested in the last chapter on *Piers Plowman,* poet or narrator and Dreamer have become less useful distinctions: waking Dreamer and waking narrator, sleeping

Dreamer and the narrator of dream action merge progressively as the poem moves toward the present, e.g. there is no longer the same need on the narrator's part to give intrusive orations in the midst of the dream action—the poet has progressively *realized* the metaphor of dreaming and waking and indeed that of the Dreamer, himself.

46 In this connection, note Seiller, pp. 71–73; "Il reste que l'âme du Christ, que l'*Homo Assumptus* fait, devant Dieu, office de suppliant, office d'intercesseur," and again of the soul of Christ, "saint Paul déclare médiateur entre Dieu et les hommes [to be] *Homo Jesus Christus.*" Seiller is insisting that the activity of the *Homo Assumptus* must remain in the "created order." To a poet his phrasing might very well prove an invitation to allegory. The emphases of Scotus's views invite such phrasing.

47 This is a good example of the simultaneity of will and knowledge in action.

48 Cf. Frank, pp. 90–92; Erzgräber, pp. 194–202.

49 The C-text clarifies the fact that "lele loue" is human: "Til that loue *and by-leyue* leelliche to hym blowe" (xx.190: my italics).

50 On Piers's new role as Peter, consider Adam, *The Christ of Faith*, p. 226: according to Scotus's explanation of the concept of person, "The moment a created being united to a higher hypostasis (i.e. the Hypostatic Union] is released from this higher hypostasis, it would promptly return to being a person again." Adam raises the traditional Thomist objection to Scotus's concept of person, an objection which Scotus himself and his proponents, past and present, directly deny is valid. Yet Adam's statement is highly suggestive with respect to Langland's practice. Langland characteristically treats doctrine imaginatively ("*vix*"!); this is only to say that it is vitally alive for him. Langland did not have to believe the charges of Scotus's opponents, for example, to have them highlight the imaginative possibilities for a symbolic continuity which are actually present in Scotus's views. In the poem, of course, Piers does not "become" St. Peter in an unqualified way. He becomes an image alluding to Peter; the historical Peter never appears in the poem except as an aspect of Piers, not vice versa.

51 Cf. *PP*, Pro. 100–11.

52 Cf. C. Hieatt, *Dream Visions*, p. 93.

53 I have profited from Frank's discussion of Need, which remains a challenge to the one presented here (pp. 113–14). Frank reads Need's speech as "really a warning against the life of need" and therefore as heavily ironic throughout. Cf. Bloomfield's denial of irony in the speech: *Fourteenth-century Apocalypse*, pp. 104–05, 135–40.

54 Contrast Frank, p. 114. The way in which Frank's readings of Need's two appearances are to be reconciled is unclear to me.

CHAPTER 7

1 See Aristotle and Aquinas, n. 3, below; Richard Hooker, "A Learned Sermon of the Nature of Pride," *Works*, 3: 616–17; Cicero, *De Officiis*, trans. Walter Miller (London: Loeb, 1913), Bk. I. xliii.153–55; Sir Thomas Elyot, *The Boke named The Gouernor*, ed. H. H. S. Croft (London, 1883), 2: 187; Rosemond Tuve, *Allegorical Imagery: Some Mediaeval Books and Their Posterity* (Princeton, 1966), p. 66.

2 Gilson, *Thomas Aquinas*, pp. 306–07.

3 Aristotle, *Nic. Eth.* v.i.1130a 1–15. Cf. Aquinas, *Summa Theologica*, pt. II–II, q. 58, a. 2, 12.

4 Gilson, *Thomas Aquinas*, p. 309. Cf. *Summa Theologica*, pt. II–II, q. 58, a. 10.

5 With the following discussion, see K. Williams, *Spenser's Faerie Queene*, pp. 190–96; and Humphrey Tonkin, *Spenser's Courteous Pastoral: Book Six of the "Faerie Queene"* (Oxford, 1972), esp. chap. 1.

6 On the Beast's ancestry, see Jane Aptekar, *Icons of Justice: Iconography and Thematic Imagery in Book V of "The Faerie Queene"* (New York, 1969), chap. 12.

7 It hardly appears coincidental to the meaning of these lines that Podalyrius is the son of Aesculapius. See chap. 5, n. 14; pp. 220–21.

8 For further discussion of the medieval background, see P. C. Bayley, "Order, Grace and Courtesy in Spenser's World," *Patterns of Love and Courtesy*, ed. John Lawlor (London, 1966), pp. 195–99.

9 E.g. *PP* III.103, VI.34, 166; C, III.164; B, XX.242, 353.

10 Cf. *PP* IV.16, XX.353, C, IX.47.

11 Chaucer's "Wife of Bath's Tale," vv. 1109–76, offers a familiar discussion of true gentleness. Richard Neuse cites Boethius's *Consolation of Philosophy* (III, metr. 6) in the same connection: "Book VI as Conclusion to *The Faerie Queene*," *ELH* vol. 35 (1968), rpt. *Essential Articles*, pp. 376–77. Cf. Dorothy Woodward Culp, "Courtesy and Moral Virtue," *SEL* 11 (1971): 46–47.

12 Paul van Buren, *Christ in Our Place: The Substitutionary Character of Calvin's Doctrine of Reconciliation* (Grand Rapids, Mich., 1957), p. 105: see *Corpus Reformatorum, Opera Calvini*, 65: 65: "Nunc igitur in nobis solummodo culpa est, nisi salutis huius participes simus. Omnes enim homines nemine dempto, ad se vocat, omnibusque Christum destinat, ut ab ipso illuminemur. Aperiamus modo oculos, ipse solus tenebras discutiet, mentesque nostras veritatis luce illustrabit" (*Commentarii in Isaiam* 42 : 6); 73: 577: "Fateor quidem, unius Dei esse caecis aperire mentis oculos, nec ad percipienda regni coelestis mysteria quemquam esse idoneum, nisi quem intus spiritu suo Deus illuminat: sed non ideo digni sunt venia, qui bruta sua caecitate pereunt" (*Commentarius in Lucam* 19 : 42). See also Calvin's *Institutes*, Bk. III.xxi–xxiv, esp. xxi.5, 7; xxii.4, 7, *10–11*; xxiii.3–5, *12*; xxiv.14, 16–17 (italicized sections are crucial).

13 Cf. Tuve, *Allegorical Imagery*, pp. 49–50.

14 One side of this tension can be seen in the Reformers' statements about "good works" and sacraments, wherein such works are broadly interpreted to imply "calling," e.g. carpentry as much as praying. Tyndale's "Exposition Uppon the v. vi. vii. Chapters of Matthew" is representative: "our works which God commandeth, and unto which he annexed his promises that he will reward them, are as it were very sacraments . . . and a sure certifying of our souls, that God hath and will do according to his promise": *Work*, p. 268; cf. the discussion of "deeds" in "A Pathway Into the Holy Scripture," pp. 18–19, 22–23; and the definition of "sacrament" in "A Table, Expounding Certain Words in . . . Genesis," p. 47. The other side of the tension, a seemingly inevitable corollary to this broader but less mysterious meaning of a sacrament, is evident in a heightened emphasis on God's inscrutability, vastness, and inaccessibility to human understanding.

15 Lucifera is the daughter of Pluto and Proserpina; her proud aspirations lead her to claim Jove as her parent.

16 See Kellogg and Steele, *Books I and II of The Faerie Queene*, p. 166 n.; and on the role of Wisdom (i.e. the Second Person) in the Old Testament, see chap. 6, n. 23, p. 225.

17   *Var.*, 1: 261; Hankins, *Source and Meaning*, p. 115, refers the more specific allusions to Revelation 17 : 6.

18   Tuve, pp. 134–43, rightly advises us against a simple identification of Arthur with Christ. Although I am more interested in the *development* of Arthur's role in *The Faerie Queene*, I have found her discussion of his significance enlightening. She defines Magnificence as the perseverance of a Christian (pp. 57–59) and describes Arthur as "the image of God's own 'form' of Fortitude, a Gift of grace with a virtue born of it" (p. 136). On Arthur's virtue, see also Hankins, pp. 5–8; Maurice B. McNamee, *Honor and the Epic Hero: A Study of the Shifting Concept of Magnanimity in Philosophy and Epic Poetry* (New York, 1960), pp. 145–59, 163, 180–81; Merritt Y. Hughes, "The Arthurs of *The Faerie Queene,*" *EA*, 6 (1953): 193–213.

19   Kellogg and Steele, p. 166 n., advance the opposite view.

20   See van Buren, *Christ in Our Place*, pp. 12–13, 38–39: *Corpus Reformatorum, Opera Calvini*, 73 : 686, 672: "praesertim vero quievit divinitas, seque minime exseruit, quoties ad implendum mediatoris officium interfuit humanam naturam seorsum operari, quod suum erat" (Commentarius in Matthaeum 24 : 36, 25 : 31); 73 : 576: "Deus erat, fateor: sed quoties oportuit doctoris officio fungi, quievit, et se quodammodo abscondit eius deitas, ne quid mediatoris partibus obstaret" (in Lucam 19 : 41); 80 : 25: "sed non prae se tulit quod erat, neque palam sumpsit in oculis hominum quod iure erat" (Commentarius in Epistolam ad Philippenses 2 : 6); 80 : 26: "Respondeo carnis humilitatem nihilominus fuisse instar veli, quo divina maiestas tegebatur" (ibid., 2 : 7); also *Institutes*, Bk. II.xiv.3. Although Calvin vigorously asserts the unity of Christ's person (ibid., xiv.1–4), his profound awareness at once of God's majesty and of human depravity leads him—not entirely consistently—to distance from Christ the sinful nature of man, which *is*, he insists, now man's nature. Calvin's tendency to rely principally on symbolic explanations and individual realizations of the Redemption, rather than on relatively more physical or generic ones, appears to reflect this tension, e.g. *Institutes*, Bk. II.xvi.6.

21   See *Institutes*, Bk. II.xvi.5–6, xvii.4–6; and van Buren, pp. 53, 143–44, et passim. My discussion of Calvin's view of the Redemption is greatly indebted to van Buren's work, which this statement paraphrases.

22   T. F. Torrance, *Kingdom and Church: A Study in the Theology of the Reformation* (Edinburgh, 1956), p. 101. See also Calvin's *Institutes*, Bk. III.ii.8, iii.9, xi.1–2, 6.

23   The phrase "Calvinist emphasis" is not meant to imply that Spenser was not a good Anglican. Calvinist and Lutheran positions were incorporated into official Anglican doctrine throughout the sixteenth century and colored to a greater or lesser extent the beliefs of individual members of the established church. The points of view of many Anglicans in this period are not readily or fully understood without reference to the beliefs—often more extremely Reformed and more categorically stated—which helped to form and continued to inform them. See E. J. Bicknell, *A Theological Introduction to the Thirty-Nine Articles of the Church of England*, rev. H. J. Carpenter (London, 1963), pp. 14, 16, 18; Virgil K. Whitaker, *The Religious Basis of Spenser's Thought* (1950; rpt. New York, 1966), pp. 5–8, 68–70, et passim; Grace Warren Landrum, "Spenser's Use of the Bible and His Alleged Puritanism," *PMLA* 41 (1926): 517–44; A. S. P. Woodhouse, *The Poet and His Faith: Religion and Poetry in England from Spenser to Eliot and Auden* (Chicago, 1965), pp. 26–27; Robert Ellrodt, *Neoplatonism in the Poetry of Spenser* (Geneva, 1960), pp. 195–209. Evans,

Anatomy of Heroism, pp. 28–29, remarks a "gradual internalisation of Christ" evident in Arthur's role as the poem develops.

24   In the context of this battle, the words *life* and *senseless* are richly ambiguous. Cf. C. S. Lewis's discussion of both words in *Studies in Words,* 2d ed. (Cambridge, 1967), chaps. 6, 10.

25   The numerous Renaissance paintings showing a wound on Christ's right side indicate the familiarity of this tradition.

26   The phrase is Berger's, *Allegorical Temper,* p. 61.

27   Arthur's shield is also unveiled in his battle with Corflambo (iv.viii.42). As in Book i, the unveiling is fortuitous; it unlooses references to Corflambo as "the Pagan," who vows by "*Mahoune*" (43–44), but is a pale, hardly apocalyptic reflection of the action in i. Corflambo himself is not even directly affected by the unveiling.

28   Cf. *FQ* v.v.20, 32.

29   *PP* xviii.325 ff. is a case in point. On the prisoner's oath, see Cicero, *De Officiis,* Bk. i.vii.23, xiii.39; Elyot, *Gouernor,* 2 : 246 ff., 260; and for additional justification, Parker, *Allegory of the "Faerie Queene,"* p. 203, n. 1.

30   See H. S. V. Jones, *A Spenser Handbook* (New York, 1930), p. 257; Elyot, *Gouernor,* 2 : 73, 80, 86; Cicero, *De Officiis,* Bk. i.xv.46, Bk. iii.xi.46–47.

31   Gilson, *Thomas Aquinas,* pp. 308–09. Cf. *Summa Theologica,* pt. ii–ii, q. 58, a. 10; q. 60, a. 1; also q. 58, a. 2, and *Nic. Eth.* v.xi.1138b 5–10. I have discussed these aspects of justice more fully in " 'Nor Man It Is': The Knight of Justice in Book V of Spenser's *Faerie Queene,*" *PMLA,* vol. 85 (1970); rpt. *Essential Articles,* pp. 463–65.

32   On Artegall's name, see Roche, *Kindly Flame,* pp. 48–49; Nelson, *Poetry of Edmund Spenser,* p. 257.

33   See *FQ* v.vii.41, v.21: the poem is inconsistent or elliptical about Artegall's armor. Arthur may simply see Artegall in armor, rather than in Artegall's old armor. The point in either case is that Artegall's real nature is disguised to Arthur's view.

34   On horse and vessel, see James Carscallen, "The Goodly Frame of Temperance: The Metaphor of Cosmos in *The Faerie Queene,* Book ii," *UTQ,* vol. 37 (1968); rpt. *Essential Articles,* pp. 356, 364–65; Anderson, "Knight and Palmer," pp. 160–61, 174.

35   Malengin is identified as the traditionally Satanic figure "Guyle" in the quatrain introducing v.ix. Kathleen Williams refers his activity to "the primal deceit of the devil" in " 'Eterne in Mutabilitie': The Unified World of *The Faerie Queene,*" *That Soueraine Light,* ed. William R. Mueller and Don Cameron Allen (Baltimore, 1952), p. 38; likewise, Aptekar, *Icons of Justice,* pp. 138–39; and T. K. Dunseath, *Spenser's Allegory of Justice in Book Five of "The Faerie Queene"* (Princeton, 1968), pp. 198–201.

36   See *Var.,* 5: 226–28; René Graziani, "Philip II's *Impresa* and Spenser's Souldan," *JWCI* 27 (1964): 322–24; Garrett Mattingly, *The Defeat of the Spanish Armada* (1959; rpt. London, 1970), passim. A passage in Machiavelli's *Prince* (chap. 19) might also have contributed the name of Spenser's eclectic symbol of his most Catholic majesty, primarily but not exclusively, Philip ii: "And you are to consider, that this State of the Souldans differs much from all the other Principalities: for it is very like the Papacy . . ." (trans. Edward Dacres, *Three Renaissance Classics,* ed. Burton A. Milligan [New York, 1953], p. 77). See chap. 3, n. 11, p. 213.

37 Hankins, p. 109, aptly cites Psalm 84: 11 as a gloss on the shield: "For the Lord God is a sun and shield.' " On the substance of the shield, see also D. C. Allen, "Arthur's Diamond Shield in the Faerie Queene." *JEGP* 36 (1937): 234–43.

38 Torrance, *Kingdom and Church,* p. 116; see p. 3, et passim; also Calvin's *Institutes,* Bk. III.xx.42, xxv.1, 4; Bk. II.xvi.16: "Since he entered heaven in our flesh, as if in our name, it follows, as the apostle says, that in a sense we already 'sit with God in the heavenly places in him' [Eph. 2:6], so that *we do not await heaven with a bare hope, but in our Head already possess it*" (my italics). (The pun on *head* is present in both the original Latin and French versions.) The Calvinist emphasis on growth, on temporal advancement, readily meshes with similar emphases in Humanism and other Renaissance movements; e.g. see Fritz Saxl's "Veritas Filia Temporis," *Philosophy and History: Essays Presented to Ernst Cassirer,* ed. Raymond Klibansky and H. J. Paton (1936; rpt. New York, 1963), pp. 196–222.

39 L. S. Thornton, *Richard Hooker: A Study of His Theology* (London, 1924), p. 48; see also Hooker, "Laws of Ecclesiastical Polity," *Works,* vol. 2, Bk. v.i.2–5, lxxvi.1–8, lvi.7–13; vol. 1, Bk. i.vi.1, xvi.4; and Arthur B. Ferguson, "The Historical Perspective of Richard Hooker: a Renaissance Paradox," *JMRS* 3 (1973): 36–37, esp. 40; 48. With Ferguson, one might argue that Hooker's view of history is not radically eschatological and yet that it is notably closer to that of the Puritans than to that of Aquinas. Hooker's thinking is influenced by, and responsive to, historical insights which derive from the eschatological perspective.

40 See Torrance, pp. 5–6, 139–43 ff., and esp. chap. 2, passim. Among the numerous passages Torrance cites, the following are representative: Luther, *Werke,* XXXIV/2, 475 ("Predigt am 2. Adventsonntag," Luc. 21: 10 Dec. 1531); LII, 16 ff. ("Am Andern Sontag [sic] des Advents," Luc. 21); XXXI/2, 506 ("Vorlesung über Iesaias, 1527–30": Is. 60); XXIV, 466 (Über das erste Buch Mose," Gen. 26: 1527); XLII, 246 ("Vorlesungen über 1. Mose von 1535–45," Gen. 5).

41 See Parker, p. 317; but conversely, Viola Blackburn Hulbert, "The Belge Episode in the *Faerie Queene,*" *SP* 36 (1939): 124–46; and Bennett, *Evolution of "The Faerie Queene,*" pp. 190–91. Whatever the precise historical referents of the Belge episode, it is obvious in canto x that Belge's emissary first seeks aid from Mercilla-Elizabeth and Arthur goes to Belge's assistance. At the very least, then, time is telescoped (Bennett, p. 190) and unhappy events—the death of Sidney, for example (Hulbert, p. 140)—are simply overlooked. Surely the Belge episode is a simplification (or an idealization), even though it is possible to argue that Leicester's campaign is neither precisely nor exclusively intended.

42 See Spenser's own account in prose of Grey's recall, in *A vewe of the present state of Irelande,* pp. 159–62 (3289–3392); and for a very different reading of the relation of history and myth in Book v, Angus Fletcher, *The Prophetic Moment: An Essay on Spenser* (Chicago, 1971), pt. 2, esp. pp. 189 ff. Cf. also Joanne Craig, "The Image of Mortality: Myth and History in *The Faerie Queene,*" *ELH* 39 (1972): 520–44.

43 *FQ* VI.i.11–12, 41; ii.16, 40, 44; iii.15, 21, 51.

44 Cf. Harry Berger, Jr., "A Secret Discipline: *The Faerie Queene,* Book VI," *Form and Convention,* pp. 50–53. I am indebted to this work. My reading of the Mirabella episode is opposed to Tonkin's (*Courteous Pastoral,* pp. 87–100) whose discussion of the traditional sources for this episode, while useful, may underestimate the extent to which Spenser modifies and reforms his sources. Cupid is said to be

"myld by kynd," a far more ambiguous phrase than Tonkin's "benevolent," especially when followed by the line "But where he is prouokt with peeuishnesse" (vii.37), and in due course by Mirabella's penance and refusal of freedom. Tonkin's reading omits Arthur's offer to free Mirabella, holding instead that he is ultimately persuaded of the rightness of Cupid's sentence (p. 93, n. 10). This is not the case unless we choose thus to interpret Arthur's total silence after Mirabella's refusal; but even in this case the reasons persuading him would prove to be heavily ironic. I must also question Tonkin's view that Timias (and Enias) lust after or love Mirabella; there is evidence in the text of Timias's rashness but of nothing more serious.

45 See *Var.*, 6 : 238; Chaucer, "The Tale of Melibee," para. 1415; Vergil's first Eclogue, in which Meliboeus is a man dispossessed of his native lands and driven into exile; Arnold Williams, *Flower on a Lowly Stalk: The Sixth Book of the Faerie Queene* (Michigan State University Press, 1967), pp. 56, 72.

46 Cf. *FQ* I.x.57: Melibee would take Contemplation's pastoral idiom literally. I think we underestimate Spenser's wit in the last two Books. See also *The Shepheardes Calender*, "Febrvarie," v. 80, and gloss, p. 27.

47 A. C. Hamilton, *The Structure of Allegory in "The Faerie Queene"* (Oxford, 1961), pp. 218–19, and Evans, *Anatomy of Heroism*, pp. 32–33, discuss the recurrence of this image at greater length.

48 Malengin in *FQ* v.ix.4–6 is a clear example; for another, see chap. 3, n. 7, p. 213. Alice Fox Blitch, "Proserpina Preserved: Book VI of the *Faerie Queene*," *SEL* 13 (1973): 18, suggests that "Spenser was aware of the connotation of 'devil' in the Italian *brigante*." Similarly commenting on Spenser's use of *brigand*, A. Williams, p. 73, links its meaning to a people in the North of England. If Spenser remembered jesting associations of Northern men with the devil, such as those in Chaucer's "Friar's Tale," vv. 1413–14, and in *Piers Plowman* C, II.115, Williams's suggestion would likewise point to a diabolical dimension.

49 *Anatomy of Heroism*, p. 224.

50 Cf. *PP* XVIII.261; " 'Prynces of this place vnpynneth and vnlouketh!' " Thereafter, vv. 313–20:

> Efte the li3te bad vnlouke and Lucifer answered,
> "What lorde artow?" quod Lucifer, *"quis est iste?"*
> *"Rex glorie,"* the li3te sone seide,
> "And lorde of my3te and of mayne and al manere vertues,
>   *dominus virtutum;*
> Dukes of this dym place anon vndo this 3ates,
> That Cryst may come in, the kynges sone of heuene."
> And with that breth helle brake with Beliales barres;
> For any wye or warde wide opene the 3atis.

Of course, the context of Calidore's entrance also suggests the myth of Hercules's binding of Cerberus, in which an analogy customarily was seen to Christ's Harrowing of Hell: see Aptekar, *Icons of Justice*, pp. 212–13.

51 See Francis R. Johnson, *Astronomical Thought in Renaissance England: A Study of the English Scientific Writings from 1500–1645* (Baltimore, 1937), passim, esp. pp. 23 n., 25, 110–11 (equinoxes); 47–50, 101–03 (planetary orbits); 87–92, 120 ff. (Cambridge University as a center of astronomical studies during Spenser's lifetime); for addi-

tional clarification of the history of theories about equinoxes and orbits—helpfully diagramed—see Stephen Toulmin and June Goodfield, *The Fabric of the Heavens: The Development of Astronomy and Dynamics* (New York, 1961), pp. 27–28, 138–41, 171–72. See also A. Kent Hieatt, *Short Time's Endless Monument: The Symbolism of the Numbers in Edmund Spenser's "Epithalamion"* (New York, 1960), passim; *Var.*, 5 : 157–60; and esp. Alastair Fowler, *Spenser and the Numbers of Time* (London, 1964), pp. 192–96.

52 Mattingly's assessment of the impact of Regiomontanus on the sixteenth century is extremely useful (pp. 159–68, 305–06). By the publication and presumably by the writing of the Proem to Book v, Regiomontanus's prophecy for 1588 had been fulfilled; the disaster it augured—not unlike the apparent eccentricities of the heavens —had turned out to be, for England, evidence of rational order, indeed of providential stability. See also Don Cameron Allen, "The Degeneration of Man and Renaissance Pessimism," *SP* 35 (1938): 202–27.

53 Cf. the "wondrous chaunce" of *FQ* vi.iii.51, and Mutability Cantos, viii.2.

54 Whether Spenser's conflation of the Theseus/Ariadne and Pirithous/Hippodamia myths resulted from his confused memory, from his freely synthesizing memory, or from a deliberate act of imagination, is at most a moot question (see *Var.*, 6: 251, and Lotspeich, *Classical Mythology*, p. 39). Ovid, Spenser's probable source, suggests whichever of these possibilities we choose to argue. The echo of iv.i.23 in vi.x.13 offers a likely reason for the conflation, and its likelihood is strengthened both by K. Williams's reading of the Ariadne myth as traditionally a tale of "repeated and undeserved suffering" and "of the apotheosis of human weakness and grief" (*Spenser's Faerie Queene*, pp. 217–18; see also Cheney, *Spenser's Image of Nature*, pp. 231–35); and by the traditional interpretation of the Centaurs as figures of bestiality and evil (*Var.*, 4: 168–69; Natalis Comes, *Mythologiae sive Explicationis Fabularum, Libri decem* [Geneva, 1651], Bk. vii.4).

55 The name *Gloriana* is used by Spenser only in *FQ*.

56 Quotation from Whitrow, *Natural Philosophy of Time*, p. 111. See Plotinus, *The Six-Enneads*, trans. Stephen Mackenna and B. S. Page (Chicago, 1952), *En.* iv.iii.24–32, iv.1–8; also my discussion of Artegall, " 'Nor Man It Is,' " p. 463.

57 Tonkin's commentary on Calidore is excellent but posits a greater distance between Calidore and the poet than perhaps is warranted: *Courteous Pastoral*, p. 141.

58 Cheney, p. 229 n.; *Var.*, 6: 247; *OED*, s.v. *Overlook v.*: (1.b *fig.*) "To rise above," [2] "To look over and beyond and thus not see . . . to take no notice of, leave out of consideration," [4] "To look down upon; to survey . . . from a higher position (b) To afford or command a view of."

59 *Poetry of Edmund Spenser*, p. 293.

60 Cf. *FQ* vi.ix.25, and *Colin Clouts Come Home Againe* (hereinafter *CCCHA*), vv. 668–75:

> Therefore I silly man, whose former dayes
> Had in rude fields bene altogether spent,
> Durst not aduenture such vnknowen wayes,
> Nor trust the guile of fortunes blandishment,
> But rather chose back to my sheep to tourne,
> Whose vtmost hardnesse I before had tryde,

> Than hauing learnd repentance late, to mourne
> Emongst those wretches which I there descryde.

One of the most provocative comments ever written on *CCCHA* is W. L. Renwick's (*Var.*, 7: 448): "There is throughout the poem a sort of oscillation between the complete pastoral disguising and the straightforward personal story—between Virgil and Wordsworth—between the tradition of objective poetry and the newfound self-importance of the poet." We find in *CCCHA* the diversity of voices (roles) which Spenser faces more explicitly in Book VI.

61 Perhaps in view of the "simplicitie and meannesse" of *Mother Hubberds Tale* (dedication), of its publication in 1591, and of the fact that the passage relevant to Book VI appears to be a late interpolation (Nelson, *Poetry of Edmund Spenser*, pp. 12–15), we are justified in recalling its bitter lines about the Suitor's life, which break into the narrative with an intrusiveness worthy of Langland's Visio; see vv. 891–914 of *MHT*, esp. "And will to Court for shadowes vaine to seeke" (912).

62 Consider J. V. Cunningham's discussion of literary tradition and form: a literary form "is a scheme of experience recognized in the tradition and derived from prior works and from the descriptions of those works extant in the tradition. It is, moreover, a scheme that directs the discovery of material and detail and that orders [or contributes to the order of] the disposition of the whole. . . . a literary form may vary somewhat from work to work, since it is only a summary description [not an Idea] of those elements of the tradition that entered into the conception and realization as into the appreciation by a qualified reader of the particular work" ("Convention as Structure," pp. 221–22).

63 *CCCHA*, whose dedication is dated 1591, was published in the year before the second installment of *The Faerie Queene*. It would presumably have settled any remaining mystery about the authorship of *The Shepheardes Calender*, which, though technically anonymous and ascribed to one Immerito, was hardly a well-kept secret: "Lo I the man, whose Muse whilome did maske, / . . . in lowly Shepheards weeds."

64 Since this passage is corrupt in Crowley as well as in Skeat, I note the Kane-Donaldson correction for the reader's convenience: instead of *venym*, read *vertu*.

65 For *as thorw*, Kane-Donaldson reads *as þe gilour þoru3* and for *man . . . bigyled* reads *bigiled man formest*.

66 For *bigan . . . sleighte*, Kane-Donaldson reads *bigan al make a good ende / And bigile þe gilour, and þat is good sleighte.*

CHAPTER 8

1 My interpretation of the Cantos has been influenced by Harry Berger, Jr., "The *Mutabilitie Cantos*: Archaism and Evolution in Retrospect," in *Spenser: A Collection of Critical Essays*, ed. Harry Berger, Jr. (Englewood Cliffs, N.J., 1968), pp. 146–76.

2 See Cheney, *Spenser's Image of Nature*, p. 240; C. S. Lewis, *Spenser's Images of Life*, ed. Alastair Fowler (Cambridge, 1967), p. 15.

3 Spenser uses *vaine*, an archaic form of the adverb *vainly*, in *FQ* v.vii.34, and perhaps also in II.vi.50.

4 E.g. *Institutes*, Bk. III.x.2.

5 See *Var.*, 6: 315–16; Kellogg and Steele, *Books I and II,* p. 436 n.; Don Cameron
   Allen, "On the Closing Lines of *The Faerie Queene*," *MLN* 64 (1949): 93–94;
   L. S. Friedland, "Spenser's Sabaoth's Rest," *MLQ* 17 (1956): 199–203. Spenser had
   at least one year of Hebrew at the Merchant Taylor's School.

Index

The index does not record references to *Piers Plowman*, *The Faerie Queene*, Langland, Spenser, Will, Dreamer, poet, and narrator; these are omnipresent. With the exception of works cited more than once, material in the notes is indexed only if it provides substantive information, and is noted by number only when it is difficult to locate. The index attends especially to the characters and episodes of *Piers Plowman* and *The Faerie Queene*.